War at the End of the World
Douglas MacArthur and the Forgotten Fight for New Guinea
1942–1945

The Sinking of Laconia *and the U-Boat War*
Disaster in mid-Atlantic

Target: America
Hitler's Plan to Attack the United States

Hitler's Secret Pirate Fleet
The Deadliest Ships of World War II

Target Hitler
The Plots to Kill Adolf Hitler

Hitler Slept Late
And Other Blunders That Cost Him the War

Lincoln's Admiral
The Civil War Campaigns of David Farragut

Czars
Russia's Rulers for Over One Thousand Years

RETURN TO VICTORY

RETURN TO VICTORY

MacArthur's Epic Liberation
of the Philippines

JAMES P. DUFFY

hachette
BOOKS

NEW YORK

Hachette Books
Hachette Book Group
1290 Avenue of the Americas
New York, NY 10104
HachetteBooks.com
Twitter.com/HachetteBooks
Instagram.com/HachetteBooks

First Edition: March 2021

Published by Hachette Books, an imprint of Perseus Books, LLC, a subsidiary of Hachette Book Group, Inc. The Hachette Books name and logo is a trademark of the Hachette Book Group.

The Hachette Speakers Bureau provides a wide range of authors for speaking events. To find out more, go to www.hachettespeakersbureau.com or call (866) 376-6591.

The publisher is not responsible for websites (or their content) that are not owned by the publisher.

Library of Congress Cataloging-in-Publication Data
Names: Duffy, James P., 1941- author. Title: Return to victory : MacArthur's epic liberation of the Philippines / James P Duffy. Other titles: MacArthur's epic liberation of the Philippines
Description: First edition. | New York : Hachette Books, 2021. | Includes bibliographical references and index. | Identifiers: LCCN 2020042412 | ISBN 9780306921926 (hardcover) | ISBN 9780306921919 (ebook) Subjects: LCSH: World War, 1939-1945—Campaigns—Philippines. | MacArthur, Douglas, 1880-1964. | World War, 1939-1945—Naval operations, American. | World War, 1939-1945—Ariel operations, American. | World War, 1939-1945—Amphibious operations. | Philippines—History—Japanese occupation, 1942-1945. | Philippines—History, Military—20th century. Classification: LCC D767.4 .D84 2021 | DDC 940.54/2599—dc23 LC record available at https://lccn.loc.gov/2020042412

ISBNs: 978-0-306-92192-6 (hardcover); 978-0-306-92191-9 (ebook)

Printed in the United States of America

LSC-C

Printing 1, 2021

To the memory of Thomas J. Fleming—
historian, author, adviser, and friend,
who urged me to write about
General MacArthur
Thanks, Tom

Contents

Maps

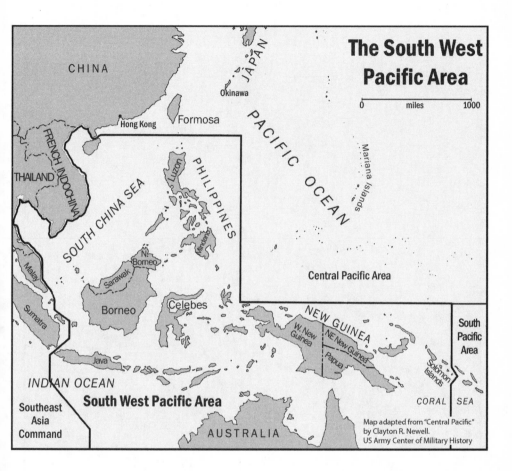

The South West Pacific Area

CHINA

JAPAN

Okinawa

Hong Kong

Formosa

PACIFIC OCEAN

FRENCH INDOCHINA

THAILAND

Luzon

PHILIPPINES

Mindanao

SOUTH CHINA SEA

Mariana Islands

0   miles   1000

N. Borneo

Sarawak

Malay

Sumatra

Borneo

Celebes

Central Pacific Area

Java

NEW GUINEA

W. New Guinea

NE New Guinea

Papua

South Pacific Area

Solomon Islands

INDIAN OCEAN

South West Pacific Area

CORAL SEA

Southeast Asia Command

AUSTRALIA

Map adapted from "Central Pacific"
by Clayton R. Newell.
US Army Center of Military History

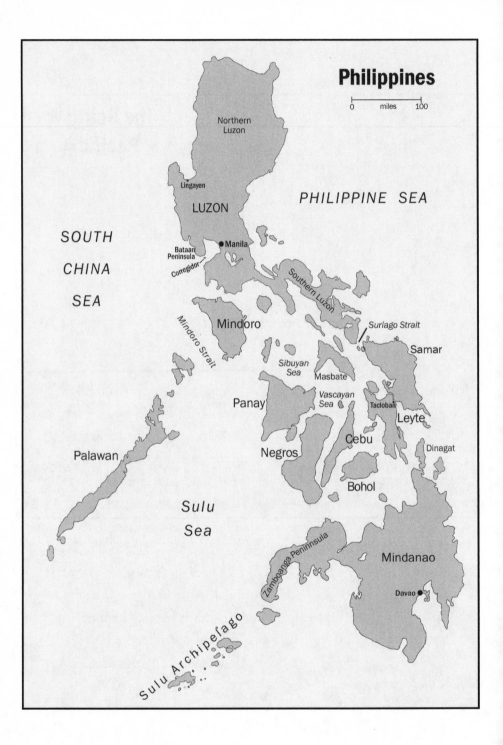

Philippines

0 miles 100

Northern
Luzon

PHILIPPINE SEA

Lingayen

LUZON

SOUTH

CHINA

SEA

Bataan
Peninsula

Corregidor

● Manila

Southern Luzon

Mindoro Strait

Mindoro

Suriago Strait

Samar

Sibuyan
Sea

Masbate

Vascayan
Sea

Panay

Tacloban

Leyte

Palawan

Negros

Cebu

Dinagat

Bohol

Sulu

Sea

Zamboanga Peninnsula

Mindanao

Davao ●

Sulu Archipelago

THE PROMISE

The spring of 1942 was glorious for the Empire of Japan. By the end of the year, the Japanese Empire ruled over 350 million people, although in some places, such as the Philippines, their hold over the population was tenuous. The empire's boundary ran from the islands of Attu and Kiska in the arctic region through the Solomon Islands in the South Pacific then west across a portion of the jungles of New Guinea to the India/Burma border.[1]

The nation's 124th emperor, Hirohito, ruled over one-seventh of the earth's surface. His reign reached nearly five thousand miles in most directions from his imperial palace, far exceeding that of any of his predecessors. In what British prime minister Winston Churchill called "the largest disaster and worst capitulation in British history," Imperial Japanese forces conquered Singapore in February. US General Jonathan Wainwright surrendered all Allied forces in the Philippines in May. The previous Christmas Day the British, Canadian, and Indian troops at Hong Kong laid down their arms, although bands of Chinese continued fighting a small guerrilla campaign against the Japanese occupiers in the area called the New Territories.

Triumphant Japanese forces occupied large sections of mainland China, the entire Malayan Peninsula, Borneo, the Dutch East Indies, Wake Island, Sumatra, the Gilbert Islands, Guam, a large portion of the Solomon Islands, Siam, French Indochina (Vietnam, Laos, and Cambodia), Celebes, Timor, the Bismarck Archipelago off the northeast coast of New Guinea, and a portion of the north coast of New Guinea. They also controlled many of the over seven thousand islands of the Philippines.

Thinking themselves unbeatable, many Japanese military leaders suffered from what several of them would refer to after the war as "victory fever." Although sixteen US Army Air Forces B-25 bombers flying from the deck of the USS *Hornet* had attacked Japanese cities, including Tokyo, in April, Japanese leaders remained confident and firm believers in their ultimate triumph. Their springtime confidence, however, would come to a shocking end later that year when they encountered three American officers—two admirals and one general—who were equally resolved to defeat them.

Admiral Chester Nimitz, military commander of the newly created Pacific Ocean Area, carefully planned for the inevitable confrontation with the Imperial Navy, which was determined to destroy the American aircraft carriers that had not been at Pearl Harbor when the Japanese attacked in December. In the Battle of Midway, fought over several days in June 1942, the Japanese suffered the sinking of four aircraft carriers, *Hiryu, Kaga, Akagi,* and *Soryu.* The heavy cruiser *Mikuma* also sank. Badly damaged was a second cruiser, *Mogami.* Two destroyers, *Asashio* and *Arashio,* suffered extensive damage. All three warships limped to Truk for repairs. Also lost were 248 carrier aircraft and 3,057 personnel, including 110 irreplaceable pilots. American losses were limited to the sinking of one carrier, USS *Yorktown*, one destroyer, USS *Hammann*, 150 aircraft, and 307 personnel.

Admiral William F. "Bull" Halsey, the aggressive commander of an aircraft carrier force in the Pacific, was hell-bent on taking the fight to the Japanese after Pearl Harbor. He directed forces that bombed Tokyo and ordered early raids on the Japanese bases on the Gilbert Islands. In October 1942, he took command of the South Pacific Area built around the Solomon Islands. American forces were having difficulty dislodging the Japanese from the islands, especially the most strategically valuable, Guadalcanal. The Imperial General Headquarters intended this island, with its landing field, to serve as the southern anchor of the empire. Halsey's aggressive actions and his support of the US Marines and Army troops fighting there drove the Japanese out, and by December 14, 1942, the Imperial Navy Staff was calling for the evacuation of all Japanese troops on the island.

Ordered by President Franklin Roosevelt to evacuate his headquarters on Corregidor in Manila Bay in March 1942, General Douglas MacArthur had expected to find an Allied army awaiting him in Australia. That army did not exist. It took some time for the American soldiers to reach Australia from the United States and the Australian troops to return home from North Africa. In late August and early September 1942, MacArthur's forces, at this time predominantly Australian, beat back a Japanese invasion at Milne Bay at the tip of New Guinea in the first defeat of a Japanese land force during the war.

As additional Allied troops arrived, MacArthur conducted dozens of amphibious landings along the northern New Guinea coast, either destroying Japanese units or isolating them and leaving them to surrender or starve in the jungles. After having defeated Japan's powerful Seventeenth Army there, he targeted Morotai Island, just six hundred miles from the large southern Philippine island of Mindanao.

But even before the Morotai landings took place in September 1944, MacArthur's planners had developed details for his return to Philippine territory. The original plan called for landing troops on Mindanao, but that later changed to the more central island of Leyte at the urging of Halsey, whose pilots reported minimal enemy activity there.

As the curtain began to rise on the long-awaited invasion and liberation of the Philippines, these three men would play critical roles in its success. As military planners in Tokyo sought a miracle that would save the valuable Philippines from falling from their grasp, MacArthur was planning his return, Halsey's carrier aircraft were pounding Japanese installations on the key islands, and Nimitz was sending additional forces to bolster MacArthur's army and navy.

LESS THAN two hours after his troops landed on the beaches of the Japanese-held island of Morotai, on September 15, 1944, General MacArthur waded ashore in thigh-high muddy water. The commander of the South West Pacific Area (SWPA) congratulated the officers and men on their successful landing. MacArthur then stepped off to one side, gazing intently in the direction of the nearest of the Philippine islands, and declared, "They are waiting for me there. It has been a long time."[2]

It had been a long and difficult two years and six months since he had reluctantly obeyed the presidential order to abandon his trapped American and Filipino forces on the Bataan Peninsula and slip away to Australia. It was shortly after he had arrived in Australia that he issued his promise to the people of the Philippines, "I shall return."

The people believed his promise. Their faith in him was almost spiritual. Believers painted his words on walls in Manila during nighttime. Resisters to the Japanese occupiers had them secretly printed on matchbook covers and gum wrappers, and people carried in their pockets slips of paper with the oath printed on them.

Now, standing on the shores of Morotai, he was ready to fulfill his promise.

CHAPTER ONE

DECISIVE BATTLE VS.

GUERRILLA WARFARE

The Imperial General Staff knew MacArthur would soon launch his forces against the 270,000 Japanese troops of the Fourteenth Area Army charged with occupying and defending the Philippines. In a desperate attempt to bolster their chances of resisting a large-scale American invasion, they made a last-minute decision to replace the existing commanding officer and bring in the man known as the "Tiger of Malaya." General Tomoyuki Yamashita arrived in Manila on October 7, 1944, less than two weeks before MacArthur's troops hit the beaches at Leyte.

The Philippine Islands were among the most important strongholds for the preservation of the Japanese Empire. As consequential as New Guinea had been, the empire faced inevitable defeat if the Philippines were lost to the Americans. The more than seven thousand islands of the archipelago dominated the shipping lanes that brought much-needed oil to the Japanese Home Islands from the resource-rich East Indies. Admiral Soemu Toyoda, the commander of the Japanese Combined Fleet, stressed the importance of those sea routes. He was willing, he said, to sacrifice every ship in his fleet to prevent MacArthur from regaining control of the Philippines. He told startled staff officers that the fleet would be useless without the fuel from the East Indies. Vice Admiral Takeo Kurita, commander of the Imperial Navy's powerful Second Fleet, was in full agreement when he said the Philippines were "vital to the continuation of the war."[1]

General MacArthur agreed with the Japanese admirals. In early September 1944, he told Army Air Forces General George Kenney he was anxious to get Kenney's land-based bombers to the Philippines so they could begin sinking cargo ships transporting oil, rubber, tin, and other raw materials from the Dutch East Indies to the Home Islands. Once that link was cut, MacArthur believed the Japanese would have only six months before they ran out of these vital supplies. He told Kenney the enemy understood this precarious situation and would fight desperately to hold the Philippines.[2]

The appointment of General Yamashita as commander of the Fourteenth Area Army defending the Philippines was an indication of the level of desperation felt by the Imperial High Command. Prime Minister Hideki Tojo, jealous of Yamashita's popularity after capturing Singapore, had banished him to Manchuria in July 1942. Following the fall of Saipan to American forces, Tojo was relieved in July 1944. His replacement as prime minister, Kuniaki Koiso, recalled Yamashita to the active war zone. Acknowledged as one of the best combat commanders available, Yamashita's orders were to take whatever actions necessary to prevent MacArthur from regaining control of the Philippines, especially Luzon. Yamashita swore that he would force MacArthur to surrender in the same way he forced British General Arthur Percival to surrender his forces at Singapore. Behind the public braggadocio was a general substantially less confident in the success of his mission. The Manchukuo Emperor in northeast China reported that the general wept when he received orders to go to the Philippines, telling the Chinese ruler he would never return.[3]

Japan's war was doomed from the start. Based in part on the need for the raw materials that make war possible, the nation's military leadership led the country into an overexpansion that was not sustainable. Japan's limited material and human resources could not support a long war on several fronts, so they had to conquer other countries to obtain what they needed.[4]

There was also an element of self-delusion in how and why the Japanese pulled the United States into the war. The Nazi defeat of the Dutch and French was seen as an invitation to take control of their colonies in southern Asia, which were rich in natural resources, especially oil and rubber—both important to the imperial war machine. They expected that at some point the United States would enter the war on the side of the Allies, thus exposing the eastern flank of the newly expanded empire to attack. The goal of the strike on Pearl Harbor was to cripple the American ability to send the Pacific Fleet against the imperial invasion forces heading south toward the former Dutch and French colonies. One American military historian referred to the Pearl Harbor attack as "a sideshow."[5]

Some Japanese expected that after a stunning defeat at Pearl Harbor the United States would be unable to conduct a full-scale war and would seek peace terms. Instead, the sneak attack on the American fleet aroused a population that had until then been reluctant to commit American forces to the war in either Europe or Asia. Michael Armacost, former ambassador to Japan, termed it "a fundamental miscalculation."[6]

Ignored by top military officials in Tokyo were the reports of Japanese civilians and military men who had visited the United States and described its vast size and the increasing potential of its industrial base. Five months before Pearl Harbor a Japanese army colonel recently returned from a fact-finding mission to the United States reportedly told a member of the Imperial General Staff that America had twenty times the steel production capacity of Japan and was able to produce five times as many aircraft and had ten times Japan's total war production capacity.[7]

At the start of the war, Japan's Imperial Navy was the third most formidable navy in the world. It boasted some of the most powerful warships afloat.[8] A major problem with this powerful navy was that it was structured on the doctrine of the "decisive battle." This was an outgrowth of the teaching of American naval historian and strategist Alfred Thayer Mahan. His book, *The Influence of Sea Power Upon History, 1660–1783*, first published in 1890, was required reading in the Imperial Japanese Naval Academy and Naval War College. The basis of Mahan's naval philosophy is the concentration of capital ships or ships of the line, commonly called battleships by World War II. The objective was to develop a fleet of these large and powerful ships that could destroy an enemy fleet in a single battle. It worked well for the Japanese in the May 1905 battle of Tsushima Strait against the Russian Baltic Fleet in which just ten of the original thirty-eight Russian ships managed to escape and reach safety. This climax to the Russo-Japanese War resulted in Imperial Japan becoming the first non-Western world power since the days of the Chinese emperors.

British military historian John Keegan called Mahan "the most important American strategist of the nineteenth century."[9] Therein lies the problem. Mahan, who served in the Union Navy during the American Civil War, was a man of the nineteenth century. He died in 1914, just eleven years after the Wright brothers made their historic first flight at Kitty Hawk, North Carolina. The advent of the airplane and aircraft carriers altered the way navies fought at sea. During the May 1942 Battle of the Coral Sea between Japanese, American, and Australian ships, the battle fleets never actually sighted or fired their big guns directly at each other. The fighting was aircraft to aircraft and aircraft to ship. No matter the range of the battleship guns, the enemy could remain out of reach and send aircraft to do the fighting. Once aircraft proved they could approach from over the horizon and sink a battleship, Mahan's strategy inched toward being obsolete. Along with it went the theory of the single "decisive battle" that would force the Americans to find a new way to end the conflict.[*]

Unfortunately for the Japanese, they clung to the theory through the end of the war, always seeking a head-to-head confrontation with the United States fleet. The American emphasis on constructing aircraft carriers made that virtually impossible.

When, in the first decade of the twentieth century, Japanese planners looked toward the United States as their next potential enemy following the defeat of the Russian fleet, they centered their strategy on a false premise that would come back to haunt them. The planners anticipated that American ships would have to operate with a long supply line leading back to the US west

---

[*] The forces under General George Washington faced a similar situation during the American Revolution. British General William Howe believed the only way to end the rebellion was through a "general action," similar to the Japanese "decisive battle." Washington's army spent years avoiding such a head-on collision with the enemy and instead chipped away at Britain's strength through skirmishes and small attacks until the colonists won.

coast. They expected the American fleet would have short periods to engage in battle before its supply chain was broken or the ships simply ran low of ammunition and food, forcing them into a decisive battle. Based on a powerful defensive posture, the Japanese strategy called for most battleships to remain in reserve close to home. Smaller warships such as cruisers and destroyers would sail east to attack, otherwise harass, and thin out the American fleet. Japanese plans made no provision for the possibility the United States would invade and take control of various islands in the central and southern Pacific regions and turn them into massive supply depots.

While most imperial admirals worshipped at the altar of the battleship and the decisive battle, a small number saw that the future was in naval airpower and the use of aircraft to fight surface fleets. Among them was Admiral Isoroku Yamamoto, commander of the Combined Fleet. In October 1940, Yamamoto may not have realized he was predicting just how the United States Navy would fight his country. "As I see it, naval operations of the future will consist of capturing an island, then building an airfield in as short a time as possible...moving up air units, and using them to gain air and surface control over the next stretch of ocean."[10]

Years earlier, a young Yamamoto was making enemies among the battleship believers when he claimed that, in the future, a ship that can transport and set in flight aircraft would be the most important warship afloat.[11]

One officer influenced by Yamamoto was his chief of staff, Vice Admiral Matome Ugaki, who made an April 27, 1944, entry in his diary, published after the war, questioning why the naval planners were still obsessed with seeking a decisive battle and not attacking elements of the enemy's forces that were easy to destroy.[12]

Following the costly defeat at Midway, imperial naval planners gave more credence to the importance of aircraft carriers, but never enough to allow them to supersede the battleships, as the US Navy did when it built its fleets around the carriers. They never gave up their search for the decisive battle, even when it was obvious that Japan was about to lose the war. They made one final attempt at a decisive head-on collision during the American invasion of the Philippines. The result was the almost complete destruction of the Imperial Navy as a fighting force. It was then they turned to suicide missions.

WHEN GENERAL Douglas MacArthur departed Corregidor on March 11, 1942, his expectation was to return to the Philippines soon while leading an Allied army currently forming in Australia. Before leaving, he altered the command structure of the American and Filipino armies to avoid a complete surrender to the Japanese and provide for the development of trained and armed guerrilla forces during an enemy occupation.

MacArthur divided his forces into four separate commands spread across the archipelago. All were to report directly to him in Australia. Major General Jonathan Wainwright commanded the North Luzon Force, which constituted mostly of the troops on Bataan and Corregidor. The forces on the Visayan Islands—chiefly Leyte, Samar, and Negros—were under the command of Brigadier General Bradford G. Chynoweth. General William F. Sharp Jr. was to continue in command of all Americans and Filipinos on Mindanao. General George F. Moore would remain in charge of the Harbor Defense Forces and those on the fortified islands of Manila Bay. Finally, MacArthur promoted Colonel Lewis C. Beebe to brigadier general and appointed him deputy chief of staff, reporting directly to himself.

Through this complex arrangement, MacArthur was the only general who had the power to surrender all the American and Filipino forces; his subordinate generals could only surrender the troops under their command. MacArthur considered Mindanao, the most southerly and second-largest of the Philippine islands at thirty-six thousand square miles, the key to maintaining an American foothold in the archipelago, and the location for the landing of a US Army corps. To facilitate support for such a vital landing, he instructed General Sharp that, when organized resistance was no longer possible, he should break up his forces into small groups and move their food, fuel, ammunition, and portable equipment inland out of Japanese reach.[13]

In this way, MacArthur expected that if Bataan and Corregidor fell to the Japanese, the other forces could continue fighting, and if necessary they could withdraw to the interior mountains of their command areas and engage in guerrilla warfare until his return. MacArthur had weighed the possibility of having to fight a guerrilla campaign against Japanese invaders prior to the attack on Pearl Harbor. As part of his planning, he had begun developing an underground intelligence network that could function during an enemy occupation. For this purpose, he had enlisted mine owners, plantation owners, and other businessmen whom he believed would remain loyal to America.[14]

MacArthur's plans failed for two reasons. The Japanese invasion came much quicker than he expected, and perhaps more importantly, he did not notify Army Chief of Staff George Marshall or anyone else in the War Department about his alteration in the command structure. Following MacArthur's departure from Corregidor, Marshall had President Roosevelt promote Wainwright to lieutenant general, a rank commensurate with his new role as commander of all American forces in the Philippines on

March 22, 1942. The War Department designated the new headquarters United States Forces in the Philippines (USFIP).

When MacArthur learned what had happened, he objected
and finally explained the reasoning behind his retaining command, but it was too late. When Wainwright surrendered on
May 6, 1942, he told Japanese General Masaharu Homma he
could only surrender the troops under his immediate command
and that the other regional commanders reported to MacArthur.
Homma made it clear that Japanese intelligence officers had
read the communications from Washington placing Wainwright
in command of the USFIP. He ordered Wainwright to contact
the other American generals with instructions to surrender their
forces or face the slaughter of all Americans and Filipinos on
Corregidor.

As the surrender progressed, thousands of American and Filipino soldiers slipped away from their units and went into hiding.
Many became the core of numerous guerrilla groups throughout the islands, often joined by escapees from the Bataan Death
March and various prison camps.

Understanding the growth and widespread dispersion of guerrilla bands, MacArthur immediately set plans in motion from his
new headquarters in Australia to unify as many groups as possible, assigning some to combat roles and others to intelligence
gathering. His headquarters stayed in touch with many of them
through radio units that submarines delivered from Australia,
along with arms, food, and other supplies. He also sent American officers to several islands to act as coordinators and offer
professional military leadership.

Soon after Lieutenant General Wainwright surrendered all
American and Filipino forces, a shroud of silence descended over
the Philippines. General MacArthur expected that the plans he

had developed before leaving Corregidor for a resistance movement among both Americans and Filipinos were working, but he
could not learn anything of their activities or results.[15]

The situation suddenly began to change on July 13, 1942. A
Dutch clandestine radio station hidden in Japanese-occupied Java
picked up and forwarded a message addressed to MacArthur
from a regimental radio shack near the town of Echague in northeastern Luzon that the enemy had not yet discovered. The sender
was Captain Guillermo Nakar of the 14th Infantry Regiment of
the 1st Division of the Philippine Army. When his regimental
commander, Lieutenant Colonel Everett Warner, followed Wainwright's instructions and surrendered on June 30, Nakar and two
companies refused to surrender and instead slipped away to the
nearby mountains. He told those left behind that he planned to
find a way to contact General MacArthur.[16]

MacArthur's spirits lifted when he read the message. Nakar
explained that detachments of Filipino and American units had
not surrendered and were actively attacking Japanese units and
facilities in the northeast and central Luzon regions. He closed
by telling MacArthur that his victorious return was the subject
of nightly prayers in every Filipino home. MacArthur and Nakar
kept up a conversation over the next few weeks, with the general
learning important information concerning enemy actions in
Central Luzon and the condition and locations of POWs.

In a message dated August 7, Nakar, whom MacArthur had
promoted to lieutenant colonel, explained that the Japanese were
aware of his radio station and had a large force searching for it.
That was his final contact. The following month he was captured,
evidently betrayed by a pro-Japanese Filipino, and imprisoned
in the dungeons of Fort Santiago, the notorious, centuries-old
former Spanish fort where he was eventually executed. The

roughly 1,100-man guerrilla force he left behind continued to operate through the end of the war.[17]

In short order a floodgate opened of radio contacts between American and Filipino guerrilla leaders and their commander in Australia. Radio listening posts throughout the South West Pacific Area began reporting to Allied headquarters on messages to MacArthur from all over the Philippines. Sometimes the information was startling to those in near isolation from events in the Philippines, such as when the Royal Australian Air Force informed the commander that they had received a message intended for him from a Filipino officer on the five-thousand-square-mile island of Panay in the central Philippines. Colonel Macario Peralta Jr. had been chief of operations of the 61st Division, Philippine Army, when Wainwright broadcast his order for all forces under his command to lay down their arms. Peralta decided not to obey. He now reported that he commanded a force of eight thousand men and was in control of a large portion of the island. He claimed the enemy had only eight hundred troops on Panay stationed in various cities. His army controlled the interior of the island to such an extent that supplies could be air dropped to his forces anywhere away from the occupied towns.

Peralta, who was later awarded the Distinguished Service Cross by Lieutenant General Robert L. Eichelberger, told MacArthur that his men had taken the puppet governor of the island prisoner and replaced him with Tomas Confesor, who refused to surrender to the Japanese. A court-martial had sentenced the ousted governor to death, and Peralta asked General MacArthur to confirm the sentence.[18]

The messages kept coming and often spoke of attacks on Japanese patrols or isolated posts. This concerned the general because he expected the enemy would retaliate against the civilian population, which they often did. While the raids and ambushes resulted in dead Japanese troops and required extensive searches for the culprits, they were never going to have a major impact on the occupation, at least not until they could be better organized and their activities coordinated.

MacArthur repeatedly urged his guerrilla contacts to keep military action to a minimum until the time of his return, and to focus on collecting information on troop sizes and movements. What he needed more than anything else was information, and these men, and in some cases women, could supply it provided they could avoid being captured or killed. He needed spies, hundreds of them, throughout Japanese-occupied territory.

As commander of all Allied forces in the theater, MacArthur's headquarters became the recipient of a great quantity of intelligence on the Japanese. Unfortunately, much of it was contradictory and incomplete. This was in part because each nation in the alliance had its own intelligence operation and spies throughout the theater, and in some cases each military service had its own intelligence units supplying information.

The German occupation of the Netherlands in May 1940 had left the Dutch forces in the East Indies and the Dutch portion of New Guinea to their own devises as the royal family went into exile in Britain. On December 8, 1941, Queen Wilhelmina declared the Netherlands in a state of war with Japan. The Japanese were expected to make a dash for the oil-rich resources of the Dutch East Indies, so Anglo-Dutch forces took up defensive positions to attempt to protect the oil fields and rubber plantations the enemy needed. Beginning on December 17, 1941, Japanese units from the Eighteenth Army began a series of landings in Borneo that drove the defenders back. On January 15, the Allied forces coordinated their efforts to block Japan by forming the

ABDACOM (American, British, Dutch and Australia Command). Overwhelmed by the superior Japanese naval and air forces and following a series of defeats at sea and on land, ABDACOM was dissolved on March 1.

Left behind as the Allies surrendered or fled were small groups of Dutch and native intelligence agents that soon became the Netherlands Indies Forces Intelligence Service (NEFIS). Clandestine Dutch radio stations throughout the East Indies provided MacArthur with invaluable intelligence on Japanese operations until the war's end.

Along with the Dutch, intelligence agents and spies from Britain, Australia, and America operated throughout the South West Pacific Area. To pull these many groups together, MacArthur organized the Allied Intelligence Bureau (AIB) in July 1942. Agents recruited into the AIB operated far behind Japanese lines conducting, among other things, long-range reconnaissance in support of guerrilla bands, including those in the Philippines.

It is unlikely that Japanese war planners ever expected the war for the Philippines that they started by invading Luzon on December 8, 1941, would last until their commanding general surrendered to American and Filipino forces on September 2, 1945. Virtually every island in the archipelago had a guerrilla force combating the Japanese occupiers. At least 180,000 Filipinos and Americans participated in these forces as active fighters or spies. Often led by American or Filipino officers with military training, these groups were so impactful that they prevented the enemy from effective control of 75 percent of the nation's provinces.[19]

As MacArthur's radio contacts with an increasing number of guerrilla leaders grew, he realized he needed a personal representative whom he trusted to slip into various islands and vet the leadership that had formed there. In September 1942, he reached all the way back to the United States for an old prewar friend, Charles "Chick" Parsons. Now a lieutenant commander of the US Navy Reserve, Parsons was well known and liked in Manila society. He survived the first months of Japanese occupation through a ruse that permitted him and his family diplomatic immunity as the honorary consul general to the Philippines from Panama, a neutral country. The Japanese interpreted the post as one having diplomatic immunity, which they reluctantly honored after first imprisoning and torturing him. Using his Panamanian identity, Parsons, known to all as Chick, had managed to secure passage to New York for his family.

In January 1943, Parsons arrived at MacArthur's headquarters in Brisbane where the general asked if he would be willing to return to the Philippines on a secret mission. To the stocky, swashbuckling Parsons the answer was obvious. The following month, Parsons began his first of forty-nine missions to the Philippines, most by submarine but several by air. This first mission was aboard the submarine USS *Tambor* to Mindanao. The submarine carried fifty thousand rounds of .30-caliber and twenty thousand rounds of .45-caliber ammunition, $10,000 in currency, a half dozen radio sets powerful enough to reach from Mindanao to Australia, along with spare parts, batteries, and generators. Also included were medical supplies including quinine and atabrine for fending off malaria. But the most important item carried by the submarine was Parsons himself, the personal envoy of the man all guerrillas in the Philippines wanted to hear from, General Douglas MacArthur.[20]

Parsons's destination on that first mission was along the Mindanao coast where he could contact Lieutenant Colonel Wendell W. Fertig, a civil engineer with a reserve commission in the US Army. Fertig now commanded several thousand guerrillas and with Parsons's help expanded his command to control as many as thirty-six thousand men. They set up a series of coast-watching stations to report on enemy ship movements. Many more missions would follow with Parsons in control of twenty submarines assigned to move supplies to Filipino guerrillas and transfer American intelligence agents between Australia and several islands. They also distributed hundreds of thousands of pesos of counterfeit occupation money that allowed resistance fighters to purchase food from local farmers and had the added benefit of causing chaos in the Japanese financial system.

When several guerrilla forces began fighting each other over control of various provinces or even entire islands, MacArthur stepped in and appointed commanding officers. His word was all that most guerrillas needed to fall in line and focus on what he wanted: reliable intelligence on enemy strength and movements. With several hundred radio stations delivered by submarine and in operation in early 1944, his influence on those resisting the Japanese occupiers multiplied. The general was, in a sense, fighting on two fronts at once. One was the war for control of New Guinea, and the other for control of the guerrilla forces in the Philippines.

In addition to colonels Fertig on Mindanao and Peralta on Panay, a wide array of leaders rose among the ranks of the guerrillas. Colonel Russell W. Volckmann led eighteen thousand men in northern Luzon; Colonel Ruperto Kangleon commanded all forces on Leyte, especially after MacArthur appointed him commander of the entire island. Their activities cost the lives of tens of thousands of Japanese soldiers, crippled the enemy's ability to rule the nation and make use of its natural resources, and paved the way for MacArthur's long-awaited return.

As for Parsons, he would play a vital role in support of the planned landings.

CHAPTER TWO

FDR SETTLES THE GREAT DEBATE

Two major debates within the American war effort in the Pacific had far-reaching consequences. Each involved the same protagonists: Admiral Ernest King and General Douglas MacArthur. The first dispute involved which military service would control the Pacific war. Ranking naval officers, especially Chief of Naval Operations King, considered the attack on Pearl Harbor an affront to the US Navy and reasoned that the nation should allow the Navy to seek revenge by defeating the Japanese with only minor assistance from the other services.

After reluctantly obeying a presidential order to evacuate the Philippine island of Corregidor before he fell into Japanese hands, one-time Army Chief of Staff MacArthur expected to take command of an Allied army forming in Australia. Discouraged by the absence of the promised forces, he nonetheless made a vow to the people of the Philippines that he would return to liberate them from the Japanese. As far as he was concerned, the region that included the large landmasses of Australia, New Guinea, and the Philippines was army territory.

The Joint Chiefs of Staff settled the issue by assigning the South West Pacific Area that included the aforementioned island nations to MacArthur, and the southern Pacific and central Pacific, comprising several thousand islands, to the Navy under the command of Admiral Chester Nimitz.

The pathway to the Japanese Home Islands initiated the second debate between the general and the admiral. MacArthur saw that path through the Philippines, while King and many of the officers of both services in Washington thought it best to bypass the Philippines and attack the island of Formosa (modern Taiwan) and the nearby Chinese coast. The American planners' primary goal was to cut the Japanese logistical supply line running through the South China Sea from the oil- and rubber-rich territories it had conquered in the Dutch East Indies and the southern tip of Asia. Without the fuel and food supplies carried aboard hundreds of cargo ships plying this route, a resource-poor Japan could not maintain its war footing for an extended period. Virtually everything the Japanese needed to fight such a large-scale war had to be imported.

Early recognition that seizing the Japanese Home Islands was imperative to forcing the empire's surrender made invasion the second objective. A massive bombing campaign preceding this invasion would necessitate a large number of land bases for heavy bombers within flying distance of Japan itself. The Washington strategists could identify only three options for locating such large airfields. A recognized choice was along the coast of China near a port so the Navy could ferry supplies and men to the bases. Another less popular location was the island of Formosa, just 110 miles off the Chinese coast. The Japanese had occupied this former Chinese province since 1895 and intelligence reports indicated strong defenses were in place. Third, and least favored by Washington, was the Philippine island of Luzon. These three locations formed a triangle over the South China Sea within which the bulk of Japan's supplies as well as reinforcement troops moved.

For months, MacArthur argued against Formosa. He claimed the population, which included several hundred thousand Japanese as well as indigenous people, had been under Japanese control too long to offer the possibility of support for an Allied invasion. Besides, he said, to leave several hundred thousand Japanese soldiers, as well as hundreds of aircraft and ships, in the Philippines to harass the Allies from the rear was reckless. Among his points concerning what he saw as the foolhardiness of attacking Formosa or the China coast before capturing the Philippines was the lack of airfields from which land-based bombers could assault Formosa. There was only so much that carrier-based aircraft could accomplish; land-based heavy bombers would still be needed if the Formosa operation was to succeed. This argument won the support of Secretary of War Henry Stimson for MacArthur's position that the Philippines, especially Luzon, had to be taken first.[1]

China presented a different set of problems. Most of the larger ports along the Chinese and French Indochina coast were under Japanese control and it appeared they were moving against smaller ports as well, shutting down the entire coast to the Allies. Supplying and reinforcing existing Allied forces in China required air travel over the Himalayas and landing at air bases controlled by the Nationalist Chinese forces. The situation grew worse with reports from the US Army commander in China, Lieutenant General Joseph Stillwell, that enemy attacks against air bases had increased and were overwhelming the forces available to defend them. Soon there might be no Allied air bases in China.

As opposition to MacArthur's plan began to crumble under his relentless determination, King lost some important allies, most especially Admiral William F. Halsey, formerly theater commander of the South Pacific Area and currently commander of the Third Fleet, and Rear Admiral Robert B. "Mick" Carney, Halsey's chief of staff. When President Roosevelt's closest military adviser, Admiral William Leahy, indicated his support for the Philippines course and the Joint Chiefs of Staff was unable to settle the issue, FDR decided to get personally involved. In the middle of preparing for his campaign for reelection to an unprecedented fourth term, he sailed to Hawaii and met with Nimitz and MacArthur.

Although most people expected Roosevelt to run, he delayed his public announcement until July 11, just eight days before the Democratic National Convention in Chicago. The president had been under pressure since the beginning of the year from party officials and even some people personally close to him to drop the current vice president from his reelection ticket. Their main concern, and Roosevelt understood this, was that his health issues might prevent him from serving out the full four years. They were horrified at the possibility of Henry Wallace becoming the next president. Perhaps the final straw was when loyal New Dealer Secretary of the Interior Harold Ickes told the president that Wallace could cost him three million votes in the general election. In the end, Roosevelt decided on Missouri senator Harry Truman as running mate. Bypassing the convention and a potential battle over the vice presidential nomination, Roosevelt wrote a letter to the delegates leaving the choice of running mate up to them and boarded a train headed to the west coast.[2]

The presidential train arrived in San Diego, far from the political infighting in Chicago, on July 20. While his train was at the naval base there, he observed some ten thousand Marines practice amphibious landings along the Pacific beaches and used the train's special communications car to contact the convention and make his acceptance speech.

At 9 p.m. on Friday, July 21, the presidential party boarded the heavy cruiser USS *Baltimore*. Shortly after midnight, Captain Walter C. Calhoun got underway in keeping with FDR's request, based on an old sailor's superstition about not starting a long voyage on a Friday. Six destroyers and a full complement of fighter aircraft accompanied the cruiser. Sailing under wartime conditions with its valuable cargo, the warship followed a zigzag course, maintained lights-out from sunset to sunrise, and ran lifeboat drills.[3]

The peace of calm seas and delightful weather was broken briefly on July 23 when the cruiser received a message from Vice Admiral Robert L. Ghormley, the commander of the Hawaiian Sea Frontier, that a suspected enemy task force was two hundred miles north of Oahu. Further investigation revealed the sighting to be lights from a search plane reflecting off the water.[4]

Despite efforts to keep the voyage secret, word spread of the president's mission to Hawaii. Some people wondered if the passenger occupying the captain's cabin was the president, and if so, why he was there. Was he seeking to enhance his credentials as a war-time leader before the election, with press photographs of himself with the general and the admiral? Or was this the commander in chief headed to settle a dispute over strategy in the Pacific war? Perhaps it was both. Either way, there would be sufficient photographs of the commander in chief and his two Pacific warlords.

ADMIRAL KING was visiting Admiral Nimitz in Honolulu when they learned of the president's impending arrival and his plans to meet Nimitz and MacArthur to the exclusion of him and the other Chiefs of Staff. King attributed the move as a political feat to show voters that FDR was in charge of the war effort.[5]

Whether it was ill feeling over his exclusion from the conference, or the fact he recognized that Nimitz did not strongly support the idea of bypassing the Philippines, he harbored the resentment long after the war. In his 1952 autobiography, King titled the section dealing with the Honolulu conference, "President Roosevelt Intervenes in Pacific Strategy." One can interpret this to mean the commander in chief of the Army and Navy had no right to interfere in war planning. When discussing the subject under debate, the Philippines or Formosa, King claims the Navy "favored a direct attack on Formosa without reference to the Philippine Islands."[6]

King was not entirely honest regarding the naval support for his view, especially concerning naval officers in the Pacific. Admiral Halsey tells of an encounter between King and Halsey's chief of staff, Admiral Carney, over the Philippines vs. Formosa issue. When Carney expressed his opinion that capturing the Philippines was necessary, an angry King asked if Carney wanted to turn Manila into another London—the target of bombing and missile attacks. Carney replied that he wanted to make Luzon what England had become, the base for tens of thousands of Allied troops and hundreds of American aircraft and naval warships.[7]

Perhaps seeking allies, King met with Fifth Fleet commander

Admiral Raymond Spruance, who had performed so well at the battle for Midway. Spruance was of the opinion that Formosa could not be taken without first seizing Luzon and using Manila Bay as a fleet anchorage to support action against Formosa.[8]

Before departing Pearl Harbor on July 22, King spent two days in meetings with Nimitz and Nimitz's staff. Evidently reluctant to order Nimitz to support the Formosa option when he met with the president, probably because he could see that Nimitz was not in favor of bypassing the Philippines and Roosevelt would see through his presentation to MacArthur's advantage, King tried persuasion. Nothing worked as Nimitz's staff kept returning to the need to use Luzon and Manila Bay for future operations against any Japanese targets from Formosa to the Home Islands.[9]

MEANWHILE, 4,700 miles to the southwest, General MacArthur was closely following the fighting between General Edwin Patrick's 158th Regimental Combat Team and the 219th Infantry Regiment of the Imperial Army's 35th Division on Noemfoor Island in Dutch New Guinea. He was also formulating his invasion of the Vogelkop Peninsula and the proposed conclusion of his campaign to liberate New Guinea. On July 6, he was surprised to receive an "eyes only" message from General Marshall. The Army chief of staff ordered his theater commander to arrange transport for himself to Honolulu, with an arrival there on July 26. Marshall emphasized the need for minimal knowledge of his planned departure or his destination.[10]

MacArthur responded by requesting clarification, as he knew nothing concerning the reason for the order. Marshall insisted that no further clarification of the order was required and MacArthur would not need to bring staff officers with him. Finally, he hinted at the actual purpose of the meeting by telling MacArthur that while in Honolulu he could expect to see "Leahy, etc."[11] That was all the explanation MacArthur needed, for if President Roosevelt's chief of staff, Admiral William Leahy, was going to be there, the general could be sure the commander in chief himself would be present. Marshall was of course loath to mention Roosevelt's travel plans, fearing Japanese listening posts might pick up the message. The last thing he wanted to do was make the enemy aware that Roosevelt was going to visit Hawaii.

The month previously, MacArthur requested that Marshall invite him to Washington so he could personally explain his position on the Luzon vs. Formosa debate to the Joint Chiefs of Staff and the president himself. Now FDR was doing him one better. As an alternative for an invitation to Washington, the president was going to meet MacArthur halfway. Instead of exhibiting his pleasure over the plans, the general grumbled over having to leave his theater of war for what he suspected was a political picture-taking "junket" by FDR. Supporting this view was the fact this was the first time Roosevelt traveled outside the United States without the Joint Chiefs of Staff.

MacArthur confided in his personal pilot, Captain Weldon "Dusty" Rhoades, that they would soon be flying to Hawaii and wanted to know if his usual aircraft, a B-17 with *Bataan I* painted on its nose, could make the flight. Rhoades demurred and received permission to requisition a C-54 passenger plane from Pan American Airways instead.

MacArthur's aircraft took off from the US Army Air Forces base at Amberley Field west of Brisbane in Queensland, at 8:15 in the morning on July 26. Across the international dateline it was still July 25 in Hawaii. In addition to Rhoades and the Pan American crew assigned to the aircraft, accompanying the general was

Brigadier General Bonner Fellers, MacArthur's military secretary; Colonel David Chambers, MD; and Lieutenant Colonel Lloyd "Larry" Lehrbas, the general's press aide. Rhoades had several rows of seats removed from the plane to make room for a cot in case the general wanted to nap. He suspected the general would not use it, as he knew MacArthur was a pacer when he was deep in thought. MacArthur would be priming for his meeting with the president to discuss the future of the war and his personal pledge to the Filipino people. Not knowing what to expect in Honolulu, MacArthur brought along no maps, no staff reports, nothing that he might require to make his case to the president.

Four and a half hours later, they landed for a fueling stop at Tontouta Naval Base on New Caledonia. Rhoades reported that when MacArthur stepped down from the plane onto the ground he paused and told his pilot this was the first time since the war began that he was standing on ground over which he was not military commander (New Caledonia was part of the Navy's South Pacific Area). Their plane landed again for more fuel at the US Navy–built airfield on Canton Island, a tiny coral atoll located 1,900 miles southwest of Hawaii. At the time, 1,124 American combat and support troops of the Canton Defense Command led by Colonel Herbert D. Gibson occupied the island. If anyone aboard the aircraft was looking down from one of the windows, they would have seen the one interesting feature about the bare island, the sight of the 21,000-ton cargo/passenger ship SS *President Taylor* grounded on a coral reef by a typhoon shortly after US troops disembarked on February 14, 1942. Despite the Navy's salvage efforts the ship remained there until the mid-1950s.[12]

MacArthur's plane approached the Hawaiian Islands at two o'clock in the afternoon of July 26. According to Rhoades, the general had not slept for the entire thirty-six-hour trip. He spent most of his time pacing the aisle in deep thought. Filling the sky over Pearl Harbor were American warplanes as they waited for the president's ship to arrive. The C-54 landed, as planned, at the army airbase at Hickam Field. An army car was waiting to take MacArthur the twelve miles to Fort Shafter and the home of his old friend Lieutenant General Robert Richardson. General Richardson was military governor of Hawaii and commanding general of all US Army troops in the south and central Pacific Ocean theaters. When Richardson learned of MacArthur's pending visit, he invited him to stay in his quarters.

Some critics of General MacArthur take issue with him taking the time to shave and bathe at Richardson's home before proceeding to see the president. However, one historian explains why by describing his condition following the long flight as "unshaven, unwashed, rumpled, and sleepless."[13]

SHORTLY BEFORE MacArthur's plane landed, the *Baltimore* halted at the entrance to Pearl Harbor beneath the coastal artillery batteries of Fort Kamehameha to take a pilot aboard before entering the harbor. Admiral Nimitz and General Richardson came aboard also, having ridden out on the pilot's boat. A ship's officer took them directly to the captain's cabin where Roosevelt and Leahy welcomed them. The ship, now flying the presidential flag, then eased into the harbor and docked alongside Pier 22-B. It was quickly obvious to everyone aboard the cruiser that the president's visit was no longer a secret. Thousands of sailors and civilians, screaming the president's name and waving wildly, occupied every ship rail and foot of dry land. It was virtually a sea of white since Nimitz's headquarters had ordered all naval personnel to wear dress whites for the day.[14]

Admiral Leahy described the scene that greeted the president's ship as having little evidence of the destruction wrought by the Japanese on December 7, 1941. He said Pearl Harbor was "jammed with ships of all kinds," other than warships, which were thousands of miles away fighting the enemy. Pearl Harbor, he wrote, was a "vast, twenty-four-hour-a-day operation of reinforcement and supply."[15]

Once the ship was tied up and the gangway lowered, a procession of several dozen Navy admirals and Army and Marine Corps generals, all in their full dress uniforms, boarded the cruiser to meet their commander in chief. Nimitz introduced each officer to Roosevelt, who chatted briefly and amiably with them. With the introductions accomplished and most of the officers returned ashore, Roosevelt turned to Nimitz and asked where General MacArthur was. Before the admiral could respond, the air was filled with the shrill sound of police sirens approaching the pier. Thousands of cheers followed this as the crowd caught sight of the police motorcycle escorts speeding toward the ship followed by a long open car driven by a soldier in uniform. Sitting in the rear seat was General MacArthur dressed in a clean pressed khaki uniform wearing the leather flight jacket General Kenney had given him, and his trademark crushed Filipino field marshal's cap with its gold scrambled eggs on the visor. He smiled and waved to the cheering throng as his car neared the gangway.

When the vehicle, which FDR's speechwriter Samuel Rosenman described as the longest open car he had ever seen, came to a stop, MacArthur stepped out and strode purposely toward the gangway. Dashing halfway up the passageway, he stopped to turn and acknowledge the renewed cheers of the soldiers, sailors, and civilians with a snappy salute and a broad smile, then continued up to the deck, which he also saluted as is customary.

The president, who appreciated the theatrics of a grand entrance himself, accepted MacArthur's salute. Reaching his hand out with a broad smile that only Roosevelt could have for the man he once described in 1932 as one of the two most dangerous men in America, he said warmly, "Hello, Doug."[16]

Admiral Leahy, who was a friend of MacArthur's of many years, jokingly asked him why he was not dressed appropriately for meeting the president, referring to the khakis and especially the nonregulation leather pilot's jacket. MacArthur replied by pointing to the skies and explaining, "It's cold up there in the sky." He made no mention of the fact he had landed an hour before the cruiser docked, and had taken the time to shave, bathe, and relax a few minutes before heading to the ship.[17]

The president, Admiral Nimitz, and General MacArthur chatted a few minutes then sat side by side in chairs on the deck for the press photographers. Although this reinforced MacArthur's comment about this meeting being a photo junket for Roosevelt's reelection, a film taken at the time shows the two of them talking amicably and even smiling. The contrast between the rather serious looking admiral in his immaculate white dress uniform and MacArthur in his khakis and leather jacket was stunning. When the photographs were finished, it was already 5 p.m., so the presidential party departed for the cream-colored, three-story Waikiki Beach mansion with an elevator loaned for FDR's use. Admiral Nimitz headed to his residence and MacArthur and Richardson left for Fort Shafter.[18]

Once in Richardson's quarters, MacArthur, pacing back and forth, resumed his complaining about having to leave his war front to sit for pictures with a president who was running for reelection. Finally, he said Roosevelt's physical appearance shocked him. He had not seen the president in seven years, when he was robust and full of vigor. Now, what he saw was a man grown so frail and thin his clothes hung on him. What MacArthur could not know at the time was that the president would suffer from a fatal stroke in nine months.[19]

Prior to his departure from Honolulu, Admiral King wrote a letter to General MacArthur with instructions that it be hand delivered to the general on his arrival. King related that during a June 1944 meeting in London of the American and British military chiefs, the British suggested that once MacArthur moved to the Philippines, British forces would assume responsibility for Australia and the oil-rich Dutch East Indies. They even presumptuously proposed the appointment of Admiral Lord Louis Mountbatten as commander of the South West Pacific Area (SWPA). A favorite of Winston Churchill, Mountbatten was Supreme Allied Commander of the South East Asia Command (SEAC). This was primarily a British war theater that included the British colonies of India, Burma, Ceylon, and Malaya. It was obvious the British Empire was attempting to reestablish itself in the region under MacArthur's control.[20]

Incensed that the British were attempting to muscle in on his territory, MacArthur responded to King, with a copy to Marshall, that he was "completely opposed" to the idea. He pointed out that all the nations fighting Japan had agreed that the SWPA forces would fight under American leadership. Now that, as he put it, "we are about to win," he could see no reason the British should supplant the American command structure and "reap the benefits of the peace." He said British naval units fighting under the current command structure would be welcome. In addition, he called attention to the fact that both the Australians and the Dutch opposed the British interference. MacArthur did not explain how he knew his allies agreed with him, but it is likely both recipients of his response concurred.[21]

At 10:30 the following morning, July 27, Admiral Nimitz and General MacArthur, the latter now wearing a regulation summer-weight army jacket, arrived as planned at the president's residence. He had invited them to join him on an extensive tour of various military installations on the island. General Richardson had arranged a crowded schedule of sights for the party to visit. Since Roosevelt preferred an open car so he could wave at the crowds and be seen by them, Richardson had limited choices of vehicles available. The one that seemed to offer the passengers the most comfort was a large black convertible. However, it belonged to the madam of the best-known brothel on the island and was easily recognizable. Richardson and Nimitz thought it would be unseemly for the president to be riding around Honolulu in the madam's car, so they decided on the much smaller convertible belonging to the city fire chief.

The president, the general, and the admiral sat in the rear seat that was likely designed for two people. MacArthur sat in the middle, with Roosevelt on his right and Nimitz on his left. In a number of photographs taken that day, it is obvious that Nimitz is sitting at an uncomfortable angle. During the daylong driving tour, Admiral Nimitz must have realized his disadvantage in the upcoming conference as his two seat mates referred to each other as "Douglas" and "Franklin," and enjoyed reminiscing about the prewar days in Washington. At one point, MacArthur asked the president what he thought of the Republican candidate Governor Dewey's chances against him in the upcoming election. Roosevelt responded that he had been too busy with war issues to think about politics, to which the two men with politics in their DNA enjoyed a hearty laugh.[22]

At 4:30, the tour concluded and the party, joined by Admiral "Bull" Halsey, sat down for dinner at the president's temporary residence. Halsey left after dinner and Roosevelt, Leahy, Nimitz, and MacArthur retired to the home's spacious living room where the conference was to take place. MacArthur entered a room that looked more like a map room at the White House. The Navy set up several large maps and other paraphernalia to allow Nimitz to make the Navy's case for bypassing Luzon. As for MacArthur, he had nothing but self-confidence concerning the Philippines and how he planned to make it happen.

This was the only presidential wartime conference for which there were no minutes. To learn what transpired we rely on the memories of the participants and those around them. They are not always in full agreement. The president started things off when he rolled his wheelchair forward, picked up a long bamboo pointer, and gently slapped it against the large map mounted on an easel in front of their chairs. "Well, Douglas," he said, "where do we go from here?" He was pointing at the southern Philippine island of Mindanao, which all parties agreed required capture before making any progress toward Luzon or Formosa. MacArthur quickly answered, "Leyte, Mr. President, and then Luzon."[23]

The meeting lasted until midnight and then resumed the following morning until they broke for lunch. Admiral Nimitz presented the Navy's view on plans to conquer Japan. The handicap for the admiral was that he was essentially presenting Admiral King's position, something he himself had been gradually pulling away from. He also had the knowledge that most if not all the Navy's ranking officers in the Pacific disagreed with King and backed moving against Luzon instead. He explained to the president that the Navy supported the idea of MacArthur invading and occupying Mindanao but not the central or northern Philippines.

The large southern island could provide airfields and harbors for the invasion of Formosa, and had tremendous strategic value in blocking the flow of oil, rubber, and other critical materials from the East Indies to Japan. Once in American hands, the island would provide air bases from which the new B-29 bombers could attack Japanese armies in China and reach the Japanese Home Islands themselves.[24]

MacArthur disagreed, claiming it would be dangerous to leave over two hundred thousand enemy combat troops and hundreds of warplanes, including heavy bombers, on Luzon behind the advancing navy. In any event, the population on Formosa had been under Japanese control since the last century and was unlikely to welcome an American invasion. The population of the Philippines did however identify themselves as American, and for the most part had spent the last few years fighting guerrilla wars against their common enemy. MacArthur knew this because he remained in touch with various American and Filipino guerrilla leaders who commanded tens of thousands of fighters who actually controlled large portions of the nation.

MacArthur discussed the strategic value of controlling the airfields on Luzon and the naval facilities in Manila Bay. He then targeted the politician in Roosevelt when he told him the American people would condemn him for abandoning seventeen million Filipino Christians and thousands of American POWs just to capture Formosa so he could turn it over to the Chinese. He contradicted a comment Nimitz made about American airfields on Mindanao being able to "neutralize" Japanese airbases on Luzon. To accomplish this, he said, American forces would have to occupy and build bases on Leyte and Mindoro, both closer to Luzon. From there, MacArthur claimed his forces could be in

Manila in five weeks from the day they landed on the beaches of Luzon's Lingayen Gulf.[25]

The president asked MacArthur about talk in Washington that liberating Luzon from the Japanese would require "heavier losses than we can stand."[26] The general responded that his losses would not be any heavier than his forces had been experiencing in New Guinea. He then told the president that modern infantry weapons made frontal assaults so deadly only mediocre commanders used the tactic. He implied he was not one of those commanders.

Writing about the conference, Admiral Leahy expressed surprise at how peaceful and friendly the discussions were. Each man presented his case for how to go forward to the best of his ability, and there was no acrimony between them despite rumors in Washington to the contrary. In his view, the meetings ended with only a "relatively minor difference"; what kind of an operation was required to retake the city of Manila. Leahy was convinced that MacArthur and Nimitz working together were "the two best qualified officers" to bring the war to an end with the surrender of Japan. Nimitz told Roosevelt he would give MacArthur all the naval support and transportation he needed. Neither man asked for anything they did not already have or have access to and pledged they would work together in full agreement. The president's chief of staff left the conference convinced they could force Japan to surrender without the need to invade the Home Islands, something everyone dreaded.[27]

The conference ended at noon, and they drove to Admiral Nimitz's residence at the Pearl Harbor Navy Base for lunch. After the meal, MacArthur gave a brief speech in which he told Roosevelt that he and Admiral Nimitz saw eye to eye on the next steps for victory and they "understand each other perfectly." With farewells said all around, the SWPA commander took a waiting car to Hickam Field where his aircraft was waiting to take him home to Brisbane.[28]

Major Rhoades met him at the field and asked if the general had gotten all he wanted, to which MacArthur responded, "Yes, we are going to the Philippines." He warned the pilot to keep this quiet, as there would be no announcement for at least several days.[29]

The following day, July 29, the president toured Hickam Field and watched as wounded men were unloaded from planes returning from Guam. He gave a brief press conference during which he was asked about General MacArthur's "I shall return" pledge and if it was about to happen. Not wanting to give anything away to the enemy, his only comment was, "We are going to get the Philippines back, and without question General MacArthur will take a part in it."[30]

By now, almost everyone understood the need to take Luzon before Formosa. Before the conference was finished, Nimitz already realized that MacArthur had won the argument. Even he was gradually coming to understand the value of taking Luzon before an attempt on Formosa or even Okinawa. Years later he told an interviewer he did not know if the president was moved by MacArthur's strategic arguments or the moral humanitarian arguments or if Roosevelt had decided to accede to the wishes of the extremely popular Republican general to avoid an embarrassing situation just before the election.[31]

Late that day the president's party reboarded the *Baltimore* and headed for Alaskan waters for an inspection tour of military facilities. By August 12, Roosevelt arrived at the Puget Sound Navy Yard in Bremerton, Washington, where he addressed a large assembly of navy personnel and navy yard workers. His speech was broadcast across the country. He recounted his cruise and arrival in Honolulu and his meeting with "my old friend General Douglas MacArthur," to discuss the "best methods of conducting the Pacific campaign." The meaning was indisputable; here was the wartime commander in chief, meeting with his popular warrior general to discuss their plans for victory.[32]

Although he had not clearly said so, it was becoming apparent that Roosevelt was favoring the Luzon invasion over Formosa. Admiral Leahy, who had started out supporting Admiral King's plan, converted before the end of the conference. One of the few people not happy with the president leaning toward Luzon was Admiral King. He blamed Nimitz for his failure to win Roosevelt's support for Formosa. He claimed Nimitz had "let me down" because he was a "trimmer," meaning Nimitz was too quick to compromise.[33]

For his part, Roosevelt evidently wanted to shore up his relationship with MacArthur. He remained concerned that the popular general might create a political problem before the election. While still traveling back to Washington, he wrote a "Dear Douglas" letter committing to "push on that plan for I am convinced that as a whole it is logical and can be done." We can easily assume that the "plan" was MacArthur's strategy for liberating Manila, although in true Roosevelt manner he does not come right out and say so. He closed the letter by predicting there will someday be a flag raising in Manila, "and without question I want you to do it."[34]

MacArthur soon replied that in his vision, Roosevelt, as commander in chief, should be the official to preside over the flag-raising ceremony in Manila.[35]

It appeared that the two old adversaries, who earlier in their careers genuinely disliked each other, had put the past behind them. The general, who returned to Brisbane and informed his staff to begin planning the return to the Philippines, and the president, who had been able to demonstrate to the voters that he truly was the commander in chief of the Army and Navy, had clearly come to terms. Some historians suspect there was an unwritten and perhaps unspoken agreement between the two that gave MacArthur what he wanted and he in turn would not speak ill of the Roosevelt administration, but the evidence for that is scanty.

Although President Roosevelt signaled that he tended to agree with MacArthur's plan for Luzon, he decided to leave the final decision to the Joint Chiefs of Staff. He relied on Admiral Leahy to report to the chiefs concerning the conference to which none of them were invited. Writing about their meeting, Leahy said the men were surprised to learn that Nimitz and MacArthur claimed they had no disagreements at the time, and they could work out their plans "in harmony."[36]

Instead of being able to make a recommendation to the president concerning Luzon or Formosa, the chiefs continued to debate the issue. General Marshall, who had earlier leaned toward Formosa, was now firmly in MacArthur's camp. Admiral King continued to insist on his Formosa plan, but perhaps reading the tea leaves and understanding the president's preference, said he would be willing to support Luzon if the invasion of Formosa would follow closely behind. To King's dismay, Marshall was beginning to wonder if an invasion of Formosa was even necessary, or if it could be bypassed and isolated. In a move of obvious desperation for their proposal, navy planners suggested occupying a portion of Formosa. Few, even in the Navy, took this seriously.[37]

Still unable to make a decision, the chiefs devised a timetable for MacArthur's forces entering the Philippines. The basics were that SWPA forces, with assistance from Admiral Halsey's Third Fleet, would invade southern Mindanao on November 15, 1944, and northwestern Mindanao on December 7. Next, on December 20, MacArthur's forces were to invade the central Philippine island of Leyte by way of Leyte Gulf. Demonstrating their continued inability to make a final recommendation, the chiefs instructed the combined SWPA and Central Pacific Forces to prepare to land on Luzon on February 20, 1945, or Formosa on March 1. They handed the final decision to the president.[38]

Then on September 12, everything changed.

CHAPTER THREE

"Bull" Halsey Changes the Plans

As MacArthur's forces battled the Japanese in the New Guinea campaign, staff members developed plans for the general's primary objective. The strategy for the invasion and liberation of the Philippines went through several dependent variables, such as the speed with which the Allies were conquering New Guinea. MacArthur did not have a definitive answer from the president about Luzon vs. Formosa, but he felt confident enough to tell members of his staff to proceed with plans for the liberation of the Philippines. The overall plan, code-named Musketeer, was divided into three areas of operation. Sequentially Mindanao was Musketeer I, Leyte was Musketeer II, and Luzon was Musketeer III.[1]

Unable to arrive at a final recommendation for the president, the Joint Chiefs, in the words of one historian, "kicked the Luzon-Formosa can a little farther down the road," and left Washington for a major conference with the British in Quebec.[2]

The Second Quebec Conference, code-named Octagon, took

place from September 12 through September 16, 1944. It was the result of Prime Minister Churchill pressing President Roosevelt for one final Anglo-American conference before the war ended. During the second day, Churchill brought up the issue of British forces, especially the Royal Navy, playing a larger role in the war in the Pacific. Admiral King, who saw this as little more than a political ploy by the British to attempt to reestablish their empire holdings in the Pacific, objected. King thought these British forces better used against the Japanese at Singapore and in support of Dutch efforts to recover their East Indies islands. He explained the logistical problems created by Royal Navy ships that were "short legged," not designed for extensive sea duty, and would need constant replenishment by United States Fleet ships. King's position was that the British had no experience in sustained carrier operations and would be a logistical nightmare for the Americans.[3]

When the prime minister pressed Roosevelt and King for an answer to his offer of the Royal Navy's participation, King tried stalling by claiming a paper was being prepared regarding the possible use of the British Fleet in the Pacific. This did not sit well with Churchill. He angrily asked, "The offer has been made. It is accepted?" There was not much the president could do except reply, "It is." There was little to be gained in causing dissension between the two allies at this late stage of the war.[4]

MEANWHILE, THE enemy prepared for the expected invasion of the Philippines. Army units throughout the archipelago received reinforcements, and several hundred aircraft arrived at the over one hundred active airfields maintained by the Japanese. Combat divisions transferred from Mongolia, Manchuria, and China to bolster the islands' defenses. Imperial General Headquarters instructed Field Marshal Count Hisaichi Terauchi to move his Southern Army headquarters from Singapore to Manila so he could better lead the defense of the vital islands. The Southern Army had overall responsibility for the entire southern Pacific and Asia theaters.[5]

Tokyo also replaced the commanding officer of the Fourteenth Area Army responsible for the defense of the Philippines, Lieutenant General Shigenori Kuroda, on September 26. While the Philippines were a backwater in the war, with only the guerrillas to be concerned about, Tokyo had looked the other way at rumors concerning the behavior of their commander on Luzon. Kuroda is described as "a quiet gentleman, who spoke English with a British accent," which he acquired while serving at posts in London and India. Gossip reached Tokyo accusing him of enjoying the life of an imperial ruler rather than a combat general. They claimed he spent most of his time playing golf or at his mansion enjoying the company of various women. He also enjoyed reading books removed from MacArthur's private library. Perhaps his worst offense was he disagreed with Southern Army headquarters's plan to distribute the troops under his command throughout the islands. He wanted to concentrate his defenses on Luzon.[6]

Kuroda's replacement was General Tomoyuki Yamashita. Called back from his post in Manchuria, he stopped first in Tokyo for a week's worth of strategy meetings, arriving in Manila on October 7, less than two weeks before the Americans landed on Leyte. Disappointed by what he found, he pronounced conditions for the defense of Luzon as "unsatisfactory." He found that the majority of his staff officers were new and as unfamiliar with the Philippines as he was. General Kuroda's chief of staff had fallen ill and evacuated to Japan. In his place, Yamashita requested an old friend from the conquest of Singapore, Lieutenant General Akira Muto, who was serving as commander of the 2nd Imperial Guards Division on occupation duty on Sumatra. Muto arrived in Manila on October 20. On being informed the Americans had landed at Leyte, he responded, "Very interesting, but where is Leyte?"[7]

In addition to his tearful "final" farewell to the puppet Manchukuo Emperor mentioned earlier, Yamashita was pessimistic about his chances for victory in the Philippines. Before reaching Manila, he told an aide, Major Shigeharu Assaed, he believed the battle for the islands was going to be another battle of Minato-gawa. This was a reference to a fourteenth-century battle fought by a samurai commander, Masashigu Kusunoki, who knew he was on a suicide mission but demonstrated his loyalty to his imperial leader by fighting to the death in a losing battle. The large equestrian statue of him that stands outside the Imperial Palace in Tokyo demonstrates Kusunoki's place in Japanese history.[8]

There had been no serious aerial attacks on the Philippines by the Allies since the islands fell to the Japanese in 1942. That changed on September 1, 1944, when fifty-seven land-based B-24s from General George Kenney's Fifth Air Force carried out attacks on airfields in the Davao area. The coastal city on the southern island of Mindanao was the farthest they could reach from their base on Owi Island off the New Guinea coast. Anticipating a strong defense, the Americans were surprised when only three fighters rose to oppose the attack. The American crews claimed that they destroyed thirty-four to thirty-eight planes on the ground, but lost two of their own to antiaircraft fire. The next day saw sixty-five four-engine bombers drop 150 tons of bombs on warehouses and docks around Davao. Three enemy aircraft went down to no losses for the Americans. Bad weather had handicapped the P-38 fighter escorts the first day, however, they played a key role on the second. The 1,300-mile round trip would have been beyond the range of the fighters if not for previous instructions about conserving fuel from civilian aviator Charles Lindbergh. General Kenney credited Lindbergh for their successful long-range flight.[9]

Seven days later, aircraft lifted off the flight decks of Vice Admiral Marc Mitscher's Task Force 38 fast carriers, part of Admiral Halsey's Third Fleet, and launched five days of air attacks against Japanese airfields on several islands. On September 9, they focused on airfields and related facilities on Mindanao. Halsey had taken a risk by sending the fast carriers in for the attacks without their usual complement of battleships. Although the slower-moving battleships provided excellent antiaircraft protection for the carriers, they would slow down their withdrawal. He took the chance the carriers could get in and out before the enemy could locate them. Halsey's gamble paid off. In addition to ground facilities, the carrier pilots reported destroying sixty-eight enemy aircraft.[10]

The Americans remained surprised at the small number of Japanese fighters they encountered during these attacks. What they did not know was the enemy was holding back on air patrols to conserve their supply of aircraft for what they expected to be a decisive battle over the American landing sites.[11]

When Admiral Halsey received reports indicating the Fifth Air Force had done an extremely effective job of "flattening the enemy's installations" prior to the carrier raids, he decided to move north for the next attack.[12]

On September 12, the fast carriers of Admiral Mitscher's Task Force 38 attacked targets in the central Philippines' Visayan Islands. These islands include Cebu, Leyte, Negros, Panay, and Samar. The ships were so close to shore they could clearly see the mountains on Samar as they launched. The pilots reported downing seventy-five enemy planes. They also claimed to destroy another 225 that had not yet taken flight. During the night, the Japanese flew in reinforcements from airfields on Luzon. The next day the Americans returned and shot down eighty-one planes and destroyed over one hundred still parked on the airfields. On the fourteenth, they returned to Mindanao but found no interceptors to combat although they did destroy a number of Japanese aircraft on the ground.[13]

Intelligence officers aboard Halsey's flagship, the battleship USS *New Jersey*, struggled to keep track of reports coming from the carriers. By their reckoning, the two days of raids on the central islands on September 12 and 13 involved 2,400 sorties. They estimated the downing of 173 enemy aircraft along with another 305 damaged or destroyed on the ground. The raids damaged or destroyed over 100 ships. Reports indicated half of them sank. The cost was nine planes and the lives of ten Americans.[14]

Field Marshal Terauchi was receiving similar reports at his headquarters in Manila. Never a fan of the strategy of conserving the army's fighters for use when the Americans landed, he was shocked at the losses that constituted roughly one-half of all combat aircraft in the Philippines. He immediately urged Imperial General Headquarters to release all aircraft so they could attack the American aircraft carriers. He rushed his operations officer, Colonel Yozo Miyama, and two other officers to Tokyo to plead his case. The headquarters staff denied the field marshal's request, citing as an excuse the difficulties in army pilots attacking ships at sea.[15]

In the predawn hours of Tuesday, September 12, a squadron of Grumman F6F Hellcat fighters bolted from the deck of the USS *Hornet* to escort bombers headed for airfields on the Japanese-occupied island of Cebu. Introduced a year earlier to carrier service, the sea-blue Hellcat replaced the Grumman F4F Wildcat that underperformed against the faster and more maneuverable long-range Japanese fighter, the Mitsubishi A6M Zero.

Among the pilots that morning was twenty-year-old Ensign Thomas Cato Tillar. A short while later, he found himself fighting off the advances of three enemy Zeros. He splashed one of the Zeros but took several hits from the others, forcing him to make a water landing as motor oil from his overheated engine washed across the fuselage. Once on the water, Tillar scrambled from the cockpit and watched the aircraft sink out of sight in less than a minute as he inflated his life raft. Settling into the raft, he assessed his condition. He was soaked in oil, his shoulder was in pain from slamming against the plane's wing as he exited the aircraft, and he had a small scratch on the rear of his neck from a sliver of the cockpit canopy that now burned from oil and salt water.

Tillar was not too worried because he assumed his squadron mates had seen his ditching and would send help. The sea was calm and the weather clear enough that he could make out a volcanic island about six hundred yards away. He suddenly caught sight of an outrigger canoe heading in his direction with Filipinos aboard, waving and smiling. Once ashore, he met a young Filipino man who said his name was Sosa. He showed the American papers identifying him as a private first class in the Philippine Army.

After Tillar ate some food the village chief and his wife had offered, two Hellcats appeared overhead and circled the island, indicating they knew the downed pilot was there. A few minutes later an outrigger came ashore from another island with a man Sosa identified as a lieutenant in the Philippine Army and an active guerrilla fighting the Japanese. The lieutenant told Tillar he was glad to have seen the American ships in the area and was wondering if the pilot could arrange a shipment of medical supplies and arms, both of which his guerrillas were in need of to more effectively battle the enemy. Tillar, who was by now experiencing exhaustion and was focused on searching for a rescue plane, responded that he would tell his superiors of the request. He asked the lieutenant how many Japanese were on Cebu. The man told him about fifteen thousand and even fewer on Leyte.

A Curtiss-Wright floatplane from Admiral Turner Joy's flagship, the heavy cruiser USS *Wichita*, arrived to rescue Tillar. Once aboard the cruiser, he told the admiral what the Filipino lieutenant had told him about enemy forces on Cebu and Leyte. Allowing the exhausted pilot to sleep in his own bunk, Admiral Joy passed the information to Admiral Halsey.[16]

Aboard the *New Jersey*, Admiral Halsey had been questioning where all the enemy planes had gone when he received the report concerning Ensign Tillar. He was unsure whether the enemy was doing a good job of hiding them or if the raids from his fleet had truly crippled Japanese aviation. He surmised that Japanese air defenses in the southern and central Philippines might be "a hollow shell." Standing on the bridge of the battleship shortly before noon on September 13, he discussed the situation with his chief of staff, Rear Admiral Robert "Mick" Carney, and his flag secretary, Commander Harold Stassen. They concluded that the central Philippines were vulnerable and the war could be shortened by canceling the planned invasions of the Yap island group and the Palau Islands east of the Philippines and transferring those central Pacific troops to MacArthur, who would cancel his planned invasion of Mindanao and go directly to Leyte instead.[17]

The existing strategy developed by the planners at the Joint Chiefs of Staff was that MacArthur's first invasion of Philippine territory was to take place at Sarangani Bay on Mindanao on November 15. As a prelude, an October 15 amphibious landing would secure the Dutch East Indies island of Talaud. The Imperial Army was using Talaud as a rest and recuperation site, but United States Army engineers saw it as an ideal location for an air base to provide cover for the Mindanao landings.

After Mindanao, the next assault was to take place on the central Philippine island of Leyte on December 20. The Joint Chiefs left open the following step, which they identified as an invasion of either the main Philippine island of Luzon or Formosa.

Halsey told Carney and Stassen he was considering sending a message to Admiral Nimitz recommending the cancellation of the Yap, Palau, and Mindanao invasions, and that MacArthur move up the Leyte landings from December to October 20. After reviewing all the variables, both men agreed that Halsey should make the recommendations. It was a bold move, and such advice was above his rank, but he decided to "stick my neck way out."[18]

Halsey then dictated a radio dispatch to Nimitz at Pearl Harbor. He outlined the reports from his pilots concerning the lack of a strong air defense, and described the photos from reconnaissance flights showing smashed ground installations and burned aircraft all neatly in rows. He told Nimitz he believed they had dealt the enemy a devastating setback. In his opinion, the Japanese were "operating on a shoestring" in the central Philippines. He also recounted Ensign Tillar's intelligence on Japanese forces on Leyte.[19]

Admiral Nimitz decided there was merit in Halsey's recommendations with the exception of canceling the Palau landings that were to begin in less than twenty-four hours. Minesweepers were at that moment combing the landing zones, and frogmen were already in the water off the target landing sights searching for underwater obstacles that could block landing craft carrying the 1st Marine Division. He decided he could forgo the Yap landings. He forwarded Halsey's dispatch to the Joint Chiefs in Quebec, offering to make the troops intended for Yap, Major General John R. Hodge's XXIV Army Corps, available to MacArthur if he agreed to the Halsey recommendations. Nimitz also said he would put the Marines of General Roy S. Geiger's 3rd Amphibious Force at MacArthur's disposal for a landing at Leyte.[20]

General Marshall radioed General MacArthur's headquarters from Quebec, asking his opinion of Halsey's recommendations. Unfortunately, MacArthur was not available for this most important decision. He was aboard the cruiser USS *Nashville* heading to the invasion of Morotai. Because the ship was in enemy waters, it was observing radio silence. MacArthur's chief of staff, Lieutenant General Richard Sutherland, received Marshall's dispatch. Unable to reach the general and reluctant to make the decision Marshall asked for, Sutherland gathered together General George Kenney, Brigadier General Stephen Chamberlin, and several senior staff members to discuss how to handle Marshall's request. They questioned Halsey's claim that the central Philippines was "wide open," since they had intelligence reports that said there were at least thirty-five thousand Japanese soldiers on Leyte.[21]

Pressed for time, they decided that MacArthur would leap at the opportunity to return to the Philippines earlier than planned. There was also the possibility Admiral King would revive his Formosa plan if they hesitated until MacArthur could be reached. So they responded, in MacArthur's name, explaining that if they had two infantry divisions from the XXIV Corps they could make the Leyte landings on October 20. Sutherland's message arrived at Quebec while the Chiefs of Staff were having dinner with some Canadian officers. When a staff officer brought the message, Marshall, King, Leahy, and Air Chief of Staff Arnold excused themselves to read and discuss "MacArthur's" reply. Within ninety minutes, both Nimitz and MacArthur's headquarters had new orders to cancel several intermediate landings and prepare for invading Leyte on October 20.[22]

General Sutherland sent one final message to Quebec. "Subject to completion of arrangements with Nimitz, we shall execute Leyte operation on 20 October. ... MacArthur."[23]

In his report to the secretary of war, Marshall said that it took MacArthur two days to prepare for the invasion of Leyte on October 20 instead of December 20. He called it "a remarkable administrative achievement."[24]

Months later, on January 6, 1945, President Roosevelt, who always loved a good story, told the country what had happened in his State of the Union address. He told how Halsey had concluded an attack on Leyte was feasible and how MacArthur had agreed to Halsey's recommendation to alter the war plans, and it "all took place in one day." It was his way of demonstrating the "teamwork and cooperation, skill and daring" of America's military leaders.[25]

All were amazed at how quickly MacArthur could change plans. What no one outside of his headquarters knew was that he had people working on a landing at Leyte well before Halsey made his recommendation.

CHAPTER FOUR

PASSAGE TO LEYTE

MacArthur was in good spirits when he returned to the Hollandia headquarters in New Guinea following the successful landings at Morotai. He was in full agreement with Sutherland and the others as he read the cables regarding the change in plans. After a brief vacation with his wife and son in Brisbane, MacArthur flew to Canberra on September 30, 1944, for a final, emotional farewell to Australian prime minister John Curtin. His wartime ally and strong supporter told MacArthur that he had an incurable disease and this was probably the last time they would be together. The prime minister would die of heart disease in July 1945.[1]

During this time, MacArthur and Nimitz received notices that the Joint Chiefs of Staff had concluded that an invasion of Formosa would require more troops than the United States had available, at least until the Germans were defeated. In consequence, MacArthur was directed to begin the liberation of Luzon on December 20, two months after the invasion of Leyte, and

Nimitz was instructed to provide fleet coverage and support for the invading force.[2]

MacArthur flew to Port Moresby where he conferred with the Allied Land Forces commander, Australian General Sir Thomas Blamey, concerning Blamey's troops replacing American units surrounding bypassed Japanese units. MacArthur's relationship with Blamey was not as compatible as it had been earlier in the war. The Australian general had favored sending his army's First Corps, under an Australian corps commander, as part of the Philippines invasion forces. MacArthur said he would rather have two Australian infantry divisions, each attached to a different American army corps. Blamey and the Australian cabinet turned this down, so no Australian army units took part in the Philippines campaign, limiting Australian participation to navy and air force units.[3]

Throughout this time, MacArthur remained in close touch with the staffs working on the plans for organizing the fleets and the landings on Leyte. He returned to his Hollandia headquarters on October 15 and spent the afternoon and evening meeting with Kenney and other commanders reviewing last-minute details of the voyage and the invasion.

THE PREVIOUS plan for landing on the southern section of Mindanao, code-named King I, was originally scheduled for November 15, and was to be followed on December 20 with landings on Leyte, code-named King II. With only a few weeks remaining before the new Leyte schedule of October 20, everyone scrambled to develop plans to move nearly two hundred thousand men and hundreds of ships across more than a thousand miles of ocean and arrive at their target on time.

Organizing the movement of all these troops, along with millions of tons of supplies and the ships to carry them and protect them, was a logistical nightmare. A contributing factor that exacerbated the effort was that the ships were departing from nine locations, including Hawaii, Hollandia in New Guinea, and Manus in the Admiralty Islands.[4]

Leyte is an island 115 miles long. At its northern section it is roughly 40 miles wide; the southern portion is roughly 30 miles wide, while its center is only 15 miles in width. A four-thousand-foot mountain range divides the northern half of the island, making travel between east and west difficult. Leyte's population was slightly less than one million people, many of whom could be expected to welcome and aide the American invaders as the island had several active guerrilla groups.

Leyte safeguards the eastern approaches to the Visayan Sea in the central Visayas, the islands composing the central Philippines. It is north of Mindanao and southwest of Samar. The waters of Leyte Gulf wash its entire east coast. Entrance to the gulf from the south is through the Surigao Strait from the Mindanao Sea. Ships entering from the Philippine Sea to the east must pass a series of small islands including Dinagat Island, Suluan Island, and Homonhon Island.[5]

Leyte presented several major problems for MacArthur's air force commander, General George Kenney. Kenney's land-based bombers and their fighter escorts could reach southern Mindanao from airfields on Morotai and several other New Guinea locations, but Leyte was beyond their range. He had hoped that soon after landing on Mindanao, Major General Hugh J. Casey could repeat the incredible work he had achieved in New Guinea. Casey had been MacArthur's former chief engineer and was now in command of the Army Service Command (ASCOM) with responsibility for quickly building airstrips and roads where there had been few or none, and repairing preexisting ones damaged by bomber raids. Casey's troops followed closely behind the combat units, accomplishing their vital work so Kenney's aircraft could land soon after and support the ground forces. Kenney was concerned that the invasion force could be at risk by relying solely on carrier planes for coverage without his land-based bombers. MacArthur told him he was going back to the Philippines this fall even if he had to paddle a canoe with Kenney flying overhead in his personal B-17.[6]

The site selected for the landings was along the east coast of Leyte, inside Leyte Gulf. The Allied Geographical Section (AGS) completed terrain studies of airfields, landing beaches, and roads in the area. MacArthur ordered the formation of the AGS on July 19, 1942, after realizing that large sections of the South West Pacific Area were not only unexplored but largely unmapped. He needed terrain and geographical information before sending troops into these areas to battle the Japanese. Many of the troops aboard the transports heading to Leyte were carrying pocket-size booklets prepared by the AGS that contained important information such as maps, locations of their objectives, and the topography they would encounter. These booklets proved invaluable guides for the troops. Major General Charles Willoughby, MacArthur's intelligence chief, called the AGS the "unappreciated work-horses of the war."[7]

The AGS considered the Leyte landing beaches satisfactory although photographs taken on September 14 confirmed obstacles such as swamps and lagoons were present. The plan bypassed these obstacles by leaving gaps where the troops were to land. General Kenney was unhappy about the existence of only four airfields on the island, all near Leyte Gulf on the eastern side of the island. This side was prone to bad weather and much of the territory had poor drainage. The airfields were originally prepared for light commercial planes, not for American P-47 and P-38 fighter planes with full bomb loads. With the need to place fighters and even heavier bombers on Leyte, the general requested a simultaneous assault on the western side of Leyte. This would provide the army engineers with flat dry land with good drainage on which to construct their airfields.[8]

The obsolete plan for the December 20 invasion of Leyte included a parachute drop by the 11th Airborne Division on the western side of the island to seize the required land. Unfortunately, that changed with the revised plan to meet the October 20 target date. MacArthur was fully aware of the challenges facing General Casey's engineers in attempting to build facilities on the muddy, often water-logged ground along the east coast, especially with the onset of the rainy season. He himself had examined the same territory in 1903 as an army engineer. Despite this, he told the ASCOM commander he needed airfields that could handle two fighter groups, one night fighter squadron, one medium bomber group, three patrol bomber squadrons, one photo squadron, and one Marine reconnaissance squadron, all by the fifth day following the landings.[9]

The departure of ships of the great invasion fleet had to be staged based on their cruising speed and their assigned duties once off Leyte. The entire invasion fleet was divided into various task groups (TGs) based on the tactical mission of the ships in the group. First to begin the voyage were the minesweeper and hydrographic ships of TG 77.5 under Commander Wayne R. Loud aboard the high-speed minesweeper USS *Hovey*. This group consisted of twenty minesweepers, two minelayers, a destroyer escort, an Australian frigate, and an Australian Harbor Defense

Motor Launch (HDML). The latter was similar in length and construction to a US Navy PT boat and conducted many of the same functions. Drawing only five feet, it was able to get closer to a coral-infested shore than many of the larger vessels. They carried a crew of twelve, two cannons, and machine guns as well as six to eight depth charges. TG 77.5 sailed from Manus in the Admiralty Islands off the New Guinea coast on October 10. The minesweepers were responsible for clearing the waters first around a group of islands near the entrance to Leyte Gulf, then the wider waters of the gulf approaching the landing beaches. The hydrographic vessels were to survey the waters of the gulf to supplement the old and possibly outdated charts the Americans used for planning the invasion.[10]

On October 12, the Dinagat Attack Group (TG 78.4) sailed from Humboldt Bay in Hollandia, New Guinea, to begin the 1,300-mile journey to Leyte Gulf. Commanded by Rear Admiral Arthur D. Struble, the eight destroyer-transports carried five hundred members of the 6th Ranger Battalion led by Lieutenant Colonel Henry A. Mucci. Two destroyers, two frigates, and the fleet tug *Chickasaw* accompanied them. The Rangers, along with a company from the 21st Infantry Division, were responsible for invading several islands guarding the gulf, killing the Japanese soldiers there, and planting navigation lights for the invasion fleet. Philippine guerrillas had informed MacArthur's headquarters that at least one enemy radar station was operating on the islands. Rear Admiral Robert W. Hayler's Support Group, consisting of the light cruisers *Denver* and *Columbia* along with four destroyers, escorted the troop carriers.[11]

The following day both task groups rendezvoused as planned and refueled from waiting tankers during a raging storm and high seas. Meanwhile, other groups of transports and warships departed from Hollandia and other New Guinea ports. Among the 738 ships of all sizes and functions heading to Leyte Gulf was the troop transport USS *John Land*. On October 15, the ship received a message for its most illustrious passenger, Sergio Osmena, president of the Philippine Commonwealth since the death of President Manuel Quezon in July. President Roosevelt, who had personally urged Osmena to accompany the invasion force, sent his best wishes for a successful operation.[12]

Vice Admiral Thomas Kinkaid commanded the entire armada from his flagship USS *Wasatch*, a ship specially designed and built to serve as a command center for a large-scale naval amphibious operation. Among those joining him when the ship sailed from Hollandia on October 15 was Lieutenant General Walter Krueger, the commanding officer of the Sixth Army, meaning all army troops headed to Leyte from any direction. The gruff, Prussian-born general had entered the United States as a child following his father's death. Unlike many of his contemporaries, he never graduated from high school and did not attend West Point. Krueger rose through the ranks from a private in the Spanish-American War to army commander. He racked up an impressive record since taking command in New Guinea in February 1943 and had MacArthur's complete confidence.

Kinkaid commanded all Allied naval forces in the South West Pacific Area since November 1943, and was commanding officer of the US Seventh Fleet that the press had taken to calling "MacArthur's Navy." During almost a year of fighting along the coast of New Guinea, Kinkaid never had an aircraft carrier under his command. Admiral King had forbidden it despite repeated requests from Kinkaid and MacArthur. The best he would do was to allow one or two Pacific Fleet carriers to support a landing operation. Now, Kinkaid had eighteen aircraft carriers on more or less permanent loan. Of course, none were a full-size fleet carrier such as those commanded by Admiral Halsey. They were the much smaller escort carriers and light carriers that were on loan from the Pacific Fleet under the command of Rear Admiral Thomas Sprague. By comparison, the carriers of the Third Fleet supported an average of ninety aircraft; the escort carriers had only twenty-four and the light carriers thirty-three.

Kinkaid was barely five hours into his passage to Leyte when he received a message from Admiral Halsey. The Third Fleet commander informed him, and by copies Admiral Nimitz and General MacArthur, that he was preparing for what he expected to be a major action against a large Japanese fleet, and would be unable to provide the promised air cover from his fast carriers until further notice. Kinkaid discussed the situation briefly with his staff and came to the conclusion that if Halsey had done as much damage as his pilots claimed to the enemy airpower in the Philippines, then his escort carriers could probably handle the air cover over the landing sites pending the arrival of Halsey's aircraft. He messaged Halsey, Nimitz, and MacArthur that he was proceeding with the operation as planned. He then ordered his escort carrier commanders to beef up their planned operations in the absence of the Third Fleet.[13]

The greater part of the ships steaming toward Leyte made up two amphibious task forces. Rear Admiral Daniel Barbey, who had led most of the 7th Amphibious Force landings throughout the New Guinea campaign, commanded Task Force (TF) 78, also known as the Northern Attack Force. Aboard its ships, anchored near Hollandia, were the Sixth Army's X Corps headquarters of Major General Franklin C. Sibert and the 24th Infantry Division commanded by Major General Frederick A. Irving. Once at sea, they were joined by the transports of Rear Admiral William M. Fechteler's San Ricardo Attack Group (TG 78.2) carrying Major General Verne D. Mudge's 1st Cavalry Division. The expanded convoy contained fifty-three thousand troops.

The Southern Attack Force or TF 79 was on loan from the Navy for the Leyte campaign. Its commander was Vice Admiral Theodore Wilkinson, who had also led a series of highly successful amphibious landings in the South Pacific. His ships were transporting 51,500 troops of Major General John R. Hodge's XXIV Corps originally known as the Yap Attack Force before the cancelation of that operation in favor of the Leyte landings. Its major combat components included the 96th Infantry Division under Major General James L. Bradley and Major General Archibald V. Arnold's 7th Infantry Division. Two reserve divisions, the 77th and the 32nd, held another 28,500 men at the ready.

Both task forces were under the overall command of Vice Admiral Kinkaid's Central Philippine Attack Force, or TF 77. Naval fire support and air cover from the escort and light carriers were the responsibility of TF 77. Its submarine groups included the Minesweeping and Hydrographic Group, the Beach Demolition Group, the Fire Support Group, and other service and support groups among its 183 ships. TF 77 was composed of mostly combat ships that included older battleships, heavy and light cruisers, destroyers and destroyer escorts, escort carriers, gun and mortar boats, minesweepers, and a wide range of auxiliary vessels that carried underwater demolition teams.[14]

Not a part of either amphibious task force and overlooked in most histories are the ships that serviced the ships; they were part of Rear Admiral Robert O. Glover's Service Force, TG 77.7. This group included tanker ships delivering fuel oil, gasoline, and lubricants to carriers and other ships in the fleet. The fuel came from as far away as Aruba in the West Indies and the Persian Gulf via commercial tankers to holding tanks in Australia and New Guinea. Glover's fast fleet oilers then delivered this invaluable commodity to keep the ships and planes moving. The crews of these vessels were indispensable to victory as they managed to refuel combat ships and transports alike in mid-ocean and often under attack by enemy aircraft. For the Leyte invasion, the Seventh Fleet had six of these fast oilers: USS *Ashtabula*, USS *Salamonie*, USS *Saranac*, USS *Schuylkill*, USS *Suamico*, and USS *Tallulah*. Added to these was the gasoline tanker USS *Kishwaukee* that did its best to keep close to the escort carriers. Ammunition was another commodity vital for success. This highly dangerous cargo was usually carried into the war zones in former civilian cargo ships or Liberty ships converted for the purpose. Also part of Admiral Glover's TG were an array of specialized repair ships and refrigerated ships carrying meat, eggs, vegetables, and every-thing else required to feed thousands of sailors and troops both at sea and once they were ashore.[15]

SHORTLY AFTER 11 a.m. on October 16, General MacArthur left his Hollandia headquarters and boarded his flagship USS *Nashville* in a driving rain. He took a barge from the shore to the ship's landing platform at the bottom of the cruiser's ladder. Everyone aboard, including the four correspondents who were joining the general's return to the Philippines, watched as he stepped from the barge to the platform. Suddenly a surge of water, perhaps from the wake of a passing boat, knocked him off balance and he fell face down on the platform. A gasp erupted from those watch-ing at what appeared to be a potentially embarrassing moment, but MacArthur got right to his feet and climbed the ladder as if nothing happened. Stepping off the ladder, he saluted the quarterdeck, as is naval custom.[16]

His chief of staff, Lieutenant General Richard Sutherland, and his air force commander, Lieutenant General Kenney, joined MacArthur aboard the *Nashville*. Colonel Courtney Whitney was also present, as was MacArthur's personal physician and aide-de-camp Colonel Roger O. Egeberg, press officer Lieutenant Colonel Lloyd Lehrbas, and several other staff officers. Included was the commanding general's pilot, Captain "Dusty" Rhoades, who called it one of the happiest days of his life.

A short while after MacArthur settled in, the cruiser weighed anchor and, along with several destroyers acting as escorts, headed toward the Philippines. At first, they maintained a speed of 25 knots until they joined the main body of the convoy, then they slowed to 12 knots. Soon afterward, a message came from Admiral Halsey that he was reducing the number of fast carrier groups from the Third Fleet that were to afford air cover over the Leyte landings from four to two. MacArthur was genuinely concerned about this 50 percent drop in air cover. He realized that Halsey, for whom he had great respect, was under the impression that his pilots had crippled the enemy air units to the point they would not be a serious threat to the landings. The general had his doubts about that. He told Kenney he wished they had their own air support and blamed the Joint Chiefs of Staff for allowing the Navy to pressure them to sideline Mindanao. Landing there, he would have air cover from Kenney's Fifth Air Force fields in New Guinea. Then after quickly establishing bases on Mindanao, Kenney could provide air cover for the Leyte landings. Now he was without his own cover and reliant on the Navy.[17]

More bad news arrived that evening. Filipino guerrillas on Leyte reported the Japanese were sending reinforcements to the island

and that there were now eight thousand of them along the gulf coast between Tacloban and Dulag, exactly where the Americans were going to land. The following day the guerrillas raised their estimate of Japanese strength on Leyte to twenty thousand. On the eighteenth, they increased it again to twenty-three thousand. Kenney remarked that based on these reports, the enemy forces waiting for their arrival would be very close to the thirty-five thousand that US intelligence agents had estimated.[18]

MacArthur spent his time alternating between reading reports and strolling on the portion of the bridge reserved for his use. Leaning on the railing looking out at the vast sea, he puffed on his corncob pipe or the occasional cigar, chatting with one or two staff officers, including Colonel Whitney. In one conversation, Whitney asked him if having such a great fleet under his command gave him a sense of power. The general responded that he could not stop thinking about "the fine American boys who are going to die on those beaches."[19]

Years later General MacArthur wrote a description of the scene that surrounded him. "Ships to the front, to the rear, to the left, and to the right, as far as the eye could see. Their sturdy hulls plowed the water, now presenting a broadside view, now their sterns, as they methodically carried out the zigzagging tactics of evasion."[20]

During the evenings, alone in his cabin, General MacArthur worked on two speeches he intended to deliver. The first he planned for the day he and his troops would land on Leyte's beaches; the other was for the day soon after when he would announce the restoration of the Filipino government. On the evening of the nineteenth, the day before the landings, he reviewed the speeches with colonels Egeberg and Lehrbas. All was well until he got to a point where he said, "And the tinkle of

the laughter of little children will again be heard on the streets."
Egeberg, who usually gave his commander and patient his due,
was shocked. He told MacArthur it was a timeworn sentimental
cliché. With a hurt look, the general made a feeble attempt to
defend his words as any author might do, but then realized
Egeberg was correct and drew a line through the phrase.[21]

October 19 was a dark night with no moon when the *Nashville*
approached the entrance to Leyte Gulf and dropped anchor at its
assigned position at 11 p.m. MacArthur was in his cabin working
on two letters, one to his wife telling her he was fine and looking
forwarding to doing his duty the next day. The other was a draft
of a letter to President Roosevelt that Colonel Lehrbas had helped
him prepare. He planned to take it ashore with him, write the
final copy while on Leyte, and arrange for mailing the next day.
In this letter, MacArthur wrote, "This note is written from the
beach, near Tacloban, where we have just landed. It will be the
first letter from the free Philippines and I thought you might
like to add it to your [stamp] collection." He closed the letter by
urging that the Philippines gain their independence as quickly as
possible following the liberation, and urged FDR to preside over
the ceremony personally.[22]

Before laying his head on his pillow, this commander of nearly
two hundred thousand men read two of his favorite passages
from his old family Bible and said a brief prayer asking the Lord
for the impossible: to safeguard every one of those men about to
go into combat.[23]

CHAPTER FIVE

"In The Dragon's Jaws"

During July 1944, the Japanese Imperial General Headquarters wrestled with the question of where to expect an American invasion after the fall of New Guinea. As their strategists in Tokyo saw it, there were four possible places for enemy landings. The result of this uncertainty was the development of a master defense plan dependent primarily on airpower called Sho-Go, or Victory Operation, with four subplans. Sho-Go-1 was to defend against MacArthur landing in the Philippines, Sho-Go-2 if the American target was Formosa, Sho-Go-3 if it was Kyushu at the southern end of the Home Islands, and Sho-Go-4 if an attack took place at the Kurile Islands at the northern end.[1]

The plan appeared powerful on paper, but never approached the level of the formidable American forces it intended to destroy. To defend against an invasion of the Philippines, Sho-Go-1 consisted of the First Air Fleet (naval land-based) commanded by Vice Admiral Kimpei Teraoka and the Fourth Air Army under Lieutenant General Kyoji Tominaga. Based in Manila, they had a combined strength of roughly 440 aircraft of which 198 were fighters. On Formosa, Vice Admiral Shigeru Fukudome commanded the Second Air Fleet and the Third Air Fleet with 737 aircraft including 223 fighters. Between October 10 and October 14, 516 reinforcement aircraft arrived at Formosa and Manila from air bases in China and Japan as well as an additional 172 transferred from carriers to Formosa.[2]

This complicated plan was born of necessity since the imperial planners could not pinpoint where MacArthur would strike. A diminishing number of available aircraft for both the Imperial Navy and Army also added to its complexity. The combat deaths of hundreds of experienced pilots, especially those familiar with carrier-based operations, exacerbated the strategy. The loss of those carrier pilots prompted the Navy to partially strip its few remaining operational carriers of aircraft and send them to Formosa. It was a risky move because it downgraded the carriers to the function of lightly armed surface vessels. It also minimized the range of the aircraft once they were tied to a land base. Justifying the situation, commander of the Combined Fleet Admiral Soemu Toyoda pointed out that many of the remaining carrier pilots had not completed their training. So, while they could take off from a carrier at sea, "they were not able to successfully always get back to the carrier."[3]

Following its devastating defeat at the Battle of the Philippine Sea in June 1944, in which three of the five participating fleet carriers sank, and over six hundred carrier and land-based aircraft were destroyed, the much-feared Imperial Japanese Navy surface forces withdrew from the area of likely combat to await developments. Vice Admiral Jisaburo Ozawa took the remaining carriers along with two old battleships, several light cruisers, and ten destroyers to Kure Naval Base on the Inland Japanese Sea.

He hoped to locate badly needed aircraft for his carriers and to train new pilots to replace those lost in the Philippine Sea. He was never able to garner more than one hundred carrier planes for his fleet.

Faced with the possibility of fuel shortages, the major surface warships, commanded by Vice Admiral Takeo Kurita, left Kure and sailed to Lingga Anchorage on the east coast of Sumatra. Known as the First Striking Force, it included the world's two largest and most powerful battleships, the *Musashi* and the *Yamato*—each displacing 68,000 tons, five other battleships, ten heavy cruisers, and an assortment of light cruisers and destroyers. Here they could be close to the source of fuel in the Dutch East Indies and have repair work done. In an effort to bolster their capabilities, battleships and cruisers received radar equipment. To improve their defenses against enemy fighters and dive-bombers, extra antiaircraft guns found a home on every ship with available space.[4]

THE AMERICANS contributed to the Japanese confusion with a series of deceptions concerning mostly amphibious operations. On November 3, 1943, the Joint Chiefs requested Lieutenant General Simon Bolivar Buckner Jr., commanding officer of the Alaska Defense Command, to develop a plan that might deceive the Japanese into believing the United States was preparing to launch an invasion of the Kurile Islands from Alaska. They hoped to draw Japanese forces from other theaters to a place they had no intention of invading.[5]

General Buckner's plan instituted a growing radio traffic that would lead Japanese intelligence specialists to predict that American and Canadian forces shipped to the American base at Attu in Alaska's Aleutian Islands intended to invade two of the Kurile Islands, Shimushu and Paramushiro. The deception included issuing arctic clothing to American troops passing through the Seattle area in case Japanese spies were watching. Named Operation Wedlock, the deception succeeded in convincing the enemy to enhance their troop level in the Kuriles from twenty-five thousand in late 1943 to seventy thousand by the fall of 1944, and to begin building massive defense facilities. They also increased their airpower in the Kuriles from 38 planes to 590. Japanese intelligence reports indicated that the American buildup reached 100,000 men from five infantry divisions that were in truth nonexistent. The 108th, the 119th, the 130th, the 141st, and the 157th composed the phantom force.[6]

Japanese listening posts continued picking up and deciphering coded radio traffic indicating the movement of troops and supplies to Alaska, as well as the assignment of warships to the area. There was even an indication that a fast carrier force left Pearl Harbor for Alaskan waters. The operation to draw away Japanese combat units remained in effect until the end of October 1944, well after MacArthur's forces were on Leyte.[7]

THROUGHOUT SEPTEMBER, aircraft from Admiral Halsey's Third Fleet as well as army land-based planes attacked a wide range of targets from the China coast to the Philippines to suppress enemy airpower that could be used against the invasion fleet.

Just after dawn on Saturday, September 2, aircraft began taking off from the deck of the light carrier USS *San Jacinto*, part of Rear Admiral Ralph E. Davison's Task Group (TG) 38.4. A primary target that day for the ship's torpedo bombers was one of a group known as the Bonin Islands, located some 620 miles directly south of Tokyo. Less than nine square miles, Chichi Jima was an important Imperial Army and Navy base that served as a communications center with long-range radio stations. The island also had a seaplane base and was home for several mine-sweeper, subchaser, and gunboat units. Earlier attacks had failed to destroy the radio towers because the unusually powerful anti-aircraft batteries hidden in the mountainous terrain drove them off. During the attack that morning by four torpedo bombers and several Hellcat fighters, the plane piloted by twenty-year-old Lieu-tenant (jg) George Bush swept in over the heavy enemy flak and headed for the radio towers. Before reaching his target, Bush's plane received several hits and immediately caught fire. Rather than turn away he managed to reach the target and dropped his payload. He then turned his burning aircraft out to sea and warned his two crewmen to prepare to bail out. Bush's two crew-men were lost, but a nearby submarine rescued the pilot. He received the Distinguished Flying Cross for his actions that day, his fifty-seventh mission. Bush went on to become the forty-first president of the United States.[8]

One week later, the primary targets of Halsey's carriers were air bases on the island of Mindanao. On September 12, the Americans attacked air bases in the central Philippine Islands known as the Visayas. Two days later, they returned to Mindanao. Intelligence reported the destruction of over two hundred Japanese aircraft in the attacks, most while still on the ground. That night, additional aircraft arrived from Manila to bolster Mindanao's defenses, but once again, over two hundred Japanese planes faced destruction on the ground or in the air. On the fourteenth, American pilots reported no enemy opposition in the air and could find barely a dozen planes on the ground to destroy. The bulk of these aircraft were destined to be used to attack MacArthur's landing forces and were now nonexistent.[9]

The area around Manila and Manila Bay came under intense attack from the carrier force on September 21 and 22. After a one-day break, the Americans returned to the Visayas. The attacking pilots were surprised at the lack of airborne resistance they faced, especially around Manila. The weeklong series of attacks had destroyed 1,000 aircraft and sunk 150 ships of all types.[10]

ANOTHER ATTEMPT to deceive the Japanese took place on October 9 at a remote coral-ringed tiny island in the northwestern Pacific known as Marcus Island. Located 1,148 miles southeast of Tokyo, the one-square-mile, triangular-shaped island was home to a 742-man naval guard unit commanded by Rear Admiral Masata Matsubara and 2,005 army troops of the 12th Independent Mixed Regiment under the command of Colonel Yoshiichi Sakata. Three infantry battalions formed the core of Sakata's force, which also included a field gun company manning three 75mm guns, a tank company with nine type 95 light tanks, and a signal company. A single airstrip ran across the entire width of the broadest section of the island. Aside from occasional bombing raids from American aircraft, the island and its well-defended beaches lined with trenches remained isolated from the war. Using a narrow channel cut in the coral, submarines made regular supply runs.

That semi-peaceful existence was about to change with the arrival of the United States Navy TG 30.2 commanded by Rear Admiral Allan E. Smith. Comprising three heavy cruisers, *Chester*, *Salt Lake City*, and *Pensacola*, as well as six destroyers, *David*

W. Taylor, Cummings, Ellet, Dunlap, Fanning, and *Roe,* their assignment was to shell the island from dawn to dusk "with great fanfare," to convince the enemy it was a prelude to an amphibious landing by American troops. Floats with dummy radar targets lifted from the ships into the skies, and smoke bombs exploded on the horizon to give the impression of another approaching fleet. By day's end, the warships had fired 889 8-inch shells and 1,933 5-inch shells and received heavy and sustained fire from the Japanese forces on the island. Despite this, there was no damage to any of the ships.[11]

The deception might have worked had not another incident attracted Japanese attention. A few minutes before 9 a.m. on the very same day, October 9, a Japanese naval patrol plane from the Kanoya Naval Air Base in southern Kyushu vanished while patrolling the Pacific to the east. When the aircraft did not respond to radio calls, the commander of the Sasebo Naval District, Vice Admiral Teruhisa Komatsu, assumed an enemy plane from a nearby aircraft carrier had shot down the craft. He quickly sent a message to naval units in Kyushu, the southernmost of the Home Islands, and the Ryukyu Islands, the chain of islands including the largest island in the chain, Okinawa. The warning declared there might be an American carrier force approaching. In fact, an army bomber from Tinian in the Mariana Islands downed the patrol plane and the nearest American carriers were 225 miles away.[12]

Despite Admiral Komatsu's warning, the forces on the Ryukyus were ill prepared for what Admiral Halsey's Third Fleet was about to throw at them. Halsey's goal was to destroy as much of the enemy's airpower as possible before MacArthur's troops landed at Leyte, preferably while they were still on the ground. He wanted the United States Navy to own the skies over the landing sites. Halsey's powerful fleet included four Task Force (TF) 38 Fast Carrier Groups commanded by Vice Admiral Marc Mitscher. The four groups had a total of nine fleet carriers, eight light carriers, five battleships, four heavy cruisers, ten light cruisers, fifty-eight destroyers, and a large assortment of auxiliary vessels such as oilers and tugboats. The task group commanding officers were TG 38.1 Vice Admiral John S. McCain, TG 38.2 Rear Admiral Gerald F. Bogan, TG 38.3 Rear Admiral Frederick C. Sherman, and TG 38.4 Rear Admiral Ralph E. Davison.[13]

In the early morning hours of October 10, aircraft from the Third Fleet swept over Okinawa and several of the nearby islands, most of which contained military airfields. The 1,396 sorties flown against the island cost the enemy over one hundred aircraft and several dozen ships, including midget submarines, mine-sweepers, and at least four cargo ships. American losses were twenty-one aircraft. The Balao-class submarine *Sterlet* rescued six of the downed airmen. This was the closest American aircraft had come to the Japanese Home Islands since the Doolittle Raid in April 1942.[14]

The following day, aircraft from TG 38.1 and TG 38.4 conducted raids against the Engano airfield and shipping in the bay near the municipality of Aparri on the northern tip of Luzon. With only sixty aircraft involved, the raids were enough to keep the enemy grounded. Confusion about where the big American strike would be remained as well. Meanwhile the main body of TF 38 received fuel and replacement planes and pilots.[15]

Halsey now turned his attention to Formosa, where Japanese naval air forces—a threat to the landing force—were based. With fueling operations completed a few minutes before 6 p.m. on the eleventh, the entire Task Force turned north-northwest from their fueling position and raced toward Formosa at 24 knots. They were anxious for the carriers to reach their assigned positions, some fifty to ninety miles east of Formosa, and launch their one thousand aircraft before dawn exposed their position and strength. A few minutes before three o'clock that morning, a flight of Japanese radar equipped Kawanishi H6K5 Type 97 reconnaissance aircraft from the 901st Flying Boat unit found four large groups of enemy ships. They reported the enemy's presence about 160 miles southwest of Cape Garambi at the southernmost tip of Formosa to the Takao Naval Guard District on Formosa. The District commander, Vice Admiral Fukuda Ryozo, issued an alert concerning the approaching enemy fleet.[16]

One hundred and ten miles off the southeast coast of China is the 190-mile-long and 50-mile-wide island of Formosa. The island resumed the pre-Japanese occupation name of Taiwan following the war. In 1544 Portuguese sailors, surveying the island from their ship, called it "Ilha Formosa," which translates to Beautiful Island. Because of this, most Westerners referred to the island as Formosa until the end of the Second World War. During the seventeenth century, Spanish and Dutch colonists occupied portions of the island until the Dutch drove off the former in 1642. Forces from China's Ming Dynasty, in turn, ousted the Dutch, in 1662. The Ming rule lasted twenty-one years until the Qing Dynasty took control. Following the April 1895 Qing defeat by the Empire of Japan in the First Sino-Japanese War, the island was ceded to the Japanese. Resistance by local Qing forces resulted in establishing the Republic of Formosa in May 1895. By October of that year, the nearly one hundred thousand Japanese troops sent to the island defeated the Republican forces and began an occupation that lasted until 1945. The Japanese reverted to the name given the island by Westerners, Formosa.

The Japanese did all in their power to instill in the Formosans a feeling of belonging to the Japanese Empire. This included a new education system and the encouragement of altering family names to Japanese names. During the Second World War over two hundred thousand Formosans served in the emperor's armed forces. The island became the strongest permanent Japanese base outside of the Home Islands with over thirty major military airfields.[17]

The importance of Formosa to Japan was made obvious by the fact that most of the Fourteenth Army troops that invaded the Philippines in December 1941, as well as the air forces that bombed American bases on Luzon, were from Formosa.[18]

Although the Japanese expected an attack from the American fleet, they did not expect it so soon. In fact, Admiral Toyoda, commander of the Combined Fleet, had left Tokyo for an inspection tour of the Naval Air Service units first on Luzon then Formosa. His deputy chief of staff, Rear Admiral Toshitane Takata, a naval air expert who was attempting to completely restructure the Japanese Naval Air Service, accompanied Toyoda. This effort came on the heels of their costly defeat at the Battle of the Philippine Sea, which he considered a "total loss" in experienced carrier pilot strength.[19]

Also joining Toyoda was Captain Mitsuo Fuchida, who had earned an empire-wide reputation as the lead pilot in the attacks on Pearl Harbor and Darwin, Australia. The two experienced officers were evidently there to lend support to the instructions Toyoda delivered to the pilots from Imperial General Headquarters: that their primary goal when an enemy invasion fleet approached was to sink transports and not attack warships. This was a radical change in naval doctrine, as pilot training had always focused on sinking warships. Toyoda probably needed the assistance of Takata and Fuchida because he was not highly regarded by many in the Navy due to his lack of combat experience. There was concern at headquarters that the change in combat doctrine might have a demoralizing effect on the pilots who wanted the glory of sinking powerful enemy ships and not just transport vessels.[20]

Admiral Toyoda and his party left Manila and flew to Formosa on October 9. They met with navy pilots and their officers that evening and planned to fly on to Japan the next morning. Their flight scheduled for early the next morning failed to take off when word reached the airfield about the attacks on Okinawa, which was in their flight path home. They remained on Formosa.

Toyoda was at his temporary headquarters at Shinchiku Airfield in northern Formosa when Admiral Ryozo issued his alert. In fact, Toyoda was in a predawn bath to prepare for a day he knew was going to be difficult when aircraft from the USS *Bunker Hill* attacked the airfield. Torpedo bombers from the USS *Intrepid* soon joined them. Dripping with soapy water, Toyoda threw on a bathrobe and rubber-soled sandals and ran into the operations room shouting, "Chase them! Chase them!"[21]

Meanwhile, once the bombing began, Admiral Fukudome moved his headquarters to an underground cave outfitted as a command center. An hour later American bombs destroyed the administration building in which he had been working.[22]

Fukudome ordered all available fighter aircraft into the air to attack the incoming enemy. All 230 planes on Formosa took to flight. As he watched the sky filling with aircraft of various types, he saw what he thought were American planes falling to the ground in flames. "Well done! Well done!" he cried as he clapped his hands in approval. The admiral's demeanor quickly changed when he realized the planes crashing in flames were not American, but his own. He later described the situation: "Our fighters were nothing but so many eggs thrown at a stone wall of the indomitable enemy formation."[23]

With communications between Toyoda and Tokyo headquarters unreliable, it fell to his chief of staff, Vice Admiral Ryunosuke Kusaka, to issue the orders to execute Sho-Go-1 and Sho-Go-2, which he did on the morning of October 12. He sent additional instructions to Admiral Ozawa to send his newly reformed air units to Okinawa under the command of Admiral Fukudome. Ozawa was not happy about losing the small air force he had worked so hard to rebuild. His carriers were now virtually without any aircraft so he would begin again to try to acquire some.

Over the next three days, the United States Navy's Third Fleet and the Imperial Navy and Army air forces on and around Formosa fought a grueling battle that Admiral Halsey described as a "knock-down drag-out fight between carrier air and shore-based air."[24]

At six that first morning, all four task groups launched aircraft for a fighter sweep across the length and breadth of Formosa to drive out any enemy fighters that dared to meet them. The Japanese did take to the air, but unfortunately for them, their air fleet included less-experienced pilots with incomplete training and no actual combat experience. Their training included watching films of simulated air warfare. Many of the American pilots had the experience of the Philippine Sea battle behind them. The first wave of American fighters found the Japanese forewarned and over two hundred fighters loomed in the sky. The one-sided dog-fights sent at least one-third of Fukudome's navy and army pilots to their graves. Their ranks thinned so dramatically, the second American wave encountered less than forty Japanese fighters. Ground support facilities and ships became their primary targets. By the time the third wave of attacks arrived, there were no enemy aircraft to challenge them, although antiaircraft shooting had improved. On that first day, Third Fleet aircraft flew 1,378 sorties, annihilating over one hundred Japanese planes in the air and on the ground at a cost to the Americans of forty-eight aircraft.[25]

Rear Admiral Sherman reported on the fourth and final strike of the day by aircraft from his Task Group 38.3, which included the fleet carriers *Essex* and *Lexington,* and the light carriers *Princeton* and *Langley.* He made note of the increasingly bad weather that hampered visibility and reported his planes focused on ships, railroad facilities, rolling stock, and smaller airfields discovered to be hiding a few enemy planes.[26]

Admirals Toyoda and Fukudome ordered planes to Formosa from wherever they were. That evening Fukudome called out a special force comprised of navy and army pilots with special training for night attacks as well as attacks in bad weather. This was the Typhoon Attack Force, or TAF, which was equipped with mostly torpedo attack bombers. He had decided it was time to stop relying on defense and take the fight to the enemy ships. Admiral Fukudome considered the TAF "the cream of my fleet strength."[27]

Late that afternoon over one hundred planes lifted off from fields on Kyushu and Okinawa. In command of the TAF was Captain Shuzo Kuno, who Fukudome described as one of the last of the surviving first-rate veterans among the senior naval aviators. The force's mission was to fly directly to the American carriers and launch their torpedoes and bombs in darkness on their unsuspecting targets. This was the first time American ships came under attack by planes using Air Mark VI radar although the Americans knew the equipment existed. US troops first discovered abandoned sections of it at Hollandia, on New Guinea and on Saipan. This radar made it much more difficult for combat air patrols to protect their ships because it operated at frequencies below that covered by American jamming equipment.[28]

On completion, the TAF was to land at airfields on Formosa. Captain Kuno complained that his valuable aircraft would be subjected to bombing and strafing the next day and requested they find a better place to house his planes during the daylight. His request was rejected.

As darkness enveloped the ships of the Third Fleet, the TAF aircraft sped toward their targets. The Imperial Navy pilots were flying Mitsubishi G4M twin-engine medium bombers, known as "Betty" to the Americans. The army pilots were flying twin-engine medium bombers previously unknown to the Americans, Mitsubishi Ki-67s that were soon nicknamed "Peggy." Heavy rain hindered the effectiveness of their aiming as they tried to fend off the defending Hellcat night fighters from the USS *Independence* and USS *Cabot*.[29]

Generating smoke to cover their positions, the warships maneuvered to keep the attackers astern and make smaller torpedo targets while the Hellcats made good use of their onboard radars to blast the bombers from the sky. In all, between the night fighters and the antiaircraft fire from the surface vessels, forty-two of the attackers plunged into the sea, leaving the American warships unscathed. A destroyer from TG 38.4 on picket duty unwittingly mistook the destroyer *Pritchett* from TG 38.3 for an enemy ship and put it under heavy 40mm machine-gun fire. Explosive shells pierced the hull and several bulkheads and entered the Combat Information Center. Sixteen crew members were injured, one fatally. Despite some structural damage, the *Pritchett* remained on duty for three days then sailed to Manus in the Admiralties for repairs.[30]

At dawn the following day, October 13, fighters raced off the American flattops with a low cloud ceiling and heavy rainsqualls and hit targets throughout Formosa and the nearby Pescadores Islands off the Formosan coast. The number of Japanese planes that rose to defend the empire was substantially less than the previous day. Targets for the American pilots were primarily ground installations that supported the air services. These included hangars, fuel and ammunition storage facilities, repair shops, and parked or disabled aircraft. They flew 974 sorties for the day. Task Force commander Admiral Mitscher restricted that day's attacks to three instead of the original planned four because he wanted all aircraft safely aboard the carriers when the radar-equipped night raiders returned, as he was sure they would. Only combat air patrol Hellcats took off after 2 p.m. in the afternoon. Pilots on the third wave of the day reported the sky over the targets empty of enemy planes.[31]

At 4:30 that afternoon, radar operators reported a flight of unidentified aircraft approaching the American fleet from the south at approximately seventy miles out. Interceptors rushed out to investigate. The ships of the four task groups maneuvered into the antiaircraft disposition, known as Special Cruising Disposition 5-Victor, to prepare to battle the incoming enemy. Fighters from the *Enterprise* shot down six of the approaching enemy. Over the next few hours as both darkness and rainsqualls reduced everyone's visibility, the radar-equipped TAF planes led others into the fleet in small groups of from one to three planes. Once again, the ships attempted to cover themselves by making smoke and radical maneuvering.[32]

One ship that came in for special attention by the Japanese attackers was Admiral Davison's flagship, the fleet carrier *Franklin*. Five of the Imperial Navy "Bettys" made passes at the huge ship while it was in the process of landing eight of its combat air patrol aircraft for refueling and restocking ammunition. Spacing themselves about one minute apart, the Japanese twin-engine bombers raced at the carrier flying less than one hundred feet above the water. Nearby destroyers turned their guns on the first enemy plane and forced the pilot to veer away from his target. The carrier's 40mm guns hit the next attacker several times, setting it ablaze. When his burning aircraft was about five hundred yards from his target, the pilot released a torpedo, which passed harmlessly under the ship's stern. The flaming aircraft crashed onto the carrier's flight deck just behind the vessel's island, slid across the deck, and splashed into the sea where it exploded. As it fell from the deck pieces of the plane caused minor damage to three 20mm guns. The following two attacking planes were shot down, while the final one headed toward the *Franklin*'s bow and fired its torpedo. The ship simultaneously turned away and reversed to allow the racing missile to pass fewer than fifty feet from the bow. The plane, burning fiercely, exploded as it passed over the bow and plummeted into the water.[33]

At about 6:30 another group of ten enemy bombers, this time Imperial Navy twin-engine Yokosuka P1Y Gingas, known as "Frances" to the Americans, focused their attention on the two fleet carriers and three light carriers of Admiral McCain's TG 38.1. Their arrival was a surprise since they were flying so close to the water that the ship radars did not detect them. With visual contact made, every ship in the task group opened fire on them. In quick succession, three of the bombers were set afire or exploded from the impact of the antiaircraft shells and crashed without harming any ships. Four others managed to avoid serious damage, although the heavy defensive fire forced them from their target, the carrier *Wasp*. They headed directly toward Captain Alexander

R. Early's heavy cruiser *Canberra*. Defensive fire from the ship downed three of them, but the fourth kept on coming despite numerous hits. Before crashing some 1,500 yards astern of the cruiser, the pilot launched his torpedo. This aircraft typically carried an eighteen-foot-long Type 91 torpedo with approximately 500 pounds of high explosives in its warhead. It struck the starboard side of the hull about eighteen feet below the waterline and just below the ship's armor belt.[34]

The *Canberra* was unusual in that it was the only United States Navy warship named for a foreign ship and a foreign city. It was President Roosevelt's idea as a way to honor the Australian Allies and remember the HMAS *Canberra* that fought alongside US Navy ships and was lost in the battle of Savo Island.

The torpedo pierced the hull and exploded in a fireball that shot up the side of the ship to the height of its mast as 4,500 tons of seawater poured into its engine rooms, bringing the vessel to a stop and killing twenty-three members of the crew instantly. It was dead in the water and a sitting duck for Japanese pilots.

Aboard his flagship, the battleship *New Jersey*, Admiral Halsey received word of the cruiser's condition at a little after 6:30 as he was preparing to order the Third Fleet to withdraw from the area and make ready to cover General MacArthur's landings on Leyte. The admiral and his staff looked over the chart covering the cruiser's position. It did not look good. The *Canberra* was 1,300 miles from the nearest allied base at Ulithi in the Caroline Islands. To make matters worse, the ship was 90 miles from Formosa, 300 miles from Aparri Airfield on Luzon, and 400 miles from Naha Field on Okinawa, all capable of sending Japanese aircraft after the wounded ship. That was when Halsey realized the cruiser was "squarely in the Jap dragon's jaws and the dragon knew it."[35]

In the meantime, Admiral McCain, TG 38.1 commander, ordered another of his ships, the heavy cruiser *Wichita*, to close with the *Canberra* and prepare to take it in tow if that was Halsey's decision. Every senior officer in the battleship's bridge knew that accepted procedure in such a situation was to remove the surviving crew and sink the cruiser so it did not fall into enemy hands. That did not sit right with the admiral they called "Bull." He ordered the light cruiser *Houston* to separate from Admiral Bogan's TG 38.2 and join McCain's TG 38.1, which was now short two cruisers. Halsey was going to take the gamble that he could save that cruiser, and keep the enemy away from it long enough for it to be out of their range. At less than 4 mph, which was the maximum speed the *Wichita* could make pulling the *Canberra* along, it was going to be some time before they reached relative safety—and thirteen days before they reached Ulithi.[36]

To relieve the *Wichita* for combat duty, Halsey ordered the fleet tug *Munsee*, commanded by Lieutenant Commander John F. Pingley, to take up responsibility for towing the *Canberra* to Ulithi. When the tug took over towing the cruiser, it put a salvage crew aboard to help the cruiser's crew begin making repairs. Their first objective was to make temporary repairs to the hull and begin pumping the seawater out. As work progressed, the *Munsee*'s salvage officer, Ensign P. S. Criblet, died while diving inside the flooded engine room to inspect repairs made to leaks in preparation for pumping out the compartment. The accident added one more sailor to the list of those who died because of the attack on the *Canberra*.[37]

Halsey then changed the Third Fleet's plans for the following day: instead of leaving the area near Formosa, he instructed all carriers to make fighter sweeps of airfields on Formosa and Luzon to keep enemy activity down. Meanwhile Admiral Fukudome had received several hundred replacement aircraft and committed them to the fight for Formosa. Most of the pilots manning these planes had not even completed their training. The Imperial Naval Air Service was scraping the bottom of the barrel.

On the morning of October 14, fighters launched off the decks of every Third Fleet carrier and swept the skies over Formosa and Luzon of the few enemy planes that rose up to meet them. The objective was to suppress Japanese airpower expected to attack the slow-moving *Canberra* and *Munsee* and the cruisers and destroyers Halsey had assigned to escort them. Contact with the enemy was minimal until the early evening, when imperial warplanes swarmed around the perimeter of the task force ships and began attacking. Once again, experience counted as combat air patrol fighters reported downing seventy-five enemy planes that approached the ships they were protecting. Halsey's diary for the day states that his pilots reported to have shot down eleven aircraft over land targets and destroyed fifty-five on the ground; shipboard antiaircraft fire accounted for another twenty-one.[38]

The day brought a gift courtesy of the United States Army Air Forces from Xinjin Airport in the southwestern section of the Chinese city of Chengdu in Sichuan Province. The gift consisted of 118 B-29 Superfortresses of the 58th Bombardment Wing of Major General Curtis E. LeMay's Twentieth Air Force. The four-engine heavy bombers dropped 675 tons of bombs on an aircraft maintenance facility at Okayama about twenty miles north of Takao and the harbor facilities at Takao. Returning bomber pilots reported no enemy fighter opposition and described ground anti-aircraft fire as "meager and inaccurate."[39]

Determined to smash the enemy fleet, Admiral Fukudome managed to assemble several hundred planes, mainly from the Home Islands, Okinawa, and bases in China, to enable him to launch large-scale attacks on the ships in the early evening. Among these were the remnants of the TAF force. A great many never made it past the antiaircraft guns of the picket ships and the fighters of the combat air patrols. One that did was a twin-engine bomber racing toward the light cruiser *Houston*, which Halsey had sent to replace *Canberra* in TG 38.1. Because it was flying too low for the ship's radar to detect, the aircraft was only two thousand yards out from the cruiser's forward starboard when the gun crews saw it and opened fire. Despite several hits, the enemy plane kept coming at full speed until it reached 1,500 yards distance and the pilot launched his torpedo. At 6:45 p.m., the torpedo smashed into it amidships when the cruiser proved unable to turn away fast enough. Two other enemy planes headed for the *Houston* and fired their torpedoes, but neither hit home. All three planes were shot down by the ship's gunners. Pillars of steam rose from the cruiser's two smokestacks as both the forward and aft engine rooms and electric power went off. The warship was dead in the water with only emergency power functioning.

Because it was turning when the torpedo hit, the ship started listing to starboard as seawater filled the lower spaces and the crew's efforts to seal up portions proved unsuccessful. The reports Captain William W. Behrens received were spotty but indicated the ship was perilously close to turning over and sinking. At 8:30, he decided to issue an order to abandon ship while damage control efforts continued. Nearby destroyers closed in and managed to take 752 sailors and officers from among the 1,255 crew members aboard in the next one and a half hours. Meanwhile, Captain Behrens ordered the executive officer, damage control officer, and gunnery officer to inspect various sections of the lower decks and report to him. Their conclusion was that the ship was not in immediate danger of sinking. At 10 p.m., Behrens canceled further abandoning efforts and the damage control crews among the men still aboard the cruiser continued to make what temporary repairs they could. One half hour later the heavy cruiser *Boston* took the *Houston* in tow and gradually moved southeast to get out of range of the enemy planes.[40]

Aboard his flagship, *New Jersey*, Admiral Halsey was in a difficult situation. He had two seriously disabled cruisers under tow by two other cruisers moving at less than 4 mph while waiting for the tugboats to meet them. The tug *Pawnee* was on its way to take over the job of getting the *Houston* to safety. Halsey was concerned that the four ships would remain sitting ducks unable to maneuver if Japanese aircraft attacked. He was also anxious to fulfill his commitment to General MacArthur that the Third Fleet would provide plenty of air cover for his landings at Leyte on the twentieth. Trying to protect these two ships could hamper his ability to carry out his promise to MacArthur.

Halsey's inclination was to cut his losses, sink the two damaged cruisers, and head toward the Philippines to begin quelling enemy airpower on Luzon. During a conference with his staff, he was convinced the Third Fleet could spare a few ships to protect the cruisers returning to Ulithi and still meet its obligations to the Army. As a result, he created a new task group, called 30.3, under Rear Admiral Lloyd J. Wiltse, specifically for that purpose. His command consisted of two light carriers, *Cowpens* and *Cabot*, six cruisers, twelve destroyers, two fleet tugs, and the two crippled cruisers. Rear Admiral Wiltse's flag was on the *Boston*.

IMPERIAL NAVY pilots flying from bases on Formosa conducted daytime attacks, while night raids launched from Kyushu made greater use of army pilots. These pilots were not only less experienced, but had minimal training in bombing and torpedo-ing moving targets, and especially in identifying the type of ship they attacked. Admiral Fukudome found that among these army pilots, even those in the elite TAF, "there was virtually no one...who could tell exactly which ship was of what type." He asked each of these pilots if they had ever seen a submarine: "There were many who never had."[41]

Because of this poor training, the pilots reported a destroyer as a cruiser, a cruiser as a battleship or even an aircraft carrier. Their reports were, in the words of Fukudome, "inclined to be exaggerated."[42]

A former US Army historian described the reports of these inexperienced pilots: "A near miss becomes a hit; a hit becomes a fatal blow. Two or more planes attacking a single target might each claim to have struck a different ship. Sometimes the bursting of a bomb or the flare of antiaircraft fire was mistaken for a shipboard explosion."[43]

Arriving back at Kyushu, the excited surviving pilots told of sinking and damaging a great number of enemy ships. In fact, it appeared to officers at the Imperial General Headquarters that the attacking aircraft had destroyed most if not all the warships in the enemy fleet. This self-deluding information even reached the emperor himself who congratulated the Army and Navy on their great success. He then declared a national holiday to celebrate the victory. It was the first such holiday in over two years.[44]

Radio Tokyo reported the glorious pilots of the emperor had sunk eleven enemy carriers, or nineteen, depending on which report listeners chose to believe, along with two battleships and three cruisers. Many others were floating in flames. It seemed as if each successive report grew in exaggeration until the radio told the nation "the enemy task forces lost the majority of their strength and were put to rout."[45]

Japanese newspapers outdid the radio broadcasts with headlines that screamed, "Desperately Fleeing Enemy Warships Completely Destroyed," and "Triumphal Song Rings."[46]

Authorities reported that during the battle of Formosa, the Imperial Navy had sunk over 500,000 tons of shipping, destroying "60 percent of America's effective naval strength," and that twenty-six thousand American sailors perished.[47]

In the view of Admiral Fukudome, these greatly exaggerated claims resulted in the Imperial General Headquarters arriving at an erroneous estimate of the current war situation and the future. It also "made the nation indulge in a false celebration and created the illusion that the empire could turn the tide of the war."[48]

When Halsey and his staff listened to the English language broadcast of Tokyo Rose proclaiming the great victory, they were dumbfounded. They knew the truth: of the hundreds of Japanese aircraft that had attacked the fleet in the last few days, many crashed into the sea. The only serious damage inflicted on the Third Fleet was that to the *Canberra* and *Houston*, both of which were in tow to safety. Then Rose said something startling. She revealed that the Navy High Command had ordered a fleet out from the Inland Sea to destroy the "remnants" of Halsey's fleet. This is the kind of information considered a valuable top secret, yet the Japanese were telling the world they were sending a fleet to attack whatever was left of the American task force.

INCREASINGLY CONCERNED about supporting MacArthur's landings on Leyte on the twentieth, Halsey was again leaning toward sinking the two American cruisers and "run beyond the range of the Japs' shore-based-air before a worse disaster struck us." But his staff, led by chief of staff Rear Admiral Robert "Mick" Carney, convinced him otherwise. They reasoned that if the Japanese believed—as they seemed to—that the small division protecting the two injured cruisers, what the wags were calling CripDiv 1, was all that was left of the Third Fleet, they might be able to use that misconception to their advantage and lure the enemy fleet steaming from the Inland Sea into a trap. Halsey, always a fan of pulling dirty tricks on the enemy, liked the idea. He ordered most of his ships to sail east just over the horizon and out of sight of enemy reconnaissance planes. He added a few more ships to what they were now calling BaitDiv 1, since those ships were now bait to lure the enemy within range of the carrier aircraft, and instructed Admiral Wiltse to fill the airwaves with distress messages that would make his force appear to be an easy target. In the meantime, Halsey sent Nimitz a message telling him, "The Third Fleet's sunken and damaged ships have been salvaged and are retiring at high speed toward the enemy."[49]

Vice Admiral Kiyohide Shima, commanding officer of the 2nd Diversionary Attack Force, steamed from the Inland Sea with two heavy cruisers, one light cruiser, and seven destroyers. East of Okinawa, Shima stopped to take on fuel. Then, depending on whose report you believe, his force came under attack by two carrier-based American aircraft, indicating to him the enemy still had carriers at sea, or a reconnaissance plane caught site of the American fleet and reported it to Shima. When Halsey received word the fleet had turned back to the Inland Sea, he was disappointed. He was hoping for a clash with enemy ships that would destroy a portion of what was left of the imperial fleet, but would have to wait for another day.

The ships of BaitDiv 1 came under several attacks by enemy

aircraft flying out of Formosa. Antiaircraft gunners and pilots from the two light carriers shot most of them down. One did manage to get through the protective screen and put a second torpedo into the *Houston*. At first it appeared to be a fatal blow, but the hard work of the damage control crews kept it afloat. At the other end of its towline, the tug *Pawnee* flashed a signal, telling the cruiser, "We'll stand by you." The tough little ship did and the two damaged cruisers arrived at their destination on October 27.[50]

HALSEY'S "KNOCK-DOWN drag-out fight" came at a heavy cost for the Japanese Empire. It came close to eliminating the Naval Air Service and most of its trained carrier pilots. Over five hundred Japanese planes were lost, as were several hundred ships of varying sizes. But the most costly loss was the pilots with carrier experience or training. These pilots and their aircraft would not be available to provide air cover for the imperial fleet in the coming naval battles around the Philippines. The battle cost the Third Fleet less than ninety aircraft and seriously damaged two cruisers. Rescue submarines plucked many of the pilots from the sea.

CHAPTER SIX

The "Special Attack Corps"

Throughout Japan's history, its warriors were often eager to sacrifice their lives for their emperor. Suicide missions by Japanese aircraft pilots and officers on midget submarines were not an entirely new phenomenon by the time the Philippines became the number one target of the Allies. There were several instances of pilots attempting to crash their planes into US warships with some limited success. None of these were planned or ordered by competent commanders, but were spur-of-the-moment decisions made by the pilots themselves. Since none of them survived, we have no clear understanding of why they chose to do what they did other than to die for their emperor.

One of the earliest recorded suicide missions to attack American ships was on September 13, 1944, although there is no indication it was successful. Author John Toland reports that several Imperial Army pilots belonging to the 31st Fighter Squadron on the Philippine island of Negros decided on their own volition to strap 100kg bombs to two of their aircraft. Taking off just before dawn,

First Lieutenant Takeshi Kosai and the second pilot vanished after takeoff. Since there were no reports of a plane crashing into American Navy warships that day, it is likely both fell victim to enemy patrol aircraft.[1]

The turn to officially sanctioned suicide missions by Japanese pilots was a sure sign of desperation. Attacks on US Navy carrier task forces proved unproductive since these most valuable targets were defended by a large array of ships with antiaircraft guns as well as their own aircraft flying defensive patrols above them.

The man responsible for sending so many Imperial Navy pilots—for most suicide pilots were navy flyers—to their deaths was Vice Admiral Takijiro Onishi. In July 1944, Onishi was already advocating what he called "body-crashing" into Allied ships and B-29 bombers. He claimed that pilots who would conduct such attacks were "god-like soldiers."[2]

Onishi called these men "Shimpu" although they became more infamous to Westerners as "kamikaze." Both versions originate with Japanese translations of "divine wind," based on two incidents occurring in the thirteenth century. In the first, the Mongol emperor Kublai Khan, grandson of Genghis Khan, sent an invasion fleet estimated between five hundred and nine hundred ships carrying forty thousand men to force the Japanese emperor to submit to rule by the Mongols. After initially defeating the defending Japanese troops, the Mongols withdrew to their ships anchored in Hakata Bay to prepare for the next day. However, during the night a powerful typhoon struck the bay and sank most of the Mongol ships, taking tens of thousands of soldiers to the bottom. The few remaining ships sailed away.

The khan ordered a new and larger fleet built for his next attempt to conquer Japan. In the meantime, the Japanese were busy constructing seven-foot-high walls along the coast to prevent an invasion. In 1281 over four thousand Mongol ships with over one hundred thousand troops entered Hakata Bay and searched for a landing site. They searched in vain for a place to go ashore, until on August 14 they once again fell victim to a large typhoon that devastated the fleet, forcing the surviving ships to withdraw. In Japanese mythology, the two storms were a divine wind sent by the gods in response to the prayers of the Japanese emperor.

Once Onishi formalized the suicide missions, the Tokyo propaganda machine began referring to the pilots as the "Divine Wind," a force that would once again drive away an enemy fleet attacking the homeland. Despite opposition from several other admirals, Onishi wasted no time when he arrived on Luzon as the new commander of the First Air Fleet charged with defending against MacArthur's impending assault. Shocked at finding his fleet had been reduced by enemy air strikes to only about one hundred operational aircraft, the short, stocky naval officer with a reputation for abrasive manners decided he knew how to best use those limited resources. Instead of fighting off enemy aircraft or attacking enemy ships, he would urge his pilots to slam their aircraft onto the flight decks of American aircraft carriers.[3]

Two days after arriving at his new post from Tokyo, Onishi had himself driven to Mabalacat Airfield, part of the former American Clark Field Air Base fifty miles northwest of the capital of Manila. There he met with Commander Asaichi Tamai, the executive officer of the 201st Air Group. The air group's commanding officer, Captain Sakae Yamamoto, was hospitalized with a broken leg, so Tamai was acting commanding officer. Also present were Captain Rikihei Inoguchi, senior staff officer of the First Air Fleet, and several senior pilot officers of the air group.

The admiral began in a serious low tone, telling these men what they already knew: the situation for Japan was grave. The

American ships reported off the coast of Leyte was a clear indication that MacArthur was determined to fulfill his pledge to the Filipino people to return and drive the Japanese out. He then explained that the fate of the empire rested on the success of the Sho-Go-1 plan, the defense of the Philippines. He told them that what remained of Japan's main battle fleets were even then sailing toward the Philippines from their anchorages. The First Air Fleet had the privilege of providing air cover for the approaching warships since they no longer had operational carriers capable of doing so. The men in the room and their pilots were to "neutralize" the enemy carriers for at least one week. This was to give Vice Admiral Kurita's fleet with the world's two largest battleships, *Musashi* and *Yamato*, time to reach Leyte Gulf and destroy the American invasion forces.

As they listened to Onishi, the men wondered how they were going to accomplish such a mission with barely one hundred planes against hundreds of enemy aircraft and an unknown number of powerful aircraft carriers. Then the admiral reached the heart of his message. It was his opinion that the only way they could stop the enemy now was through suicide attack units. He proposed to attach 550-pound bombs to Zero fighters and crash them onto the decks of the American carriers to temporarily put them out of service. And so, on that day, the First Shimpu Special Attack Corps was born.[4]

When asked, the pilots of the 201st Air Group all volunteered for the suicide missions. In coming months, kamikaze pilots would be young and inexperienced with minimal training, but enough to enable them to take their bomb-laden aircraft off the ground, fly to a target, and aim the craft at the target's flight deck. But the pilots of the 201st were among the best the Imperial Navy had left after losing nearly a thousand of them the previous June in the Battle of the Philippine Sea, which American pilots called "the great Marianas turkey shoot."

Three days after Onishi's visit to the 201st, the first formal kamikaze mission took off from Mabalacat Airfield in search of the enemy fleet reported approaching Leyte. Commanded by Lieutenant Yukio Seki, they spent several days searching for the enemy without success. On October 25, six Zero fighters that had been stripped of all unnecessary equipment but with a 500-pound bomb attached, along with four Zeros flying escort, found a group of American escort carriers off Samar and attacked. In the resulting forty-minute melee, one escort carrier, *St. Lo*, had its flight deck penetrated by one of the bomb-laden Zeros. The bomb exploded in the hangar belowdecks where sailors were busy refueling and rearming several aircraft. Gasoline was set ablaze which resulted in a series of explosions, including in the bomb storage magazine. In thirty minutes the burning ship sank, taking with it 113 men of its 889-member crew. An additional thirty crew members died from their wounds. Two other escort carriers received damage serious enough to take them out of the war: one, *Kitkun Bay*, for two months; the other, *Kalinin Bay*, never returned to combat.[5]

The Americans who witnessed these first kamikaze attacks were horrified and shaken, but it was only the beginning. Suicide missions by Japanese pilots would quickly become a vital part of the defense of the Philippines, followed later by the defense of Okinawa. Although accurate numbers are hard to come by, it is believed that at least three thousand Japanese pilots gave their lives for the emperor in this way. Some three hundred Allied ships received some level of damage from the planes, with as many as forty-seven sinking through the end of the war.

CHAPTER SEVEN

THE RANGERS AND THE

FROGMEN GO IN FIRST

As MacArthur's invasion fleet approached the Philippines, the first phase of the conquest of Leyte, code-named King II, began on October 17, three days prior to the large-scale landings. At the eastern entrance to Leyte Gulf where it meets the Philippine Sea, Captain Albert M. Bledsoe's light cruiser *Denver* began a shore bombardment with its 6-inch guns at 8 a.m. The target of the shelling was one of the small islands guarding the entrance. American reconnaissance aircraft and Filipino guerrillas identified Suluan Island as harboring a Japanese radio communications center and possibly a search radar unit. The island lay forty-five miles east of the main landing beaches.[1]

The previous night had been rough for the small fleet known as the Dinagat Attack Group (DAG), named for the island group. Typhoon winds had swept through the area causing some of the ships in the group to slow and fall behind. The main invasion fleet, farther out to sea, suffered considerably more damage from the storm—extremely high waters threatened to sweep the landing craft off several warships. The DAG consisted of eight destroyer transports and a collection of other landing craft commanded by Rear Admiral Arthur Struble. Included was the only Royal Navy ship to participate in the invasion, HMS *Ariadne*, a minesweeper serving as a troop transport with three hundred members of the 21st Infantry Regiment aboard. Aboard the remaining DAG ships were the five hundred men of the 6th Ranger Battalion.[2]

The battalion had previously been the 98th Field Artillery Battalion comprising one thousand troops and eight hundred mules. In early 1944, after a year of training in New Guinea during which they saw no combat, the Army decided they had no real need for the mules, so they shipped the animals to the China-Burma-India theater for better utilization. The battalion commander, Lieutenant Colonel J. M. Callicut, transferred to the 1st Cavalry Division.

Lieutenant Colonel Mucci, the battalion commander, had been in charge of a ranger tactics training camp in Hawaii. Mucci announced to the men that he was converting the battalion into a ranger outfit and would need only five hundred volunteers. He transferred many of the artillery-experienced officers and enlisted men to artillery units, keeping just five hundred of the tough mule skinners for his new battalion. They spent the next six months training for just the kind of mission they were embarking on at Leyte Gulf.

The DAG sailed with the protection of a support group commanded by Rear Admiral Robert W. Hayler made up of two light cruisers, *Denver* and *Columbia*, and four destroyers. At 6:30 on the morning of October 17, before the *Denver* started its bombardment, minesweepers began combing the waters around the islands in preparation for the landing of troops. The transports entered the gulf in single file behind three minesweepers, as everyone anticipated that the Japanese had seeded the waterway with mines.

Four companies, A, C, E, and F, plus Headquarters Company personnel and half the 21st Infantry Regiment were to land on Dinagat, the largest of the islands where five hundred enemy troops were believed to be stationed. Company B and some reinforcements from Headquarters Company were to land on Homonhon, and Company D was to land on Suluan where there was a lighthouse the enemy used for watching the gulf and as a communications center.

Japanese lookouts, probably positioned in the lighthouse on Suluan Island, saw them approaching and sent a frantic message to army headquarters in Manila: "The enemy is landing! Long Live the Emperor!" Manila passed the alarm to Admiral Soemu Toyoda, commander of the Combined Fleet, who was in Formosa at the time. Toyoda put Sho-Go-1, the defense plan based on MacArthur landing in the Philippines, into effect. He ordered Vice Admiral Takeo Kurita to prepare his powerful Second Fleet to sail from its anchorage in Borneo to the Philippines. Toyoda was waiting for reports on the sighting of the actual invasion fleet so he knew where in the Philippines to send Kurita. Most imperial planners expected the American landings to take place at Mindanao, the southernmost of the major islands.

When the *Denver* ended its twenty-minute shelling of Suluan Island, the USS *Crosby*, a destroyer that had been converted to a high-speed transport and reclassified as APD-17, lowered its boats for Company D's landing. Company commander First Lieutenant Leslie M. Gray had orders to search the lighthouse and adjacent buildings for any naval charts they could find that might show the locations of underwater mines in the vicinity. Then they were to place navigation lights on the island, destroy any radio or radar equipment they located, and kill or capture the enemy troops stationed there. The men made land about five hundred yards north of the lighthouse in a torrential rain and strong winds that reduced visibility dramatically. The weather meant no air cover from the escort carriers but also kept enemy planes on the ground.[3]

As the Americans made their way to the lighthouse, Japanese resistance was light but determined. An ambush resulted in the death of Private First Class Darwin C. Zufall, later buried in Manila's American Cemetery, and the wounding of Private First Class Donald J. Cannon. They carried the dubious distinction of being the first American ground force casualties of the liberation of the Philippines. A search of the partially destroyed lighthouse and the surrounding buildings failed to locate the navigation charts, but they did destroy radio and radar equipment the enemy had been using. The Rangers killed thirty-two of the enemy garrison that had mostly fled into the nearby bush.[4]

Company D completed its mission on Suluan Island late that afternoon and started back to their landing beach. They discovered the typhoon-driven waters had smashed their plywood landing boats and the radio equipment they'd left aboard was gone. With no radio and the storm limiting visibility to a few yards, they were unable to contact the *Crosby* to explain their situation. Anticipating they might have to spend the night, Lieutenant Gray established a defensive perimeter and waited until someone aboard the ship arrived to investigate their silence.

The following morning, October 18, the weather was gradually clearing, so Gray sent out a patrol in case enemy troops had approached during the night. A brief firefight in some tall grass resulted in five dead Japanese and the wounding of Private First Class Roscoe Dick, who died the next day of his wounds. Soon after, several boats arrived from the nearby destroyer USS *Sands* to return the men to the *Crosby*.[5]

Less than a half hour after Company D landed on Suluan

Island, the men of Companies A, C, E, F, and Company B of the 21st Infantry landed on Dinagat Island. They immediately headed toward a section that juts out into the channel leading to Leyte Gulf called Desolation Point where they planted a powerful navigation light. The invasion convoy would find safe passage by entering the gulf in the fifteen-mile space between the navigation lights planted on Suluan and Dinagat Islands. The Rangers searched for enemy troops but found evidence the Japanese had been there but fled before the Americans arrived. The commanding officer of the Dinagat Island landing force, Major Robert Garrett, sent a message to Admiral Struble indicting no enemy action, but noting the signs the Japanese had been living there. Garrett later learned the Japanese stationed on the island had been killed by a guerrilla force led by US Army Air Forces Captain Truman Heminway. The captain had escaped from Bataan before it fell and was leading a large guerrilla force in Mindanao ever since. He also provided the Rangers with hydrographic charts.[6]

The typhoon-type weather delayed the USS *Herbert*, which was transporting Ranger Company B with orders to land on Homonhon Island across the channel from Dinagat Island. Captain Arthur "Bull" Simons and his men finally got off at nine on the morning of October 18. Filipino civilians greeted their landing and told them there were no Japanese on the island. After patrols confirmed this information, they planted their navigation light on Colasi Point overlooking the channel. Disappointed at not finding any Japanese, one wit quipped, "Here we are with all these goddamn bullets and no Japs."[7]

A week later, a Filipino civilian approached Captain Simons and claimed that Japanese soldiers who had managed to avoid Company D on Suluan Island had returned to the lighthouse to massacre the local population. It took over a week, but Simons finally managed to obtain permission to go to the island. Since there were no landing craft available at the time, his men had native fishermen take them the eight miles in five sailboats. Once on Suluan, local guerrillas showed the Rangers the only approach to the sixty-foot lighthouse that stood on a high cliff overlooking the sea. It was a narrow trail with a long flight of stairs clearly visible to anyone watching from the lighthouse. The only other way up was to climb the nearly sheer coral rock–faced cliff on the west side of the lighthouse. After darkness set in, and leaving most of his men behind to deal with a security force stationed on the trail, Simons and several Rangers and Filipinos climbed hand-over-hand up the cliff that tore at their skin. A chance encounter between a Japanese soldier heading to the latrine and a Filipino set the action in motion. Most of the Japanese died in the ensuing firefight, with several even jumping off the cliff to their deaths. Trapped inside the lighthouse, the remaining Japanese perished when the Rangers set explosives around the base of the building and blew it up. The cost to the Rangers was one dead and two wounded.[8]

WHILE THE Rangers were securing the Dinagat Islands, US Navy Underwater Demolition Teams (UDT), commonly known as frogmen, searched the waters facing the beaches slated for the main landings. Because the typhoon sank several minesweepers and badly damaged others, the frogmen lacked the protection against enemy forces on the beaches that those ships usually provided. Instead, the frogmen needed to rely on a group of larger warships, primarily the battleship USS *Pennsylvania*, to use their heavy guns to force the enemy to stay under cover while the swimmers searched for mines, surveyed the landing beaches for obstacles, and measured water depth. But the threat of mines meant that these larger ships had to stay out of the gulf. They were forced to fire on unseen enemy positions, which meant many areas received little or no shelling.

Japanese snipers hidden among thick undergrowth and in small huts fired on the swimmers, as did mortar crews farther inland. The frogmen had additional problems caused by the muddy water that limited visibility to just a few inches in some sections. Because the water was so turbulent from the previous day's storm, in some places they were unable to take soundings to determine the water depth to prevent larger craft from beaching under enemy guns during the landings.

All along much of the landing beaches, the water was alive with machine-gun bullets and mortar shells as the Japanese did their best to kill the swimmers. The UDT teams succeeded for the most part in gathering the information needed by the landing crews, although they suffered three sailors killed and fourteen wounded.[9]

SEVENTEEN MILES east of Dinagat Island's Desolation Point is a reference point on the naval charts on the approach to Leyte Gulf called Point Fin. The ships of the great armada were to pass through this place on their way into the gulf. Except for the swish of water driven apart by moving bows, the night of October 19 was quiet and very dark, filled as it was with the tension and anxiety produced by over two hundred thousand soldiers and sailors knowing the next day might be their last. Other than several destroyers left inside the gulf to periodically shell known and suspected Japanese positions, the ships were all outside the gulf waiting to make their entrance shortly after midnight.

CHAPTER EIGHT

"A-Day" at Leyte, October 20, 1944

Because the once generic term "D-Day," in the public mind, had come to mean the Normandy landings of the previous June, MacArthur decided to call the Leyte landings "A-Day" to avoid confusion. The landing sites were at each end of an eighteen-mile stretch of the Leyte Gulf coast, which MacArthur divided and assigned to two forces that comprised the bulk of the US Sixth Army of Lieutenant General Walter Krueger. The Northern Force was Major General Franklin Sibert's X Corps, which contained the 24th Infantry Division along with the 1st Cavalry Division. It was to head toward the provincial capital of Tacloban and also seize control of the nearby airfield. The Southern Force, Major General John Hodge's XXIV Corps with the 7th Infantry and 96th Infantry Divisions, was to land just north of Dulag, where the Japanese were constructing a series of airfields. As in many of his amphibious landings throughout New Guinea, MacArthur's goal was to secure locations from which his Fifth US Air Force could support the ground troops with land-based air cover as quickly as possible. Seizure of the airfields was the primary objective of the Sixth Army on A-Day.

A secondary objective of the Northern Force was to close the San Juanico Strait to enemy ships. The twenty-four-mile-long narrow waterway that separates Leyte Island from Samar Island leads directly north toward the central Philippines.

One hour prior to the main landings, a much smaller force, composed of elements of the 21st Regimental Combat Team, was to land seventy miles to the south at Panaon Island. This nineteen-mile strip of land lay directly west of Dinagat Island across the Surigao Strait. This would allow the Americans to control the Panaon Strait, closing it to enemy ships that could attack the landing beaches and keeping it open for United States ships to circle around to the western shore of Leyte.

By 11 p.m. on October 19, the great armada that would bombard the enemy-controlled coast and send nearly two hundred thousand American troops ashore arrived at their assigned positions for the coming invasion. Onboard his flagship *Nashville*, MacArthur glanced around at the night and the silhouettes of hundreds of warships surrounding him. He went to his cabin where he fell asleep in his bunk reading his bible.

The three battleships of Admiral Theodore Wilkinson's Southern Attack Force (Task Force 79), *Tennessee, Pennsylvania*, and *California*, began their bombardment of the shore at 6 a.m. One hour later the *Mississippi, West Virginia*, and *Maryland*, of Admiral Daniel Barbey's Northern Attack Force (Task Force 78) started firing their heavy guns toward the shore.

At 6 a.m., MacArthur awoke to the rolling thunder sound of big guns firing aboard the nearby battleships, and the explosions on the shore. Minutes later Colonel Courtney Whitney, the senior officer responsible for organizing the Filipino resistance forces and maintaining communications with them, entered the cabin and found the commander slipping a small, old-fashioned revolver into his pocket. The weapon, which was his insurance against being captured alive, had belonged to his father many years earlier. The sudden vibrations of the ship told both generals that the cruiser was moving in closer to the coast. Two miles offshore, it stopped and dropped its anchor.[1]

MacArthur reminisced with Whitney about his visit to this very same area forty-one years earlier as a newly minted West Point graduate. As a second lieutenant of engineers, he was stationed in the Philippines in 1903 and had come under attack by local bandits. The battleships continued their shelling of the enemy shore while the two officers made their way to the ship's bridge.

On the bridge of the cruiser, Captain C. E. Coney welcomed MacArthur to a front row seat to the spectacle. The waters of the gulf were surprisingly calm following the days of storms. As the sun began to rise over the island, the general, who was also a field marshal in the Philippine Army, could make out the familiar sites of the provincial capital of Tacloban, a primary target of Major General Verne D. Mudge's 1st Cavalry Division. Along the shoreline, he could see the sand beaches stretching for several miles.

At 9 a.m., the battleships ceased firing and aircraft from the escort carriers made several hundred bombing and strafing runs. The cruisers moved up closer to shore to add their guns to the action. A half hour later the destroyers squeezed in closer to shore for their turn at shelling what they all hoped were well-hidden enemy positions. The occasional series of explosions revealed an enemy ammunition dump had been hit, or some other military target, but for the most part the gunners could not see what they were hitting.[2]

While this was happening, ships began lowering the variety of landing craft they had transported, including those armed with rockets and mortars that would lead the way toward the beaches, then part and ride on each flank of the landing craft carrying troops and vehicles. The small vessels circled around their mother ships until all were ready, then headed to the beaches to meet their 10 a.m. landing schedule.

Admiral Barbey's Northern Attack Force was comprised of two major and one minor attack groups. At its northern extreme was the San Ricardo Attack Group of Rear Admiral William M. Fechteler embarking General Mudge's 1st Cavalry Division. Their landing site was White Beach. The division's two brigades were to land abreast, with the 2nd Brigade of Brigadier General Hugh F. Hoffman assigned the most important mission of the day. They were to advance northwest onto the Cataisan Peninsula and capture the Tacloban Airfield. Following closely behind the cavalrymen were the army engineers whose job was to begin quickly repairing and improving the single north-south runway.

UNKNOWN TO all but a handful of men aboard the invasion fleet, Commander Chick Parsons and Lieutenant Colonel Frank Rawolle, a Sixth Army intelligence officer, had arrived on Leyte eight days prior to the planned landings. General MacArthur was concerned about civilian collateral damage when the ships of his fleet began bombarding the shore. He was especially worried about the thirty thousand people living in and around the Leyte capital city of Tacloban. He also wanted to be sure that guerrilla forces, which might be inclined to line the shore waiting for the Americans, remained far back in the relative safety of the jungle.

With the approval of Sixth Army commander Lieutenant General Walter Krueger, Seventh Fleet commander Vice Admiral Thomas Kinkaid, and MacArthur's chief of staff, Lieutenant

General Richard Sutherland, Parsons suggested his insertion along the Leyte coast near Tacloban in order to contact the island's guerrilla commander. Born in 1890, the slightly built, dark-complexioned Lieutenant Colonel Ruperto Kangleon had been the commanding officer of the 81st Infantry Regiment of the Philippine Army when the Japanese invaded. Briefly captured by the Japanese, he escaped and began organizing a guerrilla force on Leyte called the Black Army, but now on MacArthur's orders commanded all guerrilla forces on Leyte.[3]

The Black Army earned a reputation among friend and foe for its well-organized attacks on Japanese forces and the high number of Japanese troops killed. It was also noted for having one of the few female guerrilla leaders: Captain Nieves Fernandez, a thirty-eight-year-old Tacloban schoolteacher. She organized 110 local people into a determined subgroup of the Black Army that specialized in making homemade weapons and bombs that accounted for the lives of at least two hundred Japanese troops during the two years before MacArthur's return. Allied intelligence officers became aware of her presence among the Leyte guerrilla forces when they learned the Japanese had offered a 10,000-peso reward for her capture.[4]

In the early evening of Thursday, October 12, a Catalina Black Cat flying boat touched down on the surface of Leyte Gulf. The twin-engine plane had left Hollandia, New Guinea, three and a half hours earlier, flying close to the water surface to minimize detection. As the aircraft taxied along, Parsons and Rawolle dropped their inflatable rubber boat into the sea along with their equipment. With the passengers discharged, the aircraft lifted off and quickly headed for home.

Unable to get the boat across the extensive coral reef without puncturing it, they waved to several people standing in the growing darkness along the shore watching. Parsons assumed they were friendly, but Rawolle was not convinced until a small boat arrived with joyous locals to welcome the American officers and help them ashore. The following morning two guerrilla soldiers who had arrived during the night led them to a nearby headquarters used by Kangleon. Once there they explained their mission to the Filipino officer, emphasizing the removal of as many civilians as feasible from possible target areas, and setting up traps for the Japanese soldiers fleeing from the shore bombardment and aircraft bombings.

Over the next few days, the two American officers sent several hundred coded messages to the Allied headquarters containing invaluable information on enemy troop strength and movements, as well as identifying fuel and ammunition storage areas for targeting. They were also able to assure General MacArthur that all Japanese troops except for a few hundred had been withdrawn from Tacloban, thus saving the town and its population from being shelled or bombed.

IN A STROKE of bad luck for the enemy, Lieutenant General Shiro Makino, commanding officer of the Imperial Army's 16th Division, charged with the defense of Leyte, chose October 20 as the day to move his headquarters from Tacloban nine miles inland to Dagami. As the invasion took place, Makino was literally on the road between his old and new headquarters. The troops still in and around the capital city were primarily communications and other support units. When the Americans landed at 10 a.m. and the 1st Cavalry raced to Tacloban, these Japanese fled toward Dagami, leaving behind their communications equipment. It would not be until noon when the general was able to order reinforcements toward the beach. It would be another two days until he could reestablish a communications link with his superiors at the Thirty-Fifth Army headquarters of Lieutenant General Sosaku Suzuki.[5]

At fifteen minutes before H-hour, the time set for the invasion troops to hit the beaches, which was 10 a.m., hundreds of landing craft carrying thousands of troops raced toward the white sands fronting a line of coconut trees. Landing craft firing rockets at the shore escorted them. So began the largest amphibious landing of the Pacific war. By comparison, more men were landed at Leyte on that first day than landed at Normandy on D-Day.[6]

The invasion along the east coast of Leyte was divided into two main assaults to be conducted by two separate army corps. At the northern extremity of the landing zone for Major General Sibert's X Corps was a one-mile stretch of sand designated White Beach that extended two thousand yards south from the base of the Cataisan Peninsula near the town of San Jose. South of White Beach was slightly less than one mile of virtually impassable swamp followed by a one-mile-wide area designated Red Beach. The 1st Cavalry Division commanded by Major General Mudge drew the assignment to land at White Beach, using the 5th, 7th, and 12th Cavalry Regiments as its assault echelons. Held in reserve was the division's 8th Cavalry Regiment. Their primary target was the Tacloban Airfield.

Red Beach was the target of the 24th Infantry Division led by Major General Frederick A. Irving with the 19th and 34th Infantry Regiments as its landing force. Once ashore, they were to press about a mile inland and secure north-south Highway 1 north of the town of Palo, which sits along the Palo River.

Ten miles to the south lay a series of beaches designated Orange, Blue, Violet, and Yellow. These were the sites for the landings

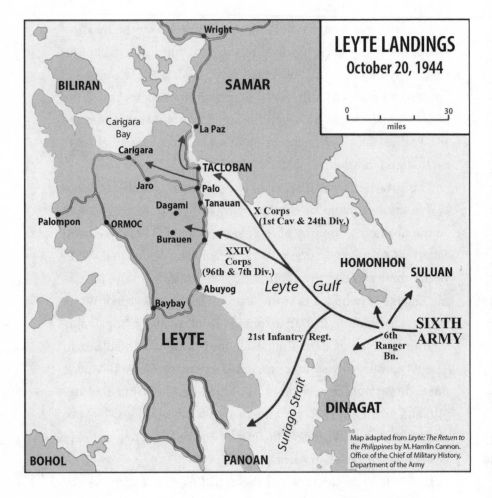

LEYTE LANDINGS
October 20, 1944

0 _____ 30
miles

BILIRAN

SAMAR

Wright

Carigara
Bay

Carigara

La Paz

Jaro

TACLOBAN

Palompon

Dagami

Palo

ORMOC

Tanauan

X Corps
(1st Cav & 24th Div.)

Burauen

XXIV
Corps
(96th & 7th Div.)

HOMONHON

SULUAN

Abuyog

Leyte Gulf

Baybay

LEYTE

21st Infantry Regt.

SIXTH
ARMY

6th
Ranger
Bn.

Suriago Strait

DINAGAT

BOHOL

PANOAN

Map adapted from *Leyte: The Return to
the Philippines* by M. Hamlin Cannon.
Office of the Chief of Military History,
Department of the Army

of Major General Hodge's XXIV Corps. The Orange and Blue Beaches, at the northern end of the corps landing zone, were the target of Major General James L. Bradley's 96th Infantry Division. The Violet and Yellow Beaches were assigned to the 7th Infantry Division commanded by Major General Archibald V. Arnold.

As THE AMERICAN troops rushed toward the beaches, in Manila General Yamashita listened to reports of the massive enemy armada entering Leyte Gulf. Much like his predecessor, General Kuroda, who considered the islands "obviously indefensible," he was pessimistic about victory in the Philippines. Added to this was the fact he had been in the country too short a time to make a true evaluation of the Army's ability to fend off an invasion. The problem of deciding where the Americans would land was another negative factor in Yamashita's decision. Since Mindanao appeared an obvious target because of its proximity to MacArthur's forces in New Guinea, several thousand troops had recently transferred to the southern island. Leyte, considered less of an American objective, relied on General Makino's twenty thousand troops for defense, many of whom were recent arrivals with little combat experience. In fact, most of them had spent the last two years on garrison duty in Manila.[7]

General Yamashita would have much preferred to concentrate his ground forces on Luzon, which he considered the most important of the islands. This strategy had also been the position of General Kuroda, who had urged his superiors to consider a negotiated peace in light of the air, sea, and ground superiority of the American forces.[8]

To Yamashita's dismay, Imperial General Headquarters disagreed, so his forces were spread from Luzon to Mindanao. The result was that no island had enough troops to defend against a massive concerted invasion, including Luzon itself. Even Emperor Hirohito weighed in on how and where the decisive battle against the Americans should be fought. After the war, he admitted he hoped for a "showdown battle" on Leyte that might inflict enough damage on the enemy forces that they would agree to open negotiations to end the war.[9]

Adding to Yamashita's woes was the fact there were troops within his command area over which he had no control. These included the Fourth Air Army commanded by Lieutenant General Kyoji Tominaga, a man with no combat experience who many considered a petty tyrant. As a result, there was minimal cooperation between Yamashita's ground forces and the air units of Tominaga.[10]

There were also some fifteen thousand men of the Imperial Navy's 31st Naval Special Base Force made up of marines and sailors. Many of the latter were survivors of warships sunk by Allied planes. These men were not under Yamashita's control, but reported to the local naval commander. Decades long bad blood between the Army and Navy resulted in a continuing lack of coordination between the two services.

On Leyte, General Makino had focused most of his defensive measures around Dulag in the southern section of the landing zone. His motive was to prevent the Americans from overrunning the airfields in the nearby Leyte Valley. Loss of the airfields to the enemy would bring in General Kenney's land-based bombers and fighters and virtually assure defeat of the entire island. Makino left the coastal area around Tacloban only lightly defended, perhaps because the Tacloban Airfield was notoriously on a flood zone and was more often than not so muddy as to be unusable, especially for the heavier American aircraft.

When the American troops began landing along the coast, for the most part they encountered only light opposition and in some places none at all. This was because the Sho-Go plan called for the Imperial Navy warships and the Army's air forces to destroy MacArthur's forces before they landed. What General Makino and his superior, General Suzuki, did not know was that Third Fleet's carrier air raids on Luzon had wiped out a large portion of the Army's aircraft on the ground. As for their navy, its ships had scattered after the Battle of Formosa, and it was left with no aircraft carriers worthy of the description. Both generals believed the Tokyo propaganda about the destruction of most of Admiral Halsey's fleet in that battle, and that it would be of little help in defending the invasion fleet.[11]

Added to the failure to comprehend that a major invasion, literally *the* major invasion of the Pacific war, was about to begin was a belief on the part of many Japanese officers that the ships reported in Leyte Gulf by naval lookouts were probably just seeking safety from a typhoon that had recently passed through. General Makino had his doubts about this although his superior, General Suzuki, recalling when white caps off Mindanao resulted in reports of numerous landing craft heading toward shore, was more complacent. Makino decided to check further and sent one of his staff officers in an observation plane to overfly the gulf. A thick fog prevented the officer from seeing any ships. This convinced the skeptical Makino that the ships, if they actually existed, had likely been the remains of Halsey's devastated fleet seeking safety from the typhoon.[12]

THE FIRST WAVE of the forces of X Corps stormed ashore from their landing craft at 10 a.m. Expecting stiff opposition, the men of the 1st Cavalry pushed past light resistance from the few enemy soldiers remaining in the area and headed to Tacloban Airfield. Following close behind was the second wave of cavalry troopers in amphibious tractors accompanied by several amphibious tanks. They moved west through swamps and thick jungle growth across Highway 1 heading to Tacloban City. Rolling over pockets of resistance, the cavalrymen occupied the airstrip and controlled their sector of Highway 1 by late afternoon. Behind them, ships unloaded additional troops as well as supplies and artillery units.[13]

To their south, the 24th Infantry Division ran into a series of pillboxes constructed of palm tree logs that slowed their advance. Although the first wave of landing craft arrived safely, the following waves came under artillery and mortar fire that sank several of the vessels and killed a number of men including a company commander. Both the 34th and 19th Infantry Regiments encountered strong opposition in these areas, but ultimately succeeded in crossing Highway 1 by the end of the day. A prime objective of the 24th Division was a hill overlooking a large section of the landing beaches known as Hill 522. Well-prepared defensive positions hidden in caves and seven-foot-deep trenches built by Filipino forced laborers allowed the defenders to dominate not only the beach but also the entire territory around the hill. Honeycombed with tunnels and rising directly from the coastal plain to a height of 522 feet with a 1,000-yard circular base, the hill served as the key to the defense of the entire area.

With a stroke of good luck, several companies from the 19th Regiment circled around the hill and discovered a route leading to the crest. The Japanese had deserted the hilltop during the naval and air bombardment. For some reason they were slow in returning to their fortified positions at the crest. The Americans beat them to it and drove off the returning defenders. The brutal, almost face-to-face combat for the hilltop lasted forty-eight hours until the Japanese finally withdrew. The battle cost the enemy about fifty killed and an unknown number of wounded. Fourteen Americans died and another ninety-five wounded. Thirty of the wounded were able to rejoin their units.[14]

Farther south, the forty thousand troops from the 96th and 7th Infantry Divisions of the XXIV Corps met stronger enemy resistance in the form of heavy mortar fire, but managed to get ashore and pushed the Japanese rear guard back. A primary objective of the 96th Infantry Division was to capture a large hill designated Catmon Hill. Rising to 1,400 feet, this hill dominated the entire countryside for miles in every direction. It was by-passed and isolated while naval gunfire subjected the defenders to periodic shelling until the hill finally fell on October 29.[15]

To the south, the 32nd Infantry Regiment of the 7th Division were halted on their way to the town of Dulag by well-positioned machine-gun nests that required recently landed tanks to clear them away. Even farther south, the 18th Infantry Regiment swept through only minor resistance and quickly occupied Dulag Air-field, their main objective.

MACARTHUR STOOD on the bridge of the *Nashville* intently watching the landing craft and other vessels moving in and out of the beaches. By 1 p.m., he decided it was time to go ashore and announce his arrival to the Filipino people. He sent a message to President Osmena and General Carlos Romulo, who had served in the Philippine Army and on MacArthur's staff, aboard the nearby transport *John Land* to prepare to land. He returned to his cabin, changed into a clean freshly pressed uniform, and adjusted his field marshal's hat. His plan was to come ashore at one of the docks, enabling him to step from the *Nashville's* motor launch onto dry land. With the dexterity of a man half his age, he climbed down into the waiting launch. Following him was General Sutherland, a half dozen officers, including General Kenney, who was anxious to get a personal look at the Leyte airfields, and a group of journalists and photographers to record the event.

When the launch pulled alongside the transport *John Land*, the Filipino president and several Filipino officers climbed aboard. MacArthur, now clearly excited to be returning, hugged Romulo, whom he considered a friend, and asked him how it felt to be home. Overcome with emotion, he could not reply as tears ran down his face. President Osmena was a little more reserved; he worried many of his fellow countrymen considered him a poor substitute for the late beloved President Quezon. Perhaps he was also thinking of the mixed messages he had received from the American government about accompanying MacArthur. President Roosevelt had urged him to return with the American general, but Secretary of the Interior Harold Ickes, whose domain included the Commonwealth of the Philippines, warned the new president to avoid coming ashore in MacArthur's shadow.[16]

As the launch made its way toward the shore, MacArthur spotted a landing craft heading back with wounded men aboard. The general told the coxswain driving the launch to hail the returning craft and it pulled alongside. Much to the surprise of the landing craft's crew, MacArthur asked where the heaviest fighting was. Somewhat stunned, one of the crew pointed to a section of Red Beach nearly straight ahead. Thanking him, MacArthur told his coxswain to head to that spot. Recalling that scene several years later, one of the correspondents aboard MacArthur's launch said that was when he knew "Douglas MacArthur was looking for trouble."[17]

About fifty yards from the shoreline, the launch grounded on the gently rising sandy bottom. One of MacArthur's aides radioed the navy lieutenant acting as beachmaster and requested an amphibious craft to take the commanding general to the dry beach. A beachmaster was the unquestioned dictator of all movement on or off the beach during landing operations, and this officer was dealing with hundreds of craft squeezing onto the beach and bulldozers unloading them. The beachmaster, probably dealing with a thousand problems at that moment, told MacArthur's aide to "Let 'em walk."[18]

MacArthur told the coxswain to drop the ramp and he stepped off into knee-deep water and strode toward the beach. This was not the first time he had waded ashore during an invasion: he had done so several times during the New Guinea campaign. Knowing the photographers would take his picture coming ashore, he probably would have preferred to do so in his clean dry uniform, but necessity prevailed.

Several of the photographers aboard the launch raced ahead of the general to take a picture of his landing. Major Gaetano Faillace took the iconic photo that raced around the world of MacArthur and his entourage walking in the knee-deep water. Despite the general's many critics, it was not a staged event and this was the only instance on that day he waded through the water to reach the beach. His expression clearly indicated that he was not overjoyed at getting his freshly cleaned and pressed trousers soaked by the brine. A combat reporter who also served as a rifleman in the 24th Division described the scene: "The small group of men is moving steadily up from the water's edge. They cross the tumultuous strip of sand, and then you notice that one of the group, the leader, wears no helmet. He wears a cap and he is smoking a corncob pipe. He walks along as if the nearest Jap snipers were on Saturn instead of in the palm trees a few hundred yards away. You stare, and you realize that you are staring at General Douglas MacArthur."[19]

MacArthur planned to make a radio address to the nation announcing his return as promised, but first he wanted to get what he called "a feel for the fighting." This was pure MacArthur, as he had done it so often before. The general strolled around the beach and a few hundred yards inland, ignoring the sniper fire around him, to ask officers and enlisted men how they were doing and to check the bodies of dead Japanese.[20]

MacArthur's pilot, Dusty Rhoades, who accompanied the general at the landing, reported that at one point MacArthur paused to watch a nearby firefight. Rhoades decided to edge toward a large palm tree for protection. When MacArthur asked if he was worried, the pilot responded he felt better near the potential protection of the tree. MacArthur told him the Almighty had a job for him and probably expected him to finish it. When Rhoades replied he was not sure the Almighty was as interested in his own survival, the general smiled and walked on.[21]

Surprised to find their commander among them, many of the soldiers just stared at him. Then a soldier from the Signal Corps arrived to tell MacArthur they'd set up their portable transmitter in a weapons carrier parked on the edge of a palm grove. The transmission went from the weapons carrier to the *Nashville*. The cruiser's equipment could broadcast it across the nation in several frequencies used by various guerrilla forces and secretly monitored by civilians.

As it began to rain, experienced radio broadcaster William Dunn turned on the microphone and gave a brief introduction of both the general and the president, ending with the words, "here is General Douglas MacArthur." Dunn handed the microphone to MacArthur who began his speech, "People of the Philippines, I have returned! By the grace of Almighty God our forces now stand again on Philippines soil—soil consecrated by the blood of our two people." He then urged them to rally in support of his forces and the guerrillas in their areas as the battlefront moved through their towns and villages to "restore the liberties of your people."

Following his two-minute speech, an obviously emotional Mac-Arthur handed the microphone to Osmena, who spoke for ten minutes about the plan to restore civilian government to the Philippines. After their broadcast, the two men walked to a nearby palm log to sit a few minutes and discuss their plans for the immediate future, which included a declaration of the reestablishment of a Filipino government with its temporary capitol in nearby Tacloban.[22]

Before leaving the area, MacArthur finished his handwritten letter to President Roosevelt, including his special note that it was the first letter from "the freed Philippines" and its stamp might be worthy of the president's collection. He told the president the landings went "smoothly," mentioned the strategic advantage of landing at Leyte, and that the Filipino people had reacted "splendidly" to the landings. He urged that following the successful conclusion of the liberation of the Philippines the nation be granted its independence. He closed by encouraging Roosevelt to preside over the anticipated ceremony of independence. Of course, he had no way of knowing that the president would die months before the liberation.[23]

MacArthur found the following message from Roosevelt waiting for him when he returned to the *Nashville*: "The whole American nation today exults at the news that the gallant men under your command have landed on Philippine soil. I know well what this means to you. I know that it cost you to obey my order that you leave Corregidor in February 1942 and proceed to Australia. Since then you have planned and worked and fought with whole-souled devotion for the day when you would return with powerful forces to the Philippine Islands. That day has come. You have the nation's gratitude and the nation's prayers for success as you and your men fight your way back to Bataan. Roosevelt."[24]

That same day, the White House issued a statement about the landings to the nation. It began: "This morning American troops landed on the island of Leyte in the Philippines. The invasion forces, under the command of General Douglas MacArthur, are supported by the greatest concentration of naval and air power ever massed in the Pacific Ocean. We promised to return: we have returned."[25]

BECAUSE THE communications units of Japan's Sixteenth Army had fled Tacloban in a rush, leaving behind much of their equipment, General Yamashita in Manila and General Suzuki on Cebu knew little if anything concerning what the enemy was doing in Leyte Gulf. Not until late on October 22, two days after the landings had begun, would they learn the true situation on Leyte.[26]

This was especially frustrating for Yamashita. Leyte was not where he wanted to fight the decisive battle the Imperial General Headquarters had decreed. He preferred to husband his resources for the defense of Luzon and especially Manila and Manila Bay. If the Americans had landed, he had no choice but to follow orders and feed troops onto Leyte as quickly and safely as possible. He would soon learn some details of the enemy forces on Leyte, and begin shipping many of his best fighting units there in support of the 16th Division. By mid-December, he had sent some forty-five thousand men to Leyte. As the fighting expanded beyond the landing zone, convoys transporting troops and supplies to Leyte would come under increasing attack. According to one Japanese general on the Fourteenth Area Army staff, nearly 80 percent of the ships bound for Leyte with men and supplies sank following attacks by American aircraft and ships. Many of these sinkings occurred close to shore, allowing most troops to swim to safety, but their equipment went to the bottom of the sea.[27]

General Suzuki, on Cebu, General Yamashita at Fort McKinley near Manila, and Field Marshal Terauchi at the Southern Expeditionary Army headquarters in Manila, were all aware that Sho-Go-1 had been declared. They were unaware that Imperial Army Headquarters in Tokyo had changed the plan for Leyte from the original holding action—to gain time to strengthen the defenses on Luzon—to fighting the decisive battle to destroy the enemy forces on Leyte. With what he learned of the approaching American fleet and the declaration of Sho-Go-1, Suzuki began ordering troops from his Thirty-Fifth Army to Leyte. He also began preparations to shift his headquarters from Cebu Island to the west coast of Leyte near Ormoc Bay.

Another Japanese general who believed Leyte would be the scene of the decisive battle was Lieutenant General Tominaga, commander of the Fourth Air Army. His air force, greatly reduced by the earlier attacks from the American Third Fleet, had less than one hundred operational aircraft with which to oppose the American landings. On that first day, his pilots flew twenty sorties with little to show for it other than the torpedoing of the light cruiser *Honolulu*. A few minutes after 4 p.m., as the cruiser stood five miles offshore waiting for fire-support calls from the troops on the beach, a torpedo plane swept down on it out of the thick mist hanging over the gulf. Captain H. Ray Thurber reacted to the sight of the torpedo hitting the water by attempting to maneuver his ship but it was too late. In less than three minutes, the deadly missile reached the light cruiser and blew a large hole in its port side. Sixty officers and men died in the explosion. Although it was able to steam to Manus in the Admiralties for temporary repairs, permanent repairs were not completed in time for it to rejoin the war.[28]

MACARTHUR WENT to sleep early that night unaware that Radio Tokyo had broadcast an announcement identifying the ship the American general was aboard, and vowing the *Nashville* and MacArthur would never leave Leyte Gulf.[29]

Ashore, the two beachheads were about one mile deep into Leyte territory. Over 50,000 men had landed that day as well as 4,500 vehicles of all types, including tanks. The operation had cost the lives of 50 Americans as well as the wounding of 192 more. At the extreme southern end of Leyte, the 21st Regimental Combat Team took control of the territory overlooking Panaon Strait, thus denying it to the enemy.[30]

At the northern end of the X Corps landing zone, the 1st Cavalry Division controlled Tacloban Airfield and was making plans to advance into Tacloban City itself. To their south, the 24th Infantry Division possessed control of Hill 522 overlooking the beachhead. In the XXIV Corps zone, the 7th Infantry Division occupied the town of Dulag, although Japanese holdouts continued an intensive defense of a portion of the Dulag Airfield about one mile west of the town. The 96th Infantry Division held Catmon Hill and all its approaches.

Before the American fleet arrived, General Makino and his staff had decided that any invasion of Leyte would be concentrated around Dulag. Knowing MacArthur's desire for land-based aircraft to arrive on the scene as quickly as possible, Makino understood how important the Dulag Airfield and three additional landing strips in the area were to the invaders. As a result,

Makino assigned the Dulag sector defense to Colonel Keijiro Hokoda's 20th Infantry Regiment supported by portions of a field artillery regiment, an airfield protection company, and the 7th Independent Tank Company.[31] (The tank company proved less than useful as most of its old 89B medium tanks suffered destruction in attempted counterattacks over the following days.)[32]

October 21, A-Day + 1, began with an attack on the ships in the gulf by Japanese bombers. In the half-light at 6 a.m., an Aichi D3A dive-bomber headed for the Australian heavy cruiser HMAS *Shropshire*, but was driven off by the cruiser's 40mm Bofors antiaircraft guns. Crippled by the gunfire, the plane turned away, dropped to a few feet above the water, and slammed into the port side of the heavy cruiser HMAS *Australia*. The dive-bomber's wing struck the cruiser's foremast and showered the bridge with flaming fuel and debris as it went overboard. Among the thirty crew members killed was the ship's commander, Captain Emile Dechaineux. The sixty-four wounded men included Commodore John Collins, the squadron commander. Witnesses and historians differ over whether the incident was a preplanned kamikaze attack or the result of a last-minute decision made by a pilot flying a seriously damaged aircraft.[33]

At 9:30 that morning, General MacArthur once again waded ashore, this time near the 1st Cavalry Division landing sector. He was anxious to have General Kenney inspect Tacloban Airfield's suitability for American fighters and bombers. He also wanted to meet 1st Cavalry commander Major General Mudge and discuss the liberation of Tacloban City. MacArthur was planning an event to take place there as soon as possible. While driving to the airfield, they passed the corpses of Japanese snipers who had been shot out of their tree nests.

Kenney was disappointed at what he found at the airfield.

American engineers were busy grading what served as a runway and filling in bomb craters. Kenney described it as "a sandspit a little over a mile long and about 300 yards wide." If it were to be useful, it would require a base of rock or coral covered over with steel mats. Kenney estimated that when the work was completed, it might be able to hold seventy-five fighters, but was unlikely to stand up to the weight of the bombers. MacArthur wanted to drive to nearby Tacloban City, but a group of Sherman tanks blocked the road. Since the tankers were still fighting their way into the town, the party turned around and headed back to the beach.[34]

The following day MacArthur and his entourage waded ashore near Dulag. They then took jeeps the short distance to the airfield. Along the way, they encountered several snipers and an enemy tank heading in their direction. An American anti-tank unit suddenly pulled alongside them and concentrated their fire on the approaching tank, setting it aflame and killing everyone inside. When they finally arrived at the airfield, Kenney was again not impressed by what he found. Although large enough for his needs, it was low country obviously inclined to flooding during the coming rainy season. He estimated it required at least a foot of rock or coral as a base on which to lay steel runway mats.

They were at the east end of the runway, and MacArthur was walking around casually chatting with troops, some of whom were engaged with the enemy. At the other end of the runway, Americans on one side of the airstrip were in a pitched battle with Japanese troops on the opposite side. Both sides used mortars and artillery. Kenney thought his commander was oblivious to the danger and was anxious to leave. When MacArthur asked if he thought it could quickly be made usable, Kenney replied he would like to inspect it under "more favorable conditions," obviously referring to the firefight at the other end of the runway.

He told MacArthur he would feel better if he were inspecting the runway from an airplane. MacArthur laughed and told him it was good for him to learn "how the other half of the world lives."[35]

Before leaving Dulag, General Kenney spoke to several Filipinos familiar with the area concerning the Burauen and San Pablo airfields still in enemy hands. They told him both filled with mud as soon as the rainy season began.[36]

October 23 was to be a big day for MacArthur, Osmena, and the Philippine people. The general left the *Nashville* at midmorning and boarded a PT boat for the landing near Tacloban. All along the beachhead, the Sixth Army was pushing the enemy back and heading toward the Leyte Valley at the center of the island. There were still the nightly raids, but the number of enemy planes was small as was the damage they inflicted. Most Japanese aircraft approaching the gulf were downed by antiaircraft fire from the ships waiting for them.

MacArthur's party arrived at the Tacloban dock about noon. The Americans were surprised when they saw that practically the entire fifteen thousand people of the town had turned out to cheer the arrival of the man they had awaited to liberate them from the Japanese. Thanks in part to the intelligence by Commander Parsons, the city had suffered little damage from the shelling and bombing.

Another thing the Americans found surprising was the scores of American flags everywhere. Some flew from hastily built flagpoles, others draped from windows and porches of almost every building and home they passed on their way to the center of the city. Hidden away during the Japanese occupation, the Stars and Stripes was now visible everywhere.[37]

As fighting continued two miles outside the city, troops from the Army Signal Corps set up a microphone on the steps of the large-columned Provincial Capitol Building to broadcast the event across the nation. Despite their enthusiastic welcoming turnout, very few citizens were there to witness the historic event now about to take place. They either had not been told about it, or thought they were not invited. MacArthur stepped to the microphone, declared the reestablishment of the civilian government of the Philippines, and named Tacloban as its temporary capital. Next President Osmena gave a brief speech followed by a bugler sounding "To the Colors" as the flags of the United States and the Commonwealth of the Philippines were raised on two flagpoles. MacArthur then awarded the guerrilla leader Colonel Kangleon, who was now part of the American Army again, the Distinguished Service Cross, and President Osmena appointed him acting governor of Leyte.[38]

MacArthur decided to move his headquarters to Leyte, so following a lead someone had given him, he went to look at a large home three blocks from the capitol building the Japanese had used as an officer's club. The cream-colored brick and concrete two-story mansion with wide verandas on both floors had been the home of Mr. and Mrs. Walter Scott Price before the Japanese occupation. An army veteran from the Spanish-American War, Walter Price founded the Leyte Transportation Company, which operated a large fleet of buses and trucks that made him wealthy and earned him the nickname the "King of Leyte." The Japanese arrested Price and sent him to Santo Tomas Prison Camp on Luzon. A month after his liberation by troopers from the 11th Airborne Division in February 1945, Price died of pneumonia.[39]

Briefly tortured by the Japanese after her husband's arrest, Simeona Price escaped with her children to a small village in the interior. When General Romulo found her and told her MacArthur was using the house, she told him she would return after the Americans were finished with it. During his 1961 farewell tour of the Philippines, MacArthur would visit Mrs. Price to thank her for her hospitality.[40]

MacArthur was not in a hurry to move into the Price House. He seemed to enjoy life aboard the cruiser, especially his nightly stroll around the bridge, watching as enemy planes attacked the fleet and got shot out of the sky for their trouble.

Japanese intelligence proved its worth when within two days of MacArthur agreeing to take possession of the Price House, Radio Tokyo announced that the large home was the general's new headquarters. The broadcast closed with the declaration that "our brave aviators will soon take care of that situation." For weeks afterward, enemy planes targeted the home. Although the building suffered only minor damage during that time, the bombing and strafing destroyed several nearby buildings, killing their occupants as collateral damage in the Japanese attempts to kill MacArthur.[41]

In a similar vein, when General Yamashita saw the photograph of MacArthur wading ashore, he assumed the scene was in either New Guinea or Australia. He could not believe the American theater commander had come ashore within hours of the landings. He told American interrogators after the war that if he knew MacArthur had come ashore, he would have sent every suicide pilot after him to kill him.[42]

MacArthur had visited all fronts since the landings. It appeared that the only division making the progress he expected was the 1st Cavalry. They captured Tacloban, the airfield, and Palo, and were driving the enemy north and west of Tacloban. They had an especially tough time at a heavily defended ridge southwest of Tacloban that was a commanding height. When they finally captured the ridge, they counted 330 dead Japanese soldiers.

An early objective of General Mudge's cavalrymen was to seize control of the San Juanico Strait. The twenty-four-mile-long waterway divides Leyte from Samar. At its northern end it flows from the Carigara Bay section of the Samar Sea down to the San Pedro Bay section of Leyte Gulf. In some places, it is less than one and a half miles wide. The mission of the 2nd Brigade of the 8th Cavalry Regiment was to prevent small Japanese vessels from transporting supplies or reinforcements to the Tacloban area from ports in the Samar Sea. Highway 1, which ran along the Leyte east coast and was at that time being crossed by troops from the landings, ended at the strait a dozen miles north of Tacloban at Guintiguian. A ferry allowed transit across the strait to La Paz on Samar where the road continued.

While celebrations were under way in Tacloban, officers from the 8th Cavalry Regiment took a landing craft up the strait to reconnoiter both sides of the waterway. They made it the full length of the strait, turning around once they had reached Babatngon at the north end of Leyte on Carigara Bay. They found no Japanese when the officers stopped and briefly inspected each side of the ferry crossing. The following day, Brigadier General Hugh Hoffman sent troops to occupy Babatngon and search Carigara Bay, where they found no enemy activity. He sent others up the waterway to occupy La Paz on Samar, and along Highway 1 to control Guintiguian on Leyte. Since they were passing through enemy territory whose strength was unknown, a platoon of light tanks and several weapons carriers supported the infantrymen. Shortly before midnight, the troops on Samar came under attack by an estimated one hundred Japanese soldiers from the 16th Division's 9th Infantry Regiment, but the Americans succeeded in driving them off. Both sides relied on machine guns, but the Americans had the added firepower of mortars. Seven days after landing, the 1st Cavalry Division's successful campaign ashore had cost the lives of 40 Americans including 4 officers, and reported 14 officers and 185 enlisted men wounded. They claimed the lives of 739 Japanese and took 9 prisoners, including 7 Japanese, 1 Formosan, and 1 Chinese.[43]

When MacArthur left Tacloban following the transfer-of-power ceremony, he visited General Krueger's Sixth Army headquarters to complain about the pace of the army getting off the beach and into the interior. He told Krueger that 1st Cavalry was the only division meetings its objectives in a timely manner. He charged that the commanders of the 7th, 24th, and 96th Infantry Divisions were not pushing their troops hard enough. The time to hit the Japanese was while they were still trying to recover from the massive shelling, before they could reestablish their defenses.[44]

The first indication that the Japanese had recovered from their surprise at the Leyte landings was the appearance of an increasing number of enemy aircraft over the gulf and the landing sites. Both day and night Imperial Army and Navy bombers and dive-bombers struck with serious results. The first of these involved fifty medium bombers escorted by army fighters that attacked the Tacloban harbor and surrounding area. They were followed a few minutes later by another thirty aircraft. US Navy combat air patrol fighters drove many of them off target but lost three of their own. One problem faced by this increase in airpower from the enemy, who were rushing in aircraft from all nearby airfields, including Formosa and Kyushu, was that they were land-based and capable of night attacks, whereas the Americans could only do battle during daylight hours. They had no place to land on Leyte as of yet, so they had to land on their carriers while there was still light enough to see them. For the most part, the carriers remained dark at night to not attract enemies.

Earlier that day, October 23, two US Navy submarines were located roughly five hundred miles to the west off the coast of

Palawan Island, where they had been patrolling the dangerous waterway between the western Philippine island of Palawan and Borneo. Dotted with numerous small islets and shoals generally named after ships that wrecked on them, it required great skill in navigating the passage. The two submarines, USS *Darter* and USS *Dace*, were sitting side by side on the surface when the *Darter*'s radar picked up a large blip near the southern entrance to the passage. The Imperial Navy was on the move.

Meanwhile General Krueger's forces continued their drive inland toward the goal of reaching Leyte Valley. Later that evening, patrols from the 96th Infantry Division of XXIV Corps were in contact with patrols from the 24th Division of X Corps. The link-up of the two corps forces secured the beachhead. The next day the commander came ashore to stay and moved into the Price House, which became SWPA headquarters and remained so for quite a while. All along the gulf coast, Admiral Barbey's landing craft of varying sizes brought supplies and reinforcements ashore.

At his headquarters near Manila, General Yamashita had read reports from Leyte with foreboding. They confirmed his worst fears and his original plan to fight only a delaying action on Leyte while building up his defenses in preparation for a decisive battle on Luzon. Shipping thousands of soldiers to Ormoc on Leyte's west coast had cost so many lives it failed to justify the effort. Every soldier that died when his transport sank or swam ashore without his equipment was one less man available to defend Manila.

On Leyte General Kenney was doing all he could to rush preparations at the airfields. Steel mats arrived at the Tacloban docks and were rushed to the muddy strip that now passed for an American airfield. The same took place at Dulag Airfield as the 7th Infantry pushed on toward additional airfields to the west.

CHAPTER NINE

THE RAGING SEA

The Imperial Navy decided its best hope to thwart MacArthur's forces was to destroy the American fleets operating in and around Leyte Gulf. Admiral Soemu Toyoda, commander of the Combined Fleet, issued orders from his headquarters in Tokyo for a massive three-pronged attack that would include most of the fleet's still-operational warships. He further ordered that the primary targets of the imperial ships were to be the troop transports in the gulf, although some of his naval officers objected to excluding American warships as targets. The result was a series of engagements over a four-day period known jointly as the Battle of Leyte Gulf, a battle so costly to the Japanese that it virtually eliminated the Imperial Navy as a fighting force of consequence for the remainder of the war.[1]

The first phase of the strategy was to use a decoy fleet to draw at least some of the American aircraft carriers north of the Philippines, reducing the enemy airpower over the gulf. Second, land-based army and navy aircraft that were in the process of moving to the Philippines would conduct surprise attacks on the American aircraft carriers to diminish their effectiveness. This would be followed by surface vessels in a surprise attack "storming" into Leyte Gulf from north and south simultaneously and destroying the enemy's transports and hindering their ability to put troops ashore. The problem no one appeared to recognize was timing. By the time the surface fleets arrived in the Leyte Gulf area, the transports had already put tens of thousands of American troops ashore, as well as hundreds of tons of supplies and equipment. Storming into the gulf was going to be too little too late.[2]

The main armada for the attack was the 1st Striking Force under the command of Vice Admiral Takeo Kurita. He had enhanced his standing in the Imperial Navy when he led a battleship division and shelled Henderson Field on Guadalcanal in October 1942, which nearly destroyed the American airfield. Toyoda's orders called for dividing the force into two fleets. The larger, known as Forces A and B under Kurita's direct command, sailed from its anchorage at Brunei on the island of Borneo and set its course for the central region of the Philippines, the Americans called this the Center Force. Kurita commanded five battleships, including *Yamato* and *Musashi*, ten heavy cruisers, two light cruisers, and fifteen destroyers. Unfortunately, several of these ships did not have the protection normally afforded imperial fleets by antisubmarine reconnaissance seaplanes due to fuel shortages and the inherent danger posed to a large ship stopped at sea to pick up its aircraft. Kurita was to approach the Philippines from the west, thread his way between several islands using the Sibuyan Sea to make for the San Bernardino Strait, then turn south directly into Leyte Gulf.[3]

Also sailing from Brunei was Force C under Vice Admiral Shoji Nishimura comprising two battleships, one heavy cruiser, and four destroyers. The Americans called this the Southern Force.

Nishimura's orders were to enter Leyte Gulf from the south by passing between the islands of Negros and Mindanao through the Surigao Strait. Assigned to follow Nishimura through the Surigao Strait, the 2nd Striking Force of Vice Admiral Kiyohide Shima sailed from the Inland Sea between Japan and China with a force of one light cruiser, two heavy cruisers, and four destroyers.[4]

Vice Admiral Jisaburo Ozawa, a leading advocate of naval aviation and the organization of the Imperial Navy's aircraft carriers, commanded a fourth fleet. Called the Main Body, the Americans termed this the Northern Force. It was perhaps the most important of the fleets heading toward Leyte. Ozawa, the highest-ranking naval officer after Toyoda, held command of the Mobile Force, which included the fleets of Admirals Kurita and Nishimura as well as his own Main Body. This fleet was unusual for two reasons: its composition and its mission. When it sortied from the Japanese home waters on the afternoon of October 20, it included one fleet aircraft carrier, *Zuikaku*; three light carriers, *Chiyoda*, *Chitose*, and *Zuiho*; two World War I–era battleships partially converted to carriers, *Ise* and *Hyuga*; three cruisers, *Isuzu*, *Oyodo*, and *Tama*; and four destroyers, *Akitsuki*, *Hatsutsuki*, *Shimotsuki*, and *Wakatsuki*. Its mission, as devised by Admiral Toyoda, was to alter the balance of power the American fleet had in aircraft by luring at least some of the American Third Fleet aircraft carriers away from Leyte Gulf. The forces of Admirals Kurita, Nishimura, and Shima had no aircraft and would have to rely on land-based navy and army aircraft from Luzon for air cover.[5]

Following the devastating defeat in the Battle of the Philippine Sea in which the Japanese lost three fleet carriers and over four hundred carrier aircraft, Ozawa brought his limping fleet home to train new pilots and rush construction of replacement aircraft.

He had less than four months before the invasion of Leyte. Handicapped by the time constraint, his carriers now went to sea with only 116 aircraft and many pilots with no combat experience. The two converted battleships were just window dressing, as they carried no aircraft. The conversion of these two old ships resulted in removing the rear turrets and replacing them with a short flight deck with catapults. The design called for allowing a dozen Yokosuka dive-bombers that the Americans called "Judy," and a dozen Aichi reconnaissance floatplanes known as "Paul." They all required conversion for catapult launching. Once the dive-bombers launched, they had to find somewhere else to land since the flight deck was not long enough. The floatplanes could put down in the water near the ship and be hoisted aboard by a crane. The result was that the front half of the ship was a battleship while the rear was an aircraft carrier of sorts.

This was not important to Ozawa, for his job was to allow the American Third Fleet to catch sight of his carrier force approaching the Philippines and then turn away. The Japanese expected that Admiral Halsey, whom they all knew to be an aggressive combat officer who saw carriers as the most dangerous warships afloat, would send at least some of his eight fleet carriers and many of their over eight hundred aircraft in pursuit, reducing the air cover over Leyte Gulf. The surface vessels of Admirals Kurita and Nishimura could then close in on the gulf from north and south and attack the enemy ships. Ozawa's decoy fleet headed toward a position northeast of Luzon.

On the evening of October 21, before departing Brunei, Kurita called a meeting aboard his flagship, the heavy cruiser *Atago*, of all division commanders and their staffs. Many of his officers had been complaining about a mission that sent the bulk of the imperial warships against troop and other transport vessels. These men recognized that the end was approaching, and many thought it was disgraceful that the imperial fleet would end the war fighting noncombat ships instead of the enemy's warships. They wanted to attack the battleships, cruisers, and carriers of the Third and Seventh fleets, not transports. They saw no honor in risking the existence of the fleet, especially the two superbattleships *Yamato* and *Musashi*, against noncombat ships when the enemy had many more worthy targets in the area. Ironically, Kurita and his chief of staff, Rear Admiral Tomiji Koyanagi, were in agreement with these men, but they had to obey Toyoda's orders.[6]

Kurita began his talk by acknowledging that many of the men were opposed to the mission. He told them the war situation "is far more critical than any of you can possibly know." He said it would be shameful if the fleet remained intact when the nation perished. He called the mission to attack Leyte Gulf a "glorious opportunity" given them by Imperial General Headquarters. He then spoke of miracles and exclaimed that no one could say their actions in Leyte Gulf could not turn the tide of the war. He ended with a rousing claim that he knew each man present will "act faithfully and well." The response was a cry of "Banzai!" from the assembled officers.[7]

The 1st Striking Force of Admiral Kurita sailed from anchorage at Brunei at 8 a.m. on Sunday October 22. It was cloudy with rain-squalls that cleared by afternoon. The fleet headed toward Palawan Passage, west of Palawan Island. Several hours later Admiral Nishimura took his ships out and made a course to the east of Palawan toward the north coast of Mindanao, heading to Surigao Strait.

It was shortly after midnight on the twenty-third when the radar operator aboard the submarine *Darter*, patrolling the Palawan Passage with the *Dace*, notified Commander David H. McClintock of a huge blip on his screen that was about thirty thousand yards distant. McClintock, senior officer of the two vessels, read the radar operator's report and used his megaphone to call over to Commander Bladen D. Claggett aboard the *Dace* to inform him of the reported sighting, closing with "Let's go!"

Remaining on the surface, both submarines went to maximum speed then found what they discovered was a large fleet of enemy warships. For some unexplained reason, Admiral Kurita had picket destroyers on each side of his two-column fleet, but none in the front. It was unusual because the passage was difficult to navigate with many dangerous obstructions, and in addition, they suspected that American submarines were in the area.

Over the next few hours, as the submarines tracked the enemy fleet, McClintock sent several updated messages on its size and speed to the commander of SWPA's submarine force, Rear Admiral Ralph W. Christie in Freemantle. Having initially reported the fleet as containing eleven heavy ships plus six destroyers, the submarine commander decided to wait for dawn to be able to make an accurate visual count and description of the ships before attacking them. While each report increased the number of ships in the fleet, they remained understated. They never reached the accurate count of five battleships, ten heavy cruisers, two light cruisers, and fifteen destroyers.[8]

A few minutes after 5 a.m. on the twenty-third, both submarines, now on opposites sides of the enemy fleet, submerged. At 5:32, McClintock, aboard the *Darter*, fired all six of his submarine's forward torpedo tubes at the leading port-side ship at less than one thousand yards distance. This was Admiral Kurita's flagship *Atago*. Kurita's chief of staff described the attack as "a complete surprise," since there were no sightings of enemy periscopes or torpedo wakes prior to their impact.[9]

The submarine turned and aimed its stern torpedo tubes at the next ship in line, the heavy cruiser *Takao*. Two of the torpedoes struck the target, flooding three boiler rooms and destroying two propellers and the rudder. Badly damaged and unable to continue the journey, the cruiser stopped dead in the water. Its triple hull construction saved it from sinking, but it was knocked out of action. Two destroyers ultimately escorted the wounded vessel to Brunei. It could not be repaired, so the cruiser was laid up at Singapore as a floating antiaircraft battery.

The *Atago*, with Kurita aboard, broke up and sank in a matter of minutes. The admiral and several surviving members of his staff attempted to transfer to the nearby destroyer *Kishinami*, but when this proved impossible, they had to swim to the destroyer. The cruiser took 360 officers and men to their watery grave. Within minutes the *Dace* fired its six bow torpedoes at the ship nearest it, which was the heavy cruiser *Maya*. The Japanese cruiser blew up and sank in minutes.

Standing on the bridge of his flagship, the superbattleship *Yamato*, Vice Admiral Matome Ugaki assumed command of the entire force until the fleet was beyond the passage. Ugaki decided there were too many friendly ships in too close proximity, the Palawan Passage being only twenty miles wide at the place of the attacks, so he ordered the fleet to increase speed to 24 knots and continue through the passage as quickly as possible. As the fleet moved north, several destroyers continued sweeping the area dropping depth charges, but the submarines had already raced toward the south out of range.[10]

A few hours later the two submarines returned to the scene and surveyed the possibility of sinking the *Takao*, which was engaged in making repairs sufficient to be able to get underway and return to Brunei. As darkness fell and the two American vessels prepared to attack the cruiser while avoiding the two destroyers watching over it, the *Takao* suddenly began to move under its own power. It headed southwest at 6 knots with the destroyers running close support. As the submarines attempted to avoid the screening destroyers and get into position to fire on the cruiser, the *Darter* suddenly ran aground on a coral reef called the Bombay Shoal a few minutes after midnight. The sound attracted one of the destroyers, but after a cursory inspection in the dark, the ship resumed its role protecting the cruiser.

Alerted to the mishap, Commander Claggett brought his submarine as close as he dared to the *Darter*, which was sitting high and dry almost completely out of the water. When all efforts to free the submarine failed, the two commanders decided to abandon it. The crew commenced burning secret papers and taking hammers to radios, radar, and other equipment. They did not want an enemy to discover anything of value on the trapped submarine. It took two and a half hours to transfer the entire crew of eighty-one by rubber rafts the fifty yards to the *Dace*. Once the last man, Commander McClintock, was aboard, the *Dace* raced away at full speed to avoid the demolition charges McClintock had set. When the explosions failed to sink it, Claggett fired four torpedoes at the submarine but all four exploded against the reef since the submarine was too high out of the water. Efforts to destroy the *Darter* using the *Dace*'s .50-caliber deck gun did pierce the former's hull, but the attempt had to stop when the submarine's radar reported an approaching enemy aircraft and it had to dive. Ironically, the Japanese bomber pilot either did not see the *Dace* or decided to attack what appeared to be an easier target. He did drop one bomb on the abandoned submarine. Later efforts to ensure the *Darter* could serve no purpose to the enemy failed to dislodge it. (A 1952 navy demolition team blew off the submarine's bow to destroy the four torpedoes housed there.)[11]

Although the encounter in the Palawan Passage cost the Americans one submarine with no loss of life, the Imperial Navy lost the services of three heavy cruisers, two destroyers, and nearly one thousand sailors including several members of Admiral Kurita's staff. The transmissions from the *Darter* warned Admirals Halsey and Kinkaid of the approach of a large enemy fleet whose location had been previously unknown.

It took the fleet nine hours to exit what they considered the submarine-infested waters of the Palawan Passage. Admiral Kurita and those staff officers with him transferred to the *Yamato* and made the superbattleship his flagship.

As WORD SPREAD of the approach of at least one major enemy war fleet, Admiral Kinkaid informed MacArthur of the situation and outlined his plan for what he assumed would be a major naval battle near the southern entrance to Leyte Gulf. He told the general he needed every available warship for the coming fight, including MacArthur's flagship *Nashville*. MacArthur responded that absolutely the cruiser should take part in the battle. Kinkaid explained that he could not send it into combat with the commander aboard. The general told the admiral not to be ridiculous, the commander should be there. He went on to explain he had never been in a major naval engagement and he was "anxious to see one."[12]

Having given up the argument that day, Kinkaid returned on the twenty-fifth and insisted as firmly as he dared that MacArthur must get off the warship so he could use its firepower. He suggested the general transfer to Admiral Barbey's amphibious flagship *Wasatch* for the night and then to Tacloban the following day. A clearly disappointed general reluctantly acquiesced to Kinkaid.[13]

With the knowledge that what they soon called the Center

Force was heading north of Palawan, aircraft from the Third Fleet searched all the western approaches to the Philippine Islands. The fast carriers launched from along the eastern side of the islands, so they had to cross over to search the waters on the west side.

Search planes from Rear Admiral Frederick Sherman's Task Group (TG) 38.3 discovered two imperial warships sailing south from Manila Bay in the early hours of October 24. They were the surviving members of Cruiser Division 16 under Rear Admiral Naomasa Sakonju, the light cruiser *Kinu* and destroyer *Uranami*. The third ship of the division and its flagship, the heavy cruiser *Aoba*, suffered severe damage in a torpedo attack from the American submarine *Bream* the day before. The torpedo struck the cruiser's No. 2 engine room, leaving it without power to move. The *Kinu* towed the stricken cruiser back to Cavite naval facility in Manila Bay and Admiral Sakonju transferred his flag to it. The two ships resumed their mission, which was to meet and escort troop transports from Cagayan on Mindanao to Ormoc on the west coast of Leyte, but were interrupted a second time by aircraft from the carriers *Essex* and *Lexington*. Although the attackers made no direct hit on either ship, close-by explosions caused minor structural damage to each. More seriously, strafing by the aircraft killed forty-seven members of the cruiser's crew and twenty-five men aboard the destroyer. Both ships continued south toward Mindanao.[14]

AT 6:30 ON THE morning of October 24, the 1st Striking Force of Admiral Kurita entered the Sibuyan Sea between the islands of Mindoro and Panay. Kurita knew it would be hard for enemy reconnaissance planes to miss his five battleships, seven heavy cruisers, two light cruisers, and thirteen destroyers, but he was counting on Admiral Fukudome's Second Air Fleet, which had just moved from Formosa to Manila for air cover against what he expected would be a large number of enemy aircraft. What he did not know was that Fukudome had only about two hundred aircraft at his disposal and decided he could best support Kurita not by flying air cover over his ships and engaging in single plane combat against an enemy that greatly outnumbered him, but by attacking the American aircraft carriers themselves.[15]

Three different imperial air forces were attacking the Americans on this day, as Kurita searched the skies above the Sibuyan Sea for his nonexistent air cover. General Tominaga's Fourth Air Army focused on the landing sites in Leyte Gulf. These attacks continued for most of the day, but did little damage at a cost of some seventy attacking aircraft. The kamikazes of Admiral Onishi proved useless at this time as bad weather and thick clouds prevented many of these less-experienced pilots from finding any targets.

It was up to Fukudome's land-based naval pilots to attempt some genuine results. Beginning at 8 a.m., they swept in from Luzon in three waves heading for the carriers of Admiral Sherman's TG 38.3. Fighters lifting off the light carriers *Princeton* and *Langley* and the fleet carriers *Essex* and *Lexington* met about 140 attacking Japanese planes, downing most of them. Shortly after 9:30 a Japanese bomber, a "Judy," raced down on the *Princeton* and dropped its 550-pound bomb directly onto the flight deck. The bomb roared through three decks and exploded. The resulting blast set several fully fueled torpedo planes in the hangar afire. The pilots of those planes were waiting to take off and attack Kurita's fleet in the Sibuyan Sea. Exploding torpedoes helped spread the flaming aviation fuel. As firefighting crews fought the flames, the light cruiser *Birmingham* passed a line to the carrier, planning to take it under tow, but a sudden explosion sent so much debris flying onto the cruiser that it killed 238 members of the crew and injured 426 others, including Captain Thomas Inglis. Also suffering damage were two nearby destroyers and another light cruiser. At 5:50 p.m., with all living crew members off the carrier, torpedoes fired from the light cruiser *Reno* sank it. One hundred eight men died on the carrier and 1,461 others were rescued. Some of the latter were pulled from shark-infested water as gunners on nearby ships drove off the predators.[16]

ADMIRAL FUKUDOME's Second Air Fleet had failed its assignment of destroying the enemy aircraft carriers. One light carrier sank, and several surface vessels were damaged enough to take them out of the fight, but his pilots had barely caught sight of the remaining two task groups. South of Sherman's TG 38.3 was Admiral Bogan's TG 38.2 off the coast of the San Bernardino Strait. Farther south, Admiral Davison's TG 38.4 was off Leyte Gulf. Missing now was Admiral McCain's TG 38.1. Before he received the report of the enemy force sailing north from the *Darter*, Admiral Halsey decided that after ten months at sea, a rest and replenishment of the ships and their crews was overdue. So, on the evening of October 22, he ordered McCain to take his TG, along with its three fleet carriers and two light carriers, to the naval base at Ulithi in the Caroline Islands for some R & R.

The submarine report of the approaching fleet containing several capital ships was a surprise to Halsey and his staff aboard his flagship, the battleship *New Jersey*. The Americans expected the Japanese to attempt to support the Imperial Army's 16th Division along the Leyte Gulf coast in the way they had done at Guadalcanal, in what was referred to as "the Tokyo express." These were nighttime runs by fast ships, usually destroyers, delivering supplies and reinforcements to Imperial Army forces battling the Americans. The runs were at night to lessen the possibility of attack from carrier-based aircraft operating mostly in daylight hours. With the submarine's report, Halsey worried the enemy was going to launch a massive attack on Admiral Kinkaid's Seventh Fleet, which was protecting the Sixth Army landing sites in Leyte Gulf. This was exactly what Admiral Toyoda planned.

At daybreak on October 24, teams of planes launched from all three Third Fleet task groups off the east coast to search for the Japanese ships. The search area was a wide arc reaching three hundred miles west and included all waterways that could give Japanese warships access toward Leyte Gulf. Each team consisted of a Curtiss Helldiver serving as a search plane, protected from potential enemy aircraft attack by two Grumman Hellcat fighters. A team from the fleet carrier *Intrepid* reported the presence of the Center Force a few minutes before 8 a.m. The Helldiver pilot, Lieutenant (jg) Russell Max Adams, quickly counted the number and type of ships that he watched off the southern coast of Mindoro entering the Tablas Strait leading to the Sibuyan Sea. Flying at nine thousand feet with mostly clear skies and unlimited visibility, Adams could clearly see the white wakes of the large ships heading east. A radio report went to another Hellcat pilot circling over the Sibuyan Sea waiting to relay it back to his carrier.[17]

The search planes did not go undetected by the radar on *Yamato*. General quarters brought all hands to their battle stations before most of the crew had breakfast. Anxious gunners aboard the warships watched the sky above them for either friendly or enemy aircraft.[18]

When Halsey received the report that the Japanese fleet contained only warships, no transports or other noncombat vessels, it was immediately clear the enemy was coming out for a fight.

This was no reinforcement or resupply run: it was a combat force that meant business. Halsey could not have been more excited. Illness had resulted in his hospitalization just prior to the Battle of Midway, forcing him to miss this most seminal sea battle to date. He was itching to tangle with the imperial fleet and it looked like his chance had arrived. He ordered all task groups to begin launching aircraft to attack the ships in the Sibuyan Sea. He radioed Admiral McCain to reverse course, refuel at sea, and return to the area as quickly as possible. McCain's TG 38.1 was about six hundred miles to the east, so it would not be able to participate until at least the following day. Aircraft from Admiral Sherman's carriers soon engaged in fighting off the attackers from Admiral Fukudome's Luzon-based naval bombers and fighters.

AT A FEW MINUTES before 10:30 a.m., fighters, bombers, and torpedo bombers from Admiral Bogan's TG 38.2 began attacking Kurita's ships. This was followed by a second, third, fourth, and fifth attack. The strikes against Admiral Kurita's ships involved 259 sorties at a cost of eighteen planes downed by antiaircraft fire. The American pilots, happy to see very little air cover over the ships, were surprised at the intensity of the antiaircraft fire directed at them. Every ship in the 1st Striking Force had extra antiaircraft guns added to compensate for what was expected to be a shortage of air cover. The first attack involved forty-five aircraft from TG 38.2's fleet carrier *Intrepid* and light carrier *Cabot*. Twenty-one fighters struck first to drive deck gunners under cover. Following immediately behind them were twelve dive-bombers and twelve torpedo bombers. Torpedoes hit two ships. The heavy cruiser *Myoko* quickly dropped behind the rest of the fleet when a torpedo severely damaged its two starboard screws and reduced its maximum speed to 15 knots. Forced out of the fight, Captain Itsu Ishihara turned his wounded ship around and headed back to Brunei, escorted by a destroyer. Admiral Kurita's force was now down by seven ships: four heavy cruisers and three destroyers. The superbattleship *Musashi* received a torpedo hit on its starboard side, but its commander, Rear Admiral Toshihara Inoguchi, reported the massive ship was able to continue at a reduced speed.[19]

Shortly after noon, as the force re-formed itself following the morning attack and continued east toward the San Bernardino Strait, the second wave of fighters, bombers, and torpedo planes attacked. The attacks continued until late in the afternoon. The American pilots looked on the two giant battleships as juicy targets and many concentrated their fire on them. Following the fourth strike, the *Musashi* had taken hits from four additional torpedoes and several bombs. The second superbattleship, *Yamato*, serving as Kurita's flagship, took several bomb hits, as did the battleship *Nagato*. Unable to maintain speed, *Musashi* received orders to turn away and head toward Manila Bay along with a destroyer escort. Following the fifth attack, as it withdrew from the area, it began to list and sent plumes of black smoke into the otherwise clear sky. During one of the later attacks, the ship's antiaircraft director was disabled, and Admiral Inoguchi suffered a bad shoulder wound.

Admiral Kurita, growing increasingly anxious over the absence of air cover, sent a message to Combined Fleet headquarters and Fukudome's headquarters in Manila at 4 p.m., explaining that he was turning around and retiring to get out of range of the American carrier aircraft that had been pounding his ships all day. His primary concern was finding his ships trapped in the narrow confines of the San Bernardino Strait as Halsey's aircraft pummeled them. Kurita also had to consider the fighting abilities of the crews of his ships. The men had been fighting enemy aircraft all day or making emergency repairs between attacks. Most had not eaten since the night before. He requested the support of land-based aircraft to fend off the enemy attackers. Admiral Fukudome later admitted he ignored Kurita's request because he believed the best support he could provide was to cripple the carriers that were launching the fighters and bombers. Heading back west, the force passed the *Musashi*, which was now dead in the water and sinking. Finally, after suffering strikes by nineteen torpedoes and eleven bombs, the mighty warship slipped over and sank shortly after nightfall, taking over one thousand members of its crew with it, including Admiral Inoguchi.[20]

Meanwhile, the day grew complicated for the Americans by additional reports of enemy fleets in the area. One was a message from Admiral Nimitz that an enemy fleet containing aircraft carriers was heading south toward the Philippines. This was Admiral Ozawa's Northern Force. Adding to the problems, planes from the *Enterprise* in Admiral Davison's TG 38.4, situated off Leyte Gulf, reported a fleet with battleships north of Mindanao heading toward the Surigao Strait and the southern entrance of Leyte Gulf. These were Admiral Nishimura's ships, which had left Brunei shortly after Kurita. They were to be the southern end of the pincer around Leyte Gulf. Following behind, and yet unseen, was the 2nd Striking Force of Admiral Shima. Combined, these two fleets had two battleships, three heavy cruisers, one light cruiser, and eight destroyers. The Americans referred to them as the Southern Force, not realizing there were actually two battle fleets heading toward the Surigao Strait. They would not be aware of Admiral Shima's force until shortly before noon when an Army Air Forces bomber reported its presence.

The lead planes, Hellcat fighters armed with .50-caliber machine guns and 5-inch rockets, swept down out of the morning sun followed closely behind by Helldiver dive-bombers dropping their 500-pound bombs. Probably due to the intense antiaircraft fire, the attack did only minor damage to the fantail of the battleship *Fuso*, but destroyed its aircraft catapult and two catapult-mounted search planes. A second bomb wrecked its No. 2 turret, killing everyone working there. The destroyer *Shigure* took a direct bomb hit on its forward gun turret, killing five men and wounding six others. The antiaircraft fire succeeded in shooting down one aircraft. A rescue team found the pilot several days later.[21]

The Japanese were at a distinct disadvantage for two reasons. One was a problem typical of imperial planners, an overly complicated plan of attack that relied on everything going as expected to maintain a tight timetable. Kurita was unable to get a reply from Fukudome concerning his air cover by the land-based naval forces, and he could not reach Admiral Ozawa to determine if his Northern Force had succeeded in drawing away any of the American carriers. The requirement that he maintain radio silence, which he already had ignored in desperation, prevented him and Admiral Nishimura from communicating concerning the timing of their joint attack into Leyte Gulf. The radio silence also prevented Nishimura from communicating with Admiral Shima, whose force was coming behind him to support his attack.

ADMIRAL HALSEY was especially concerned about the report from Nimitz of an enemy carrier force heading his way. He had instructed Admiral Sherman to send planes north in search of the carriers, but Sherman's task group was preoccupied with defending itself against the massive attacks from enemy aircraft identified as both land-based and carrier-based. Ozawa had sent the few planes he had aboard his carrier south in hopes that the Americans would follow them back to attack his Northern Force, drawing them away from attacking Kurita.

Inside Leyte Gulf, Admiral Kinkaid, commanding Seventh Fleet, ordered Rear Admiral Jesse Oldendorf to use his task group to lay a trap for Nishimura's ships as they headed toward the Surigao Strait. They anticipated the enemy would reach the Strait during the night, so everyone prepared for a night battle. Oldendorf's force consisted of six older but still effective battleships: *California, Maryland, Mississippi, Pennsylvania, Tennessee,* and *West Virginia*; four heavy cruisers, including one Australian; four light cruisers; twenty-eight destroyers; and thirty-nine PT boats. The battleships formed a virtual blockade across the strait. Against this formidable force, Nishimura had two old battleships that were so out of date they previously served for crew training, one heavy cruiser, and four destroyers.

The first line of defense was the PT boats lined up at the far end of the strait. Next were the destroyers, the cruisers, and finally the battleships. The PT boats made first contact at 10:30 the night of the twenty-fourth. Despite several hours of torpedo attacks, the Japanese ships pushed through without a single hit. They ran into trouble when they attempted to run a gauntlet of the first American destroyers firing torpedoes from both sides of the strait. By 3 a.m., both battleships received torpedo hits. The *Fuso* suffered several torpedo strikes on its starboard side and an hour later capsized. The next set of Oldendorf's destroyers fired torpedoes that sank two Japanese destroyers and forced a third to withdraw until American cruisers sank it with gunfire. The battleship *Yamashiro* (Nishimura's flagship) came under intense

MacArthur wading ashore at the Leyte assault beach on October 20, 1944. Accompanying him are left to right: Philippine president Sergio Osmena, Lieutenant General George Kenney (partially hidden), Colonel Courtney Whitney, Brigadier General Carlos Romulo, Lieutenant General Richard Sutherland, Bill Dunn of CBS, and MacArthur's aide, Staff Sergeant Francisco Salveron.

General MacArthur addressed the people of the Philippines via radio on a Leyte beach, October 20, 1944, shortly after the landings. The speech included the famous words, "I have returned." Philippine president Sergio Osmena spoke to his nation next. Both speeches were transmitted to a cruiser in Leyte Gulf and relayed using several frequencies known to be favored by guerrilla forces across the entire width and length of the Philippines, and ultimately to the United States.

Admiral William F. "Bull" Halsey, commanding officer of the US Third Fleet supporting the liberation of the Philippines. (Photo taken in 1943.)

Navy Lieutenant Commander Charles "Chick" Parsons and Army Major Charlie Smith. Both men were selected by MacArthur to oversee the smuggling of weapons and other war material from Australia to the guerrilla forces in the Philippines prior to the liberation.

General Walter Krueger and Vice Admiral Thomas Kinkaid review invasion plans aboard the latter's flagship, USS *Wasatch*, in Leyte Gulf, October 1944.

Battleships *Mississippi*, *West Virginia*, and *Maryland* in action at Leyte Gulf, October 20, 1944.

General Tomoyuki Yamashita (right), Japanese commander of the Fourteenth Area Army occupying the Philippines. He surrendered his forces on September 2, 1945, in northern Luzon. Tried by a military tribunal, the "Tiger of Malaya" was executed in Manila on February 23, 1946.

Members of A Troop of the 12th Cavalry Regiment of the 1st Cavalry Division descending nets on the attack transport USS *Har* during the assault on Ley in October 1944.

Army medics with the 3rd Battalion treating wounded riflemen from the 34th Infantry Division on the beach at Leyte, October 20, 1944.

Colonel Ruperto Kangleon (center). He led the guerrilla forces on Leyte known as the Black Army. A highly successful and well-organized force, they were widely feared by the Japanese troops.

General MacArthur and Philippine president Sergio Osmena discussing plans to establish a civilian government shortly after their radio broadcasts on Leyte.

General MacArthur visiting Major General Archibald V. Arnold, commander of the 7th Infantry Division, near the town of Dulag on Leyte, October 22, 1944.

Army engineers from 346th Engineer Construction Battalion are aided by Filipino civilians to lay metal airfield mats at Tacloban airstrip on Leyte.

American troops from the 7th Infantry Division crossing coconut log bridge near Dulag.

Men of B Troop of the 44th Tank Battalion moving through Tacloban, October 22, 1944.

General MacArthur addressing troops and civilians at Tacloban on Leyte, October 23, 1944. He announced the restoration of Philippine government control of the island; President Osmena is on the general's left.

Filipino civilian atop an American tank guiding it to a hidden enemy position spotted earlier, near Julita, Leyte, October 24, 1944.

34th Regiment vehicles bogged down in mud west of Pawling on Leyte in late October 1944.

Antiaircraft guns aboard the escort carrier USS *Sangamon* fire at Japanese dive-bombers off the coast of Leyte, November 22, 1944.

MacArthur touring Leyte battlefield while on his way to present the Medal of Honor to Major Richard Bong, who successfully fought forty air-to-air combat missions against enemy fighters, December 12, 1944.

Sixth Army commander Lieutenant General Walter Krueger (right) conferring with Major General Innis Swift, commander of I Corp (hands on hips), near town of San Fabian, Luzon, January 13, 1945.

General MacArthur, attempting a little exercise by walking around Santo Tomas on Luzon, is greeted by an admiring population on February 7, 1945.

General MacArthur and troops from the 38th Division inspecting recently killed Japanese soldiers while touring the front on Bataan, February 16, 1945.

Colonel Macario Peralta (right), leader of over 8,000 guerrillas on Panay. Prior to the liberation, his men controlled much of the island. He was awarded the Distinguished Service Cross.

Guerrilla leader Lieutenant Colonel Wendell Fertig (on left) and Lieutenant Commander "Chick" Parsons discuss their plans on Luzon in March 1945.

Infantrymen take cover from enemy snipers behind medium tanks near Damortis, Luzon. The troops were held up for several hours by enemy action until the arrival of the tanks.

American infantrymen from the 43rd Division crossing a waist-deep stream on their way to San Fabian, Luzon.

Eighth Army commanding officer, Lieutenant General Robert Eichelberger (center) reviewing the plans for parachute operations against Manila with Major General Joseph Swing (left), commander of the 11th Airborne Division, on January 21, 1945.

Luzon guerrilla leader Major Robert Lapham commanded 13,000 Filipino troops of the Luzon Guerrilla Armed Forces. So effective was his leadership that the Japanese Army put a one-million-dollar bounty on his head.

American troops halted by partially blown bridge leading to Olongapo, Luzon.

Major General Robert Beightler, commanding officer of the 37th Division, riding in an armored reconnaissance car through the town of Angeles, south of Clark Field on Luzon.

Troops of the 61st Field Artillery Battalion firing their 105mm howitzers at enemy positions in Manila on February 5, 1945.

American civilians, including children born in the prison, were freed from Manila's Bilibid Prison in early February 1945.

Exhausted troops from the 43rd Division withdrawing from Manila after sixteen days of continual building-to-building fighting.

fire from the cruisers and battleships and eventually capsized in flames and sank, taking the admiral with it. Only one ship survived: the destroyer *Shigure* limped back to Brunei for repairs. Forty miles away, Admiral Shima picked up battle reports from Nishimura's ships and decided to reverse course.[22]

In the Sibuyan Sea, Admiral Kurita's ships slowly moved west hoping to get beyond the range of the American carrier planes, which had already attacked five times. So many ships had suffered serious damage that the fleet speed had to slow down from its original 27 knots to 18 knots. They were like sitting ducks moving so slowly. As sunset approached, the admiral began to wonder why the enemy air attacks stopped. It could be he was out of their range, or perhaps Admiral Ozawa's decoy fleet, with whom he had no contact, had been effective and drawn the enemy carriers away from Leyte. The most frustrating thing for the admiral and the other ranking officers of the fleet was the silence from either Combined Fleet headquarters, Admiral Ozawa's decoy fleet, or Admiral Fukudome's land-based air fleet on Luzon. The only message Kurita received was a ludicrous warning from Combined Fleet to be alert for the strong possibility the Americans would use submarines to protect the entrance to San Bernardino Strait. The problem the fleet encountered did not come from under the sea, but in the sky above them where support did not exist.[23]

In the flag plot of Admiral Halsey's flagship *New Jersey*, the loudspeakers blasted the chatter from and between various pilots attacking the Center Force. It became obvious that the enemy fleet was in bad shape. Even allowing for the normal errors made by pilots in combat about what their weapons had hit and what had sunk, several reported hits with torpedoes and bombs on one of the superbattleships and watching it begin to settle in the water. Reports of hits on other ships rolled in one after another.

The men cheered report after report of stricken enemy ships, and then came word that the enemy had turned away and was retreating. It was almost too good to be true, and as it turned out, it was. At 6:30 as the sun was setting, Halsey's combat intelligence officer, Lieutenant Commander John Lawrence, reported that pilots from Admiral Davison's carriers reported that the Japanese fleet had turned around and were heading west.[24]

At 7:15, Admiral Toyoda finally responded to Kurita's report that he had turned his ships west: "With confidence in heavenly guidance, all forces will attack!" By then Kurita had already decided to resume sailing for the San Bernardino Strait since enemy air attacks had ceased entirely. There is strong evidence that Kurita never intended to abandon the plan to attack the ships in the gulf, but simply wanted time to rest his crews, make whatever repairs they could to his ships, and perhaps even convince the enemy he was withdrawing. The fleet passed through the strait at midnight and turned south toward Leyte Gulf, hugging the shore of Samar as they went.[25]

NOW THE SITUATION for the Americans went haywire. Halsey, believing that Kurita's fleet was in full retreat, was anxious to find and engage the enemy carrier fleet. He was prepared to pursue them once he had a clear understanding of where they were. He soon received word that search planes had found the Japanese carriers less than two hundred miles north of Admiral Sherman's task group. This supported reports from Sherman's ships that several of the planes attacking them had the telltale signs of being carrier-based. So inexperienced were the pilots of these planes that they were ordered to land at airfields on Luzon after attacking the Americans rather than attempt a carrier landing. In fact, the reports about inexperienced pilots were accurate. Admiral Ozawa's carrier force was ill equipped with planes and pilots; the only mission for his force was to lure the American carriers away from Kurita's fleet. If Ozawa was successful, Kurita would be free of air attacks to enter Leyte Gulf and destroy the American ships located there. Fearful of not being found, Ozawa had even resorted to sending out radio communications that the Americans could easily interpret as a carrier force heading their way.

Halsey's original plan was to pursue the carriers but leave behind a powerful force to guard the exit from San Bernardino Strait should the Center Force return. He and his staff prepared the plan that directed Vice Admiral Willis Lee to cover the strait with four battleships, two heavy cruisers, three light cruisers, and fourteen destroyers. These ships, all named in Halsey's plan, were from the carrier formations. They were designated Task Force (TF) 34. In support of Lee would be Admiral Davison's TG 38.4 carrier force with two fleet carriers.

The plan went to all task group commanders. Information copies went to Admiral Nimitz at Pearl Harbor and Admiral King in Washington. Not included on the list of recipients was Seventh Fleet commander Admiral Kinkaid, although his communications people intercepted it and gave him a copy. Halsey later explained that the message was a warning to the ships involved of their possible new assignment. Ensuring the task group commanders understood it was a plan only and not an actual order, Halsey sent them a follow-up message that TF 34 would be formed only when he directed it. Unfortunately, he used voice radio to communicate this, so King, Nimitz, and Kinkaid did not receive this information. All three believed the task force under Admiral Lee was formed and on duty. This was especially important to Kinkaid. If this powerful force guarded the northern entrance to the gulf, he could concentrate his assets on the southern entrance and Nishimura's ships.[26]

Once the Japanese carrier force had been located, it was designated Northern Force by the Americans. Much remained unknown about the Imperial Navy's carrier strength. Of greater importance was the size and composition of the Northern Force led by Admiral Ozawa. After Admiral Nimitz had warned that the enemy carrier fleet was approaching, two Helldivers from Admiral Sherman's TG 38.3 were sent out in the early afternoon of October 24 to establish its position. Several pilots reported sightings that were occasionally incomplete or even contradictory. They often had a hard time attempting to remain above an enemy group of ships while the latter kept up a barrage of antiaircraft fire. Ducking between clouds and the clumps of smoke from the exploding shells, they did the best they could in identifying the vessels below and counting them. The first report came in at 3:40 that afternoon: four battleships, one with a flight deck mounted on its aft that was either the *Hyuga* or the *Ise*, five or six cruisers, and six destroyers. The pilot, Lieutenant (jg) H. N. Walters, had seen the ships. He gave their position as 130 miles east of northern Luzon traveling south at 15 knots. This was Ozawa's "Group A," commanded by Rear Admiral Chiaki Matsuda and containing both of the converted battleships but no aircraft. Despite this, its official designation was Carrier Division 4. Ozawa had sent them south running parallel to his main fleet to seek enemy ships and engage them in a surface battle.[27]

An hour after Walter's report, Lieutenant (jg) Stu Crapser in his Helldiver was returning to the *Lexington* after making a three-hundred-mile-wide search to the north and east when his crewman, James F. Burns, made radar contact with what appeared to be several ships seven miles off. Flying over them, Crapser tallied three carriers, at least one cruiser, and several destroyers.

Burns transmitted that information to the *Lexington*. Crapser decided that since it was too late in the day for the carriers to send off attackers and be able to recover them before it was too dark, he would make use of the 1,000-pound armor-piercing bomb in his bomb bay, placed there because the aircraft was originally to go on a bombing mission. He headed down on one of the carriers as another sent several fighters aloft. He released his bomb and pulled up for cloud cover as antiaircraft shells exploded around them. They came under attack by several Zeros but they departed after Burns shot one out of the sky. When they returned to the *Lexington*, they found the bomb still in the bomb bay and a large hole in the underside of the Helldiver's left wing.[28]

While none of the reports on the enemy carrier fleet were accurate, they reported enough information to convince Halsey that he could now do what he had been waiting for since missing the fighting off Midway: go head to head against a Japanese carrier force. What he could not have known was just how weak that fleet was. At this time, Ozawa's force was composed of the fleet carrier *Zuikaku*, three light carriers, the two converted carrier/battleships, and ten destroyers. Following their attack on Admiral Sherman's forces, Ozawa had only a handful of planes left, mostly Zero fighters for maintaining combat air patrol.

Until he received these reported sightings, Halsey had been prepared to block the exit from San Bernardino Strait into the Philippine Sea with his battle line in case Kurita decided to resume his mission to attack the amphibious forces in Leyte Gulf. By evening, several pilots overflying the Sibuyan Sea had reported that the enemy ships had indeed turned back. Indications are these reports never reached Halsey aboard his flagship. Near exhaustion after several days without sleep, he had been thinking all along that the battle for Leyte Gulf would be a three-part puzzle. The Center

Force was one, the Southern Force was the second piece, and his pilots had now found the "missing piece," the Northern Force.

Halsey identified three options for dealing with the carrier force of Admiral Ozawa. He could separate the surface warships of the proposed TF 34 from the remaining ships and leave it to block San Bernardino Strait along with two carriers for air support and take the rest of the fleet north after Ozawa. This would be committing one of the first sins of naval warfare: dividing his forces in the face of an enemy of unknown strength. He rejected this out of concern that the Third Fleet might be defeated in detail without its full power, especially since McCain's task group was still too far away to be of help. He could maintain watches over the Northern Force while the Third Fleet waited to see if the Center Force came out to fight, but this gave the Japanese the option of where and when to strike at his forces, which would stand more or less idle waiting to see if Center Force emerged. Besides, standing by the "rat hole" waiting for the rat was not Halsey's style of aggressive warfare. Finally, he could take his entire force north to confront the enemy carrier fleet, leaving San Bernardino Strait undefended. Assuming as he did from pilot reports, that the Center Force had been badly mauled and had at least temporarily turned away, this was the option he chose.

Halsey's chief of staff, Rear Admiral Robert "Mick" Carney, reports that a great debate about the proper course of action to take concerning the enemy carrier fleet took place that evening in the New Jersey's flag plot. According to Carney, both Halsey and his chief air officer, Commander H. Douglas Moulton, believed that the Imperial Navy's effectiveness would be "hamstrung" if its tactical air arm were destroyed because they were convinced that Japan lacked the resources to replace the lost aircraft. The result of these discussions was that it was "essential this opportunity," of attacking the Northern Force, "be taken, to deprive them of their tactical air, as the principal target."[29]

Carney admits that lost in these discussions was the question of whether the Seventh Fleet was powerful enough to fend off Kurita's Center Force should it arrive. The basic assumption was that it could do so. What Halsey, Carney, and Moulton did not know at the time because it had not been communicated to them, was that many of Kinkaid's ships were running low on ammunition, especially the type required for a ship-to-ship battle, since they were originally intended to focus on shore bombardment.

His decision made, Halsey pointed to the location of the most recent reports concerning the enemy carrier fleet on a chart and told Carney, "Here's where we're going, Mick, start them north."[30]

Halsey then sent a message to Admiral Kinkaid informing him the Third Fleet was departing. Halsey's assumption was that the Seventh Fleet would be able to handle whatever portion of the Center Force still existed should it make a run for Leyte Gulf. The message appears straightforward: "Center Force heavily damaged according to strike reports. Am proceeding north with 3 Groups to attack carrier force at dawn."[31]

The confusion over who was guarding the San Bernardino Strait continued and only increased by the fact Halsey was taking three task groups with him. Admiral Kinkaid, and Admiral Nimitz who also received the message, assumed that TF 34 had indeed come to life and its battleships were remaining behind along with the fourth task group under Admiral McCain. But McCain was still too far away to play any role at this time. In fact, Halsey had not formed TF 34 and proceeded north with those ships.

Halsey's decision to pursue the Japanese carrier force relied in part on the wording of Admiral Nimitz's instructions concerning Third Fleet's responsibilities around the Leyte operation.

In addition to providing "strategic support" to the landings by destroying enemy naval and air forces threatening the operation, the instructions contained this key and later controversial phrase: "In case the opportunity for destruction of major portion of the enemy fleet is offered or can be created, such destruction becomes the primary task" of the Third Fleet.[32]

Just as the Japanese were operating in a divided command situation, so too were the two American naval forces. Admiral Kinkaid's Seventh Fleet reported to General MacArthur as part of his South West Pacific Command. Admiral Halsey's Third Fleet reported to Admiral Nimitz as part of his Central Pacific Command. Although not an overriding factor, in the coming events this divided command contributed to the confusion that might have been avoided with a single commander in charge as MacArthur had earlier requested.

Halsey viewed the Seventh Fleet as a defensive force protecting the transport ships and the landing beaches. The Third Fleet he saw as offensive in nature, which would include chasing down and destroying an enemy fleet containing a number of aircraft carriers.[33]

Admiral Halsey was not alone in what many had described as his "obsession" with the enemy carriers. In his after-action report, Admiral Sherman called the enemy carrier force "our meat," and noted that they were close enough to prevent them from escaping. He saw the race north as an opportunity to "completely wipe out" the "precious carriers," which the Japanese could not afford to lose.[34]

Third Fleet search planes found the Northern Force eighty miles away shortly after 2 a.m. They reported the presence of at least four aircraft carriers. Halsey wanted to avoid a night battle, at which the Japanese were proficient, so he slowed his fleet from 25 to 16 knots. He also was concerned about overrunning the enemy ships and allowing them to slip between Third Fleet and Luzon, giving them a straight run to Leyte Gulf. On the other hand, he feared having the enemy carriers to his east and enabling them to engage in "shuttle-bombing," meaning carrier planes would attack from the east, continue on to a Luzon airfield to quickly refuel, rearm, and attack from the opposite direction. He wanted to meet the enemy head on.[35]

At 6:30, as daylight broke, a first strike of 180 aircraft launched from the American flight decks. Over the next three hours, Halsey's pilots began reporting their successes, beginning with a fleet carrier and a hybrid battleship/carrier in flames as well as one cruiser, a destroyer seen to go to the bottom of the sea, and another cruiser and smaller carrier crippled. The jubilation in the flag plot was tempered by a series of messages from Kinkaid, several of which were delayed in the flood of messages flying everywhere concerning Leyte Gulf. The first arrived at 6:48 although Kinkaid had sent it at 4:12 a.m. The message explained that his forces were engaged in a surface battle at the Surigao Strait and inquired if TF 34 was guarding San Bernardino Strait. A somewhat surprised Halsey responded that TF 34 was with the Third Fleet carrier groups engaged in fighting the enemy's carrier fleet. Halsey was surprised because he was not aware that Kinkaid had intercepted and read his plan for TF 34.[36]

Meanwhile, Third Fleet aircraft continued pounding Ozawa's fleet, remaining out of range of the ships' antiaircraft guns as they did. The small number of planes the Japanese could put aloft found few targets and generally headed for the safety of Luzon airfields. When the fleet carrier *Zuikaku* could no longer take the beating and began to sink, Admiral Ozawa decided to go down with his flagship. When staff officers could not persuade him to move to another ship, they forcibly carried him off the carrier and transferred him to a cruiser along with his flag. The surviving ships headed north away from the enemy carrier force for several hours until Ozawa decided to try a surface battle against the Americans. After two hours, he realized he could never catch the now-retreating enemy and turned back toward Japan.[37]

MEANWHILE, THE twenty-two remaining ships of Admiral Kurita's Central Force threaded their way through the ten-mile-long San Bernardino Strait that several strategists at the US Naval War College claimed to be too shallow and narrow for large warships to pass through, leaving everyone to believe the major battle for Leyte Gulf would take place at Surigao Strait. Admiral Kurita was proving them wrong by bringing not only large warships but also the largest battleship ever built through the passage.[38]

Late on the evening of the twenty-fourth, as his ships crawled through the San Bernardino Strait, Kurita sent a message to Toyoda's headquarters boasting that his fleet intended to "charge into Leyte Gulf" the next morning "without regard for any damage we may suffer."[39]

Preparing for a fierce battle at daybreak on the twenty-fifth, the sailors aboard the Japanese ships were shocked when they found the wide sea before them empty. Kurita turned his fleet south and headed along the Samar coast toward Leyte Gulf. The lookouts on the Yamato peered nervously into the morning mist and low-hanging clouds searching for the enemy. Most had not slept in the last two days and were beginning to suffer from this. Suddenly a few minutes before seven, they reported seeing masts on the horizon less than twenty miles to the southeast. Quickly identified as being aircraft carriers, everyone cheered the opportunity to fight an enemy worthy of their efforts. They assumed they were looking at the fleet carriers of the US Third Fleet, but they were wrong.

Kurita's chief of staff, Rear Admiral Koyanagi, called it a "miracle" and a "heaven-sent opportunity" because "nothing is more vulnerable than an aircraft carrier in a surface engagement." He would later learn how vulnerable these particular carriers were, for they were not the fleet carriers Kurita expected, but the much smaller, slower, and weaker escort carriers of Kinkaid's Seventh Fleet.[40]

KNOWN DERISIVELY as "Kaiser Coffins" after the Kaiser Shipbuilding Company that constructed them quickly—and as some said, shoddily—these small aircraft carriers (also called "jeep carriers" and "baby flattops") were built on the unarmored hulls of cargo or tanker ships. Most had only one 5-inch gun for defense since their purpose was to escort troop ships by flying combat air cover over them. They were not intended to face an enemy battleship or cruiser line in a surface battle. To the sailors' and pilots' disbelief, that was exactly what they were about to do. The US Navy uses the hull designation for aircraft carriers of CV. For these specially manufactured small carriers they added the letter E, thus their designation became CVE. Sailors serving on them often referred to the official designation as "Combustible, Vulnerable, Expendable" because of their lack of armament and armor.

At the time, there were sixteen escort carriers on duty in Leyte Gulf under the overall command of Rear Admiral Thomas L. Sprague, divided into three units using their radio call signs of Taffy 1, Taffy 2, and Taffy 3. Taffy 1 was operating at the southern end of the gulf near Surigao Strait; Taffy 2 was one hundred miles north near the entrance to the gulf; and Taffy 3 operated off the shore of Samar not far from the San Bernardino Strait. The Japanese lookouts had found the escort carriers of Taffy 3. Rear Admiral Clifton "Ziggy" Sprague (no relation to Thomas) commanded them.

AS THE IMPERIAL Navy fleet moved south at 18 knots, excitement on board increased when aircraft launched from the decks and confirmed that they were approaching carriers. As a demonstration of how unreliable eyewitnesses could be, the Japanese lookouts estimated the enemy fleet was composed of four or five fast carriers, one or two battleships, and at least ten heavy cruisers. Taffy 3 actually contained six escort carriers, three destroyers, and four destroyer escorts. Kurita's four battleships, six heavy cruisers, two light cruisers, and ten destroyers outgunned them. During this time, Kurita received word that Admiral Nishimura's fleet had been destroyed and would not be joining him in Leyte Gulf.

To the men commanding the escort carriers in Leyte Gulf it looked to be another day consumed with combat air patrol, reconnaissance, antisubmarine patrols, and providing ground support for the troops on Leyte until the Army could repair and start using landing fields there. That all began to change when several pilots flying an antisubmarine patrol to the north suddenly reported the presence of Japanese warships twenty miles from Taffy 3 and approaching rapidly. This unbelievable message preceded a series of explosions on the horizon that resembled antiaircraft fire. Then came word that lookouts on several carriers reported seeing the pagoda-like masts of imperial warships. Admiral Sprague knew this could only mean Japanese battleships and cruisers.

Sprague immediately sent a signal to his ships to launch

their planes right away, regardless of what kind of ammunition they were carrying. Few if any had armor-piercing shells to use against warships since they were scheduled to attack enemy troops on land using machine guns, antipersonnel bombs, and in some cases depth charges for submarine patrol. He also ordered them to turn east into the wind to aide launching their aircraft then turn southwest away from the enemy, and instructed the destroyers and destroyer escorts to begin making smoke to cover the carriers' movements. Numerous local squalls that reduced visibility further aided this maneuver.

Anxious to close the gap between his ships and the American carriers, Kurita ordered speed pushed up to 24 knots. Not wanting to waste time re-forming his fleet into a combat formation, and wanting to hit the carriers before they could launch all their planes, he ordered a "general attack." The cruisers went first, followed by the battleships and then the destroyers. By 7 a.m., the Japanese battleships began firing shells containing colored dye. Each ship used a different color so it could track where its shells landed. American sailors were amazed at the colorful geysers splashing up around their ships until they realized what it was.

As the American carriers launched every plane they had and sought cover, the destroyers and destroyer escorts swung into action in an incredibly heroic manner, putting them at great risk to strike the powerful enemy and protect their charges. As the Japanese ships raced into action, the Americans did the best they could with their limited resources to stop them. Chaos reigned as ships fought individual actions.

At a few minutes after seven, Admiral Kinkaid was shocked to receive a message from the Taffy 3 commander that enemy warships were approaching his fleet. He immediately sent off a message to Halsey that enemy battleships and cruisers were firing on Taffy 3 from fifteen miles distance. Halsey received it at 8:22. An earlier message from the Seventh Fleet commander indicated defeat of the Japanese fleet in Surigao Strait and that he was sending ships in pursuit of stragglers. The Third Fleet commander believed the Center Force was so weakened that Taffy 3 would be able to hold them off until the Seventh Fleet's battleships under Admiral Oldendorf, which had beaten Nishimura, could come to their aid. Unfortunately, they were too far away to arrive in time and were already low on ammunition and fuel. Eight minutes later, Halsey, still focused on the enemy carrier fleet his planes were attacking at that moment, received another message from Kinkaid requesting that fast battleships be sent to Leyte Gulf urgently. Feeling he was unable to respond due to his distance from the scene and the expected coming major battle against the enemy carrier fleet, Halsey ordered Admiral McCain, who was still refueling, to rush to the aid of the forces under attack and informed Kinkaid they were on the way.

Messages seeking help kept pouring in from Kinkaid and Sprague, but Halsey remained determined to destroy the enemy carrier fleet, which was now only forty-two miles away and which he deemed the most dangerous force the Japanese had at sea.

Admiral Nimitz had been receiving copies of these messages at his headquarters and was growing concerned. He had assumed that Halsey had left TF 34 to guard San Bernardino Strait, but now had his doubts. He sent his own message to Halsey. The message, as Nimitz intended it, said "WHERE IS TASK FORCE 34 REPEAT WHERE IS TASK FORCE 34." It was a simple question, but when encrypted, as all messages were, extra words were added to the front and to the rear that had no real meaning to confound enemy code breakers. On receiving messages, the radio operators removed the extra words prior to delivery.

Unfortunately, although he removed the extra words in the front, "TURKEY TROTS TO WATER," for some reason the extra words on the rear were not, so the message Halsey received closed with the words "THE WORLD WONDERS."[41]

Halsey took the message from Nimitz as an insult, even throwing his hat on the deck and shouting incoherently concerning who Chester thought he was to second-guess the commander in the field. Everyone in the flag plot of *New Jersey* was shocked into silence by his reaction except for his chief of staff, Mick Carney. "Stop it!" Carney yelled. "What's the matter with you? Pull yourself together." The two men retired to Halsey's cabin. One hour later Halsey returned and ordered TF 34 to form and proceed to Leyte Gulf along with the carriers of TG 38.2, but he warned Kinkaid that the force could not arrive before eight the following morning.[42]

With his escort carriers under bombardment, Admiral Sprague ordered his pilots to land at Tacloban to refuel and rearm, to the surprise of Generals MacArthur and Kenney and the army engineers working on the landing strip. Planes that crashed on landing in the muddy strip were bulldozed out of the way while those still capable of flying were fueled and armed and sent on their way.

With no air cover of their own, Kurita's ships were constantly harassed by the American planes. Shortly the pilots of Taffy 2, whose carriers had sailed north to support them, joined in attacking the Japanese ships. It looked to the Japanese admiral as if more of Halsey's fleet carriers had arrived in response to the frantic messages from Kinkaid that his communications officers had picked up and sent him. He had been unable to catch the enemy carriers in a trap because of the smoke, the rainsqualls, and the relentless torpedo attacks from the destroyers and destroyer escorts. And now additional carriers and their aircraft were arriving.

After two hours of this melee, Admiral Kurita decided to call his ships together and head north. His ships were running at top speed and consuming fuel at an alarming rate. The last thing he wanted was his fleet dead in the water and getting pounded by enemy aircraft. He needed to close ranks since his ships had become widely scattered during the fighting, assess the damage they suffered, and decide if it was best to attempt to lunge into Leyte Gulf in what appeared to be a suicide mission to destroy enemy ships that for the most part had already unloaded their troops and cargo. Once inside the gulf, they would likely be trapped.

Undecided about withdrawing, Kurita circled his ships around several times, always suffering attacks from the air against which they had little defense. Shortly after 1 p.m., Kurita's Center Force headed toward San Bernardino Strait. Each ship was leaving a trail of oil behind. Had he remained much longer, he would have surely encountered battleships and several fleet carriers from the Third Fleet sent south by Halsey. As it was, Halsey's ships arrived too late to participate in the battle.

HALSEY SPENT the remainder of his life defending his decision to take his entire force north to chase what turned out to be a decoy fleet. He believed reports that Kurita's Center Force had suffered heavy damage and that Kinkaid's Seventh Fleet at Leyte could successfully challenge them. As a result, he headed north and prepared for combat. Unfortunately, pilot reports of serious damage to the Japanese fleet heading for San Bernardino Strait were notoriously overstated. Similarly, exaggerated reports from

Japanese pilots attempting to assess damage they had inflicted while engaging enemy fighters and avoiding antiaircraft fire had convinced Imperial General Headquarters of the destruction of Halsey's fleet off Formosa earlier in the month. The problem of pilots on both sides incorrectly reporting damage continued throughout the war.

Kurita came in for harsh criticism for turning away and heading west through the strait. Living in near poverty in Tokyo, he gave few interviews in his later years. When he did, each gave a slightly different explanation of why he turned away from Leyte Gulf when he did. Ten years after the event, his chief of staff, Admiral Koyanagi, wrote that the entire plan of breaking into the Leyte Gulf anchorage without any air cover was "a completely desperate, reckless, and unprecedented plan which ignored the basic concepts of war. I still cannot but interpret it as a suicide order for Kurita's fleet."[43]

The American losses in the Battle of Leyte Gulf were one light carrier to a kamikaze, two escort carriers, two destroyers, one destroyer escort, one submarine, and nearly three thousand lives. Japanese losses were three light carriers, one fleet carrier, three battleships, ten cruisers, eleven destroyers, and twelve thousand lives.

Never willing to admit defeat, the official imperial description of the battle broadcast over Radio Tokyo on October 26 claimed, "Japanese forces now have complete air and sea superiority on and around Leyte."[44]

CHAPTER TEN

BATTLING ACROSS LEYTE

As American troops poured onto the beaches along Leyte Gulf, the imperial Japanese war strategists finally came to the realization that this was the actual invasion, and it was taking place on Leyte, not Mindanao as many had predicted. Army headquarters issued a directive claiming the Philippines as "the area of decisive battle for the Japanese armed forces."[1]

It is difficult at this point to understand the Japanese attitude toward the invasion. Despite their massive losses in New Guinea and the Solomon Islands, they continued to believe they could win. Perhaps it was, as William Manchester said, that they believed their own propaganda, even when it was ridiculous to do so. Lieutenant General Sosaku Suzuki, commanding officer of the Thirty-Fifth Army responsible for security in the central Philippines, which included Leyte, reacted joyously when he learned that a massive American fleet that stretched a hundred miles back along the sea was heading his way, as if victory was a foregone conclusion. So confident of success was Suzuki that he told members of his staff that he planned to force MacArthur to surrender not only the forces he brought with him to Leyte, but also those he left behind in New Guinea.

In Manila, General Tomoyuki Yamashita, the "Tiger of Malaya," who had arrived to take command of all army troops in the country only ten days before, bragged that he would force MacArthur to surrender in the same humiliating fashion he had forced British General Percival at Singapore in February 1942.

In Tokyo, Prime Minister Kuniaki Koiso used a radio broadcast to proclaim to the Japanese people that the battle for Leyte would prove to be Japan's greatest triumph since the battle of Tennozan in 1592. The result of this important ancient battle between rival forces was a greatly unified Japan under Toyotomi Hideyoshi, leading in a direct line to the modern Japanese empire.

One army general who appeared to have doubts was Lieutenant General Shiro Makino, whose ten thousand troops of the 16th Division were battling both the overwhelming American forces to their front and the thousands of Filipino guerrillas who were ambushing his retreating soldiers. Emissaries from MacArthur and the local resistance leaders had planned the ambushes. Makino had experience dealing with the indigenous units as they had been attacking his airfield construction crews for months.

Another ranking officer concerned about the future of the war was Vice Admiral Takijiro Onishi, who had recently taken over command of the First Air Fleet on Luzon from Vice Admiral Kimpei Teraoka. Throughout August, attacks from Halsey's fleet of fast carriers had pummeled the First Air Fleet, which was responsible for the air defense of the Philippines. The rate of destruction increased when attacks from newly built airfields on Morotai by General Kenney's Fifth Air Force began. During this period, Teraoka's air fleet had suffered an 80 percent loss that reduced its serviceable aircraft of all types to roughly one hundred planes.

The change in command brought a substantial change in policy to the air defense of the Philippines. Both Teraoka and Vice Admiral Shigeru Fukudome, commander of the Second Air Fleet who had recently moved his forces to Luzon, had rejected suicide attacks on enemy ships, but Onishi was a powerful advocate of what he called the "godlike soldiers." The new commander told a group of staff officers that stopping the American aircraft carriers meant crashing bomb-carrying Zeros onto their flight decks. Soon scores of devoted pilots were lining up to be selected for the special attack groups he formed.

Meanwhile, Field Marshal Hisaichi Terauchi, commander of the Southern Expeditionary Army Group responsible for the war in Southeast Asia and the southwest Pacific, rejected General Yamashita's plan to forgo Leyte and center his defense on Luzon with the bulk of his 150,000 troops. Yamashita immediately ordered troops onto every available ship in Luzon harbors and rushed them to Leyte. Their objective was the port of Ormoc, on the northwestern end of the island, well beyond the reach of American infantry units struggling across the Leyte Plain in the island center.

Beginning on October 23 and continuing until December 11, 1944, convoys consisting of cargo ships, destroyers, naval transports, and a mix of smaller vessels made the six-hundred-mile trip from Manila to Ormoc. The imperial forces succeeded in putting forty-five thousand troops ashore on Leyte despite suffering heavy losses after American carrier and land-based planes attacked them.[2]

At about the same time, Lieutenant General Suzuki on Cebu began rounding up every available craft that could carry men and supplies. He was able to transport over six thousand men from two divisions stationed on Mindanao and Palawan to Ormoc.

Desperate to stop the American advance across Leyte, the Japanese threw everything they had at them, including dozens of kamikaze aircraft. Admiral Onishi's suicide forces swung into action from their base outside of Manila. While the ships of Admiral "Ziggy" Sprague's Taffy 3 fought off Kurita's Center Force, the escort carriers received particular attention from newly arrived land-based navy aircraft containing suicide pilots. Their brief training had been focused on crashing into the flight decks of American aircraft carriers, which is just what they began doing on arrival over Taffy 3. One of the first victims was the CVE *St. Lo*. After a kamikaze crashed through its flight deck and set off a series of fuel explosions belowdecks, it sank, taking over one hundred men with it. Also hit in the coordinated kamikaze attack were the escort carriers *White Plains*, *Kitkun Bay*, and *Kalinin Bay*. The two latter escort carriers suffered enough serious damage to take them out of the war for several months. Earlier in the day, the escort carrier *Gambier Bay* sank by shellfire from Admiral Kurita's ships. It had the misfortune to be the only US Navy aircraft carrier sunk by surface gunfire during the war. By day's end, Taffy 3 had only two of its original six escort carriers operational. This left a dramatic shortage in flight decks for returning aircraft. Over one hundred planes from the CVEs landed at Tacloban and Dulag airfields despite neither being completed. The result of the forced landings on the unfinished landing strips were numerous crashes, although most aircraft were quickly fueled and loaded with ammunition and bombs to return to the fight.[3]

Although the Battle of Leyte Gulf may have been over for the 1st Striking Force of Admiral Kurita, its agony continued as it fled the scene. The destroyer *Nowaki* stopped before reaching

San Bernardino Strait to rescue survivors from the heavy cruiser *Chikuma*, which had been attacked by planes from Taffy 3 and left dead in the water. A few minutes before 11 p.m. a scout plane from the Third Fleet reported the destroyer's position, and Admiral Halsey, now obviously angered at having missed the sea battle, rushed two fast cruisers and two fast destroyers to the scene. They caught the enemy destroyer heading for the entrance to the strait and sank it. Also attacked were the destroyers *Shiranuhi*, which sank, and *Hayashimo*, later beached as useless.[4]

THAT EVENING MacArthur, Kenney, and several staff officers sat down for dinner at Price House. The conversation soon turned to Halsey chasing after the decoy fleet and leaving the San Bernardino Strait unguarded. The admiral came in for what Kenney described as "highly uncomplimentary expressions" from the army officers who for the most part believed Halsey had abandoned their troops. Finally, MacArthur had heard enough and pounded the table, telling them, "That's enough. Leave the Bull alone. He's still a fighting Admiral in my book."[5]

General MacArthur took a liking to Admiral Halsey on the first day they met on April 15, 1943, in Brisbane to plan a series of amphibious landings in the South and South West Pacific Areas. The general's relationship with the Navy was not the best, especially since he never held back on his complaints about the Navy not providing his forces on Bataan the support he expected of them. But Halsey was an entirely different story. MacArthur considered him a "dynamic" leader and ranked him with John Paul Jones, David Farragut, and George Dewey as one of America's "great sailors" and a "battle commander of the highest order."[6]

While it may be true that Halsey could do no wrong in

MacArthur's book, the general felt uneasy about how long the carrier air support for his landings would last. On the day of the invasion, he told General Kenney, "Get the Fifth Air Force up here as fast as you can." He told Kenney that if he ever suggested another invasion without Kenney's land-based air forces for cover, Kenney should "kick me where it will do some good."[7]

MacArthur's experience on New Guinea taught him the true value of land-based bombers and fighters supporting his troops. It was not an entirely new lesson, for in 1931 he told Secretary of War Patrick J. Hurley that in the next war the nation "that does not command the air will face deadly odds."[8]

Two events bear witness to the importance of getting those Fifth Air Force planes to Leyte. On October 23, the first merchant ship to dock at Tacloban was the SS *Adoniram Judson* carrying a cargo of Marston steel landing mats to use at Tacloban Airfield and three thousand barrels of aviation fuel. While there, it came under dozens of attacks from enemy fighters and bombers. Its Naval Armed Guard and members of the crew defended the ship as its vital cargo was unloaded over six days. In the process, they shot down two Japanese planes and possibly as many as six others. The War Shipping Administration designated it "Gallant Ship," one of only nine ships with this distinction. Its captain, Charles A. Jarvis, received the Merchant Marine Distinguished Service Medal for his and his ship's service at Tacloban.[9]

Arriving on the same day as the initial landing troops were Major General Hugh Casey and a small number of his staff. As MacArthur's chief engineer, Casey had been responsible for the rapid construction of airfields in captured territory along the New Guinea coast and nearby islands. His job now was the construction of Tacloban and other airfields to house Kenney's aircraft.

Casey quickly took over a vacant home near the airfield and set up tents for engineers.[10]

Meanwhile, Lieutenant General Walter Krueger's Sixth Army fought its way toward the center of the island and the mountainous terrain in the north where the soldiers knew the enemy was preparing to make a stand to stop them.

The biggest problem for the American troops was the shortage of air cover for their operations. Third Fleet carrier groups were in dire need of rest, repair, and replenishment. In essence, they had to depart the Leyte area for some period, leaving the air cover for the escort carriers. These ships had few planes and many were required to provide combat air patrol over the fleet as Japanese attacks persisted daily. Japanese convoys continued to Ormoc, which for the most part was at the outer edge of the operational zone for the escort carrier planes. On October 25, five barges, escorted by destroyers carrying about one thousand soldiers and their equipment, landed safely at the port. The convoys continued on an almost daily schedule, often with few or no attacks from American aircraft.

The Tacloban Airfield was still a sea of mud with a thin layer of crushed coral when the steel mats arrived on October 25, and the engineers began installing them with the help of hundreds of Filipino volunteers. Land-based Japanese bombers from Luzon and Cebu harassed the workers daily and slowed progress. These attacks and the relentless rains made life miserable and highly dangerous for the Americans and Filipinos struggling to lay the mats and build an actual useable airstrip.

Two days earlier Kenney had been standing near the airstrip awaiting the arrival of six navy torpedo bombers that had requested permission to land. As the planes approached, they lowered their landing gear and turned on their running lights.

When the first plane touched down on the mud, Kenney realized that there were still six planes circling in preparation for landing. It turned out a Japanese bomber had attached itself to the end of the formation and had lowered his landing gear and turned on his lights just as the Americans ahead of him had. When it was his turn to land the pilot suddenly turned away and headed toward a large landing craft in the nearby bay. His bomb load ignited the craft's cargo: a load of gasoline-filled drums. It was a clear demonstration of the ability of many Japanese pilots to engage in night operations with a high degree of courage.[11]

The Fourth Air Army of Lieutenant General Tominaga had been quietly accumulating aircraft and pilots from airfields throughout the Pacific and Asia unknown to the Americans and even the Imperial Navy. The rivalry between the Navy and Army prevented him from alerting the naval commanders that he now had close to 2,500 aircraft at bases throughout Luzon. While the greatly diminished number of naval aircraft of Admirals Fukudome and Onishi focused on attacking enemy ships, Tominaga was more concerned with aiding the Imperial Army forces defending against the invaders throughout Leyte. The Japanese now had a huge advantage in air strikes against combat forces on the ground until Kenney could bring in his Fifth Air Force fighters and bombers.[12] Making matters even worse, the new pilots included a large number of Tokko pilots, the army version of the navy kamikazes, although it is unclear if many of them were aware of their fate. Fighter planes went to bases on Negros to be closer to the action on Leyte.[13]

Despite almost constant rain and typhoon weather in the eastern part of Leyte, and the daily air attacks that seemed to increase in intensity, the work on laying the coral base and installing the runway steel mats moved quickly. A major problem occurred when naval landing craft ran out of space to put supplies ashore at Red Beach and moved up to near the airfield. Much to their delight, the men unloading the craft found a nice hard surface at the airfield and unloaded their supplies. Despite arguments from the engineers about blocking the landing field, the landing craft continued to arrive. General Kenney rushed to the scene to find that over two dozen landing craft had dumped piles of supplies that blocked the work of the engineers. While Kenney complained to MacArthur and Admiral Barbey, the landing craft kept coming in. Kenney told the engineers that if the supplies remained where they were in two days they were to bulldoze the lot into the sea. The Navy removed the offending supplies and the work on the landing strip continued.[14]

By the evening of October 26, the engineers had managed to install close to three thousand feet of matting. Kenney thought this was enough for an experienced P-38 fighter pilot to land safely, and ordered the airbase on Morotai to send thirty-four of the aircraft up the following day. Kenney and MacArthur were having lunch on the twenty-seventh at Price House when they heard the sound of approaching airplanes. MacArthur listened carefully then asked Kenney what that was. Kenney responded they were the first members of the 49th Fighter Group arriving at the airfield. MacArthur jumped to his feet and rushed to the door calling for Kenney to follow and get into the general's car. They were driven to the field in time to see the P-38s that the Germans called "the forked-tail devils" fly over the area in formation, raising a cheer from the Americans and Filipinos on the ground.[15]

As the fighters landed, MacArthur and Kenney greeted the pilots. MacArthur told them they did not know how glad he was to see them. It appeared the Navy felt the same way. On the twenty-sixth, Admiral Halsey sent a message to MacArthur explaining that his pilots were exhausted and badly needed rest, and the carriers were running low on fuel, food, and ammunition. He wanted to know when the Army was taking over the air war over Leyte. The admiral was referring to the original invasion plan in which the Army's Fifth Air Force would assume responsibility for Leyte on the fifth day after the invasion. He was unaware of the difficulty the army engineers were having finding sites suitable for building landing strips.[16]

Although anxious to get his ships away from Leyte, Halsey remained on station as the escort carriers of the Seventh Fleet withdrew to repair the damage many had suffered during the enemy surface and air attacks. Third Fleet aircraft flew combat air patrol over the gulf and attacked enemy installations on Cebu and Luzon. One of Halsey's greatest concerns was the exhaustion of his pilots, who were now required to engage in close support action over the army troops, something for which they lacked training and experience. The situation deteriorated on October 29 when kamikazes attacked two of his carriers, *Franklin* and *Belleau Wood*, seriously damaging the flight decks of both ships and forcing them to be withdrawn to the naval base at Ulithi for extensive repairs and to replace the forty-five planes lost in the attacks. He also expressed concern to Admiral Nimitz about the large number of enemy airfields his pilots had to attack, and the Japanese rate of reinforcement of land-based fighters and bombers.[17]

Allied intelligence had difficulty keeping track of the number of enemy aircraft in the Philippines with new planes arriving nearly every day from around the empire. As the general aviation picture expanded, so too did the number of suicide pilots from both the Navy and Army. The troops on the ground were attacked almost hourly by low-flying fighters, as was Tacloban Airfield. Nightly bombing raids on the narrow airstrip became routine, as few Allied planes were able to defend against the roving enemy.

Kenney was unable to move many more fighters onto Tacloban, and the aircraft carriers were beginning to run low on planes due to enemy combat and accidents. Without a doubt, at this moment in the war, the Japanese dominated the air over Leyte.[18]

IN TOKYO, MEN who should have known better, including Imperial Army chief of staff General Yoshijiro Umezu, believed reports from navy pilots attacking the American Third and Seventh Fleets that the enemy fleets had been badly crippled and MacArthur's army was trapped on Leyte. As we have seen, this misjudgment of pilot reports resulted in their belief that the Third Fleet had been decimated off Formosa. So desperate were they to believe in victory, they ignored the earlier error and repeated it.[19]

A clear indication that Japanese headquarters remained convinced that Leyte was the site for their new decisive battle, despite General Yamashita's efforts to convince them otherwise, was the arrival at Ormoc of the best-equipped and highly regarded 1st Division of the Imperial Army. The division had fought a small but successful battle against Soviet forces along the Amur River border between Manchuria and the Soviet Union. Soon after MacArthur's landing at Leyte, the division commander, Lieutenant General Kataoka Tadasu, received orders to put the division on a train for Shanghai. From there the nearly twelve thousand members of the division and all their equipment boarded four merchant ships and several naval transports headed for Manila. After landing there, General Yamashita reviewed the troops. The general wanted to keep them for the defense of Luzon, but had to order the entire division to prepare to move to Leyte.[20]

Allied intelligence picked up no warnings concerning this and several other landings at or near Ormoc over the next few weeks.

Patrolling B-24 bombers from Morotai and P-38s from Tacloban happened across the convoy and its escorts. Their attack caused little or no damage, and the entire division and 90 percent of its equipment were unloaded. The following day, twenty-four B-24s attacked the convoy as it prepared to return empty to Manila and sank one ship. Additional convoys continued to arrive at Ormoc and many of them were attacked by the few P-38s Kenney had at Tacloban, which carried bombs.

WHILE THE WAR in the air and at sea continued, the main fighting remained on the ground. Most of the Third Fleet carriers withdrew to Ulithi for repairs and replenishment, leaving several on station to continue providing support to the ground troops until the Army could bring in enough planes to take over. One problem MacArthur and Krueger faced was the relentless attacks along the beaches, which destroyed supplies that had piled up quickly. Adding to this was the ability of the enemy to mount nighttime raids all over the island, whereas the carrier planes had to be on their ships so the carriers could maintain lights out. To rectify this, MacArthur asked Nimitz to send several squadrons of Marine night fighters from their bases on the Solomon Islands. Once the Marines arrived, the Japanese no longer owned the night skies over the battlefields.[21]

Battling torrential rains and several typhoons, the Sixth Army slogged its way west toward the Leyte Valley and the nearby mountain range. Enemy reinforcements continued to pour in despite frequent attacks on the convoys by American aircraft and ships. Soon some forty-five thousand Japanese combat troops arrived, supporting the original ten thousand men of the 16th Division.

Advance along most of the front established by the invading

troops slowed due to the weather, the thick mud, and a growing intensity of Japanese resistance. A major objective for General Sibert's X Corps was the northern port city of Carigara. General Krueger wanted this port occupied to protect his northern flank from enemy landings as they were doing at Ormoc. This became increasingly important after the deputy commander of the 7th Amphibious Force, Rear Admiral William M. Fechteler, told Krueger's assistant operations officer that there were suitable landing beaches along Carigara Bay and an enemy landing there would have the added support of land-based air cover from bases on Mindoro and Luzon.[22] Capturing Carigara would not only prevent Japanese landings along the bay, but also give American forces a direct route through the mountains to Ormoc, the ultimate goal to stop all enemy reinforcements.

Thirty-Fifth Army commander Suzuki moved his headquarters to Ormoc so he could better implement his plan for defeating the Americans. He ordered the 1st Division to man the ridges covering the route south of Carigara toward Ormoc to halt any enemy advance in that direction. This was just the plan General Krueger had once the 1st Cavalry Division and the 24th Infantry Division entered a mostly abandoned Carigara on November 1. That same day, a Japanese staff officer, who recognized that the Americans now controlled the town, had withdrawn the troops. The officer, Major Chuji Keneko, ordered all units in the Carigara area to withdraw to the nearby hills and establish defensive positions to prepare to carry out General Suzuki's plan to defeat the Americans. The general's plans called for using Carigara as an assembly point for numerous units in the northwest region of Leyte and to launch a counterattack aimed at recovering Tacloban. The following day he learned the Americans had moved so rapidly, and his own troops so scattered, that his plan was aborted.[23]

CHAPTER ELEVEN

BREAKING THE YAMASHITA LINE

Despite the devastating defeat suffered by the Imperial Navy, and his own feelings concerning the importance of defending Luzon, General Yamashita remained committed to stopping the American forces' advance across Leyte. He continued shipping troops to Ormoc on the west coast of Leyte; most who survived the hazardous journey immediately pushed into the nearby mountains where elements of the US 21st Infantry Regiment were making slow progress. Progress stalled when they encountered a ridgeline of ugly precipitous peaks that ran across the main road leading from Carigara in the northeast toward Ormoc. On November 5, the Japanese launched a series of attacks that pushed the Americans back several miles and set up a nine-mile-wide defensive line they called the Yamashita Line.

Sixth Army commander General Krueger focused on capturing Ormoc. This port was now the center of Japanese resistance on Leyte. Thirty-Fifth Army commander Lieutenant General Sosaku Suzuki had pulled a number of units out of the surrounding

mountains to provide closer and more concentrated defense as reinforcements and supplies continued to arrive, although in greatly
reduced numbers as American submarines and aircraft took a
heavy toll on the vessels arriving in Ormoc Bay. Krueger's plan
was to drive on Ormoc from two directions, forming a pincer.

General Frank Sibert's X Corps had to fight its way through
a series of tortuous ridges and rock formations through which
Highway 2, the road to Ormoc, twisted and turned. The Japanese
1st Division had about four thousand men well placed to prevent
the Americans from moving south along the winding highway.
What followed were twelve days of some of the worst fighting on
Leyte as American units attacked well-hidden enemy positions
defended with mortars and heavy machine guns. There were
no wild and reckless "Banzai" charges or yelling by these well-
disciplined troops. Instead, they often remained hidden during
the day, allowing American units to pass by, then attacked them
from the rear.

As Americans attempted to advance up the near side of a
hill, they came under devastating fire from artillery hidden in
trenches and foxholes on the reverse side. Days of continuous
rain turned the grassy hillsides into slick mud that made climbing almost impossible and slowed the Americans struggling up
under enemy fire. The treacherous steep hills quickly earned the
name "Breakneck Ridge" for its potential to do bodily harm to the
climbers. A typhoon that swept through the area on November 8
added to the misery of the Americans.

After days of little success, Major General Frederick Irving
decided his best chance of subduing the enemy was a pincer
movement around their rear. A battalion from the 19th Infantry
Regiment advanced across Highway 2 and moved south on the
Japanese right flank three miles. There, the 2nd Battalion under

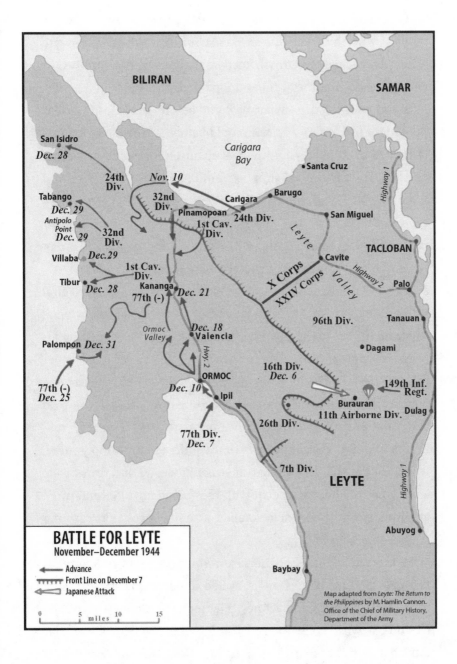

BILIRAN

SAMAR

San Isidro
Dec. 28

Carigara
Bay

• Santa Cruz

Highway 1

24th
Div.

Nov. 10

32nd
Div.

Carigara

• Barugo

Tabango
Dec. 29

Pinamopoan

24th Div.

• San Miguel

Antipolo
Point
Dec. 29

32nd
Div.

1st Cav.
Div.

Leyte

TACLOBAN

Villaba • *Dec.29*

1st Cav.
Div.

• Cavite

X Corps

XXIV Corps

Highway 2

Palo •

Tibur •
Dec. 28

Kananga

77th (-)

Dec. 21

Valley

96th Div.

Tanauan •

Ormoc
Valley

Dec. 18
Valencia

• Dagami

Palompon *Dec. 31*

Hwy. 2

16th Div.
Dec. 6

77th (-)
Dec. 25

ORMOC

Dec. 10

• Ipil

149th Inf.
Regt.

Burauran
11th Airborne Div. Dulag

77th Div.
Dec. 7

26th Div.

7th Div.

LEYTE

Highway 1

Abuyog •

BATTLE FOR LEYTE
November–December 1944

← Advance
⊤⊤⊤⊤⊤ Front Line on December 7
⊲══ Japanese Attack

Baybay •

0   5   miles   10   15

Map adapted from *Leyte: The Return to
the Philippines* by M. Hamlin Cannon.
Office of the Chief of Military History,
Department of the Army

Lieutenant Colonel Robert Spragins, who would receive the Distinguished Service Cross for his actions on this mission, struggled for two days through trackless jungle led by several Filipino scouts familiar with the area. Late in the day on November 12, forward elements reached the Ormoc Road but halted when confronted by strong enemy fire from a ridge along the opposite side of the road. Both sides decided to await daylight before launching attacks. That night the Americans, who could barely see the hard-surfaced Ormoc Road, could do nothing to stop the enemy vehicles moving north with badly needed supplies for the Japanese.

Enemy activity in the battalion's rear revealed that the Americans had been surrounded. With ammunition and food supplies running low, Spragins requested an airdrop for the following day, November 13. The day passed without a supply drop and several soldiers were reduced to eating palm hearts and rummaging through the packs of dead Japanese for food. To their great frustration, the Americans watched as the badly needed supplies began dropping from American aircraft that afternoon either behind the Japanese lines or in the no-man's-land between the opposing forces. Two days later two companies crossed the road and captured an enemy observation post atop a nearby hill. Colonel Spragins was now able to close the enemy supply route, which he did that night when his men attacked and drove back a truck convoy heading north with reinforcements. Several more attempts to run the roadblock failed with only two tanks carrying supplies making it through.

Meanwhile, the 1st Battalion from the 34th Infantry Regiment boarded landing barges and traveled along the coast to a spot two miles behind enemy lines. Lieutenant Colonel Thomas E. Clifford, a West Point football legend who earned a Silver Star during the fighting in Hollandia on New Guinea, led his 1st

Battalion men southwest toward Highway 2 with a plan to link up with the 19th Infantry's 2nd Battalion on the highway and prevent Japanese troops from retreating south. Clifford's battalion managed to secure a position atop a hill called Kilay Ridge overlooking Highway 2 from which they fought off nearly a dozen major Japanese assaults. Ordered to hold the ridge at all costs, the battalion spent the next three weeks in rain-flooded, mud-filled trenches and foxholes.

The two American units were only a thousand yards apart, although the rain caused visibility to be less than a few yards. Fighting continued over the next month as enemy forces attempted to break out and head south. By the time the fighting ended and the ridgeline was secure, Clifford's battalion of 565 men had been reduced by 26 killed and slightly over 100 wounded. A body count found nearly 1,000 dead Japanese soldiers. Both battalions received the Presidential Unit Citation for the blocking of enemy forces trying to retreat to Ormoc.[1]

FARTHER SOUTH, a company from the 7th Infantry Division of Major General John R. Hodge's XXIV Corps made its way across the Leyte Valley and the nearby mountains, reaching the west coast at Baybay, twenty-eight miles south of Ormoc. They traveled along what passed for a road in that part of the country that Japanese intelligence believed was impassable due to thick mud, bomb craters, and downed bridges. When the Americans discovered no enemy forces in or around Baybay, Lieutenant Colonel John M. Finn, commanding the 32nd Infantry Regiment, ordered two full battalions to join them. He even moved his regimental headquarters to Baybay and assigned a third battalion to guard along the road to keep it open.[2]

When the Japanese learned the Americans were at Baybay, General Suzuki ordered elements of the 16th Division at Ormoc south to prevent the Americans moving north. These troops were originally to take part in a planned attack across Leyte to attempt to capture the Burauen airfields. Guerrilla forces informed 7th Division commander Major General Archibald Arnold that the enemy was building a road through the mountains toward Burauen. A patrol sent to search for the road reported finding no trace of the Japanese doing any construction work in the area.

General Suzuki arrived along with his staff at Ormoc on November 1. He was so convinced that his reinforced army, including thirteen thousand troops that arrived that same day, would defeat the Americans that he now risked all for the fight. Suzuki's own commanding officer, General Yamashita, reluctantly sent these additional troops to Leyte despite his own opinion, and those of his staff, that they would better serve the goal of defeating MacArthur by keeping those forces on Luzon. Retaining control of Luzon, Yamashita believed, was vital to holding on in the Philippines. Leyte, in the view of the Fourteenth Area Army, was of minor importance to that overall objective.

Although fighting continued at scattered locations across Leyte, the city of Ormoc soon became the central point of conflict. Located in the northwestern sector of the island, the city had a deepwater port for the landing of reinforcements and supplies. In addition to destroyers bringing in convoys from Luzon, the port itself had several destroyers and submarines stationed there. Adding to the port's protection was a series of fortified shore positions located throughout the nearby hills with clear visibility of the Ormoc Bay below them.

Two battles were instrumental in the success of the American campaign for Leyte. First was a little-known yet important naval clash fiercely fought by destroyers, submarines, patrol boats, and armed barges. The Japanese had the added weight of numerous shore batteries in their fortified positions. The fighting took place in two narrow channels and in the bay fronting the city. Over several weeks from mid-November to early December, Japanese convoys attempted to push their way through to Ormoc Bay— sometimes successfully, other times less so. Clashes between warships of varying sizes and strength finally concluded when the Japanese realized they could no longer afford to lose any more ships and men to the enemy. This series of battles had cost them thirty-one ships. The American cost was three destroyers. By then the Japanese strength on Leyte exceeded fifty-five thousand men who had little hope of evacuation and were determined to fight to the death.

While this sea battle was taking place, General Krueger ordered a pincer attack on the Ormoc region. The Japanese had pulled together a strong defensive line of fortified positions that blocked the entire northwest area around Ormoc and the Ormoc Valley. Following weeks of grueling combat against dug-in Japanese positions, Sibert's X Corps gradually pushed south from the mountains while Hodge's XXIV Corp struggled north along the coast. The pincers around the Ormoc region gradually tightened and the Japanese focused on the enemy advancing overland from the north, east, and south.

Meanwhile, Major General Andrew D. Bruce's 77th Infantry Division boarded ships of the Ormoc Attack Group commanded by Rear Admiral Arthur D. Struble at Dulag in Leyte Gulf and sailed south. They passed through Surigao Strait and turned north along the Leyte west coast without encountering enemy forces. The division, called the "Statue of Liberty Division" because most of its men were from the New York City area, made a virtually unopposed landing some three miles south of Ormoc. Bruce himself had selected the site based on air reconnaissance and guerrilla reports of few Japanese troops in the area.

General Bruce led the 77th in a relentless drive north, crushing the confused enemy who found Americans on all sides of them. Finally, on December 11 the division pushed through the city that had become a "blazing inferno"[3] of exploding ammunition dumps, burning homes and other buildings, and linked up with members of the 184th Infantry of the 7th Division from XXIV Corps. The surviving Japanese troops slipped away during the night and fled into the northern mountains to continue the fight.

AS THE FIGHTING raged around Ormoc and Ormoc Bay, in Manila, Fourteenth Area Army commanding officer General Yamashita became increasingly concerned about losing Leyte to the enemy. Such a loss could result in cutting off the entire southwest Pacific from the Home Islands if the Americans were able to rehabilitate or construct new air bases on Leyte. Air bases would serve as home for the land-based fighters and bombers of the US Fifth Air Force. American submarines were already taking a terrible toll on cargo vessels transporting oil and rubber from the East Indies to Japan. An upsurge in land-based aircraft, if moved to Leyte from their current bases in New Guinea, would make transiting the South China Sea even more costly, perhaps prohibitive, for the Japanese.

The US Fifth Air Force could make only limited use of the airfields at Tacloban and Dulag as engineers primarily fought a losing battle against the high water table and constant floods of mud across both fields. Of even greater concern to Yamashita and his superiors in Tokyo were the three unfinished airfields the Japanese had begun building near the town of Burauen in the southern end of the Leyte Valley. Imperial General Headquarters wanted all five airfields occupied or destroyed.

To assure the security of his directive concerning the airfields, Yamashita sent a member of his staff, Major Mitsusuke Tanaka, to meet with General Suzuki. Tanaka explained to Suzuki that the orders he was relaying came from not only Yamashita, but also Imperial General Headquarters. It appears this was possibly an exaggeration on the part of Yamashita and Tanaka to inspire Suzuki to achieve the goals they set for him. Suzuki was told to "annihilate the enemy's air power" by making the airfields at Tacloban and Dulag inoperable and to either destroy the three airstrips near Burauen or gain control of them.[4]

The plan of attack had several segments. In the first, demolition teams were to fly to the Dulag and Tacloban fields in Mitsubishi Ki-57 twin-engine transport planes. They were to land with their wheels up if necessary to get their passengers to their targets. Aboard each aircraft were ten specially trained demolition teams from the 1st Guerrilla Company with orders to destroy everything they found on the ground, including parked airplanes, ammunition and fuel supplies, and buildings. Their four transports left an airfield south of Manila after dark on November 26 for the 350-mile trip south.[5]

For some unexplained reason, one of the transports separated from the others and flew to the west coast of Leyte, landing near Ormoc. Shortly before 3 a.m. on the twenty-seventh, the remaining three flew at a low level along the gulf coast with their lights on in a successful attempt to fool enemy lookouts that they were American cargo planes. As soldiers from the 728th Amphibian Tractor Battalion camped along the shore watched, one of the aircraft suddenly dropped into the gulf as if it suffered mechanical failure. Since it was only about twenty-five yards from the beach, one of the men from the tractor battalion decided to wade out to offer help. He managed to climb aboard the plane's wing when someone inside hurled a hand grenade at him. The Americans opened fire on the aircraft, killing two of the men inside, but the others managed to swim away and vanished in the darkness.

A second plane crashed near one of the airfields, killing all aboard. The final aircraft told an interesting tale. It made a soft crash-landing across a narrow river from a campsite occupied by the 11th Airborne Division. Having mistaken the craft for an American cargo plane, members of a machine-gun crew stationed along the river shouted across the waterway asking if the presumed fellow Americans needed any help. When someone aboard the plane shouted back that they were okay and required no help, the machine gunners turned their attention back toward the sky, watching for enemy aircraft. When dawn began to break, the Americans saw the red "meatball" emblem on the plane and only then realized it was Japanese. The men aboard it had long since gone but had left behind an assortment of demolition kits.[6]

Despite the shortage of serviceable landing sites on Leyte, the US Fifth Air Force still dominated the skies over the island and continued to wreak havoc with enemy attempts to land troops and supplies at Ormoc, sinking a great number of ships either on the way to Ormoc or returning to Luzon. Imperial Fourth Air Army commander Lieutenant General Tominaga decided the best way to forestall the enemy's plans to improve and expand the newer airfields was through an attack by specially trained troops who could land on the airfields and take control of them at least temporarily. In addition to destroying enemy assets at the sites, they could render the landing fields useless and hold them until the arrival of infantry troops as reinforcements. The Japanese saw these airfields as the key to regaining control of Leyte and expanding their own air operations.

The Japanese planners selected two of the three airfields around Burauen, Bayug and Buri. Both were still under construction but held promise as sufficient for Fifth Air Force use. The plan expanded from a hit-and-run mission to a coordinated assault by the air units and General Suzuki's infantry forces, who would rush from their present positions to assist the Air Army troops on retaining control of the fields. When laid out on paper, the plan for Operation Wa was rather simple without unreasonable expectation of success for Japanese officers. Preceding the assault was a general air offensive on both airfields using every available aircraft to achieve maximum damage. Then the airborne forces would be landed on the airstrips and attack all remaining targets. Meanwhile, troops from the 15th and 26th Infantry Divisions would launch ground offensives against both airfields. If all went in their favor, imperial forces could gain control of both fields and make them available for use by Japanese fighter aircraft. Regaining control of the airfields would be the first step in driving MacArthur's forces back into the sea.[7]

Beginning on November 24 and continuing through the next four days, aircraft from the Fourth Air Army's 2nd Division bombed and strafed the airfields while navy planes attacked Allied ships in Leyte Gulf.

On the night of November 26, forty members of the Kaoru Airborne Raiding Detachment boarded four transports at Lipa Airfield south of Manila and headed south toward Leyte. Commanded by Lieutenant Shigeo Naka, the detachment was mostly composed of men from a Formosan tribe recognized for their skill in jungle fighting and personal courage. Highlighting the importance of their mission, Lieutenant General Tominaga personally visited the men prior to their flight. Also aboard the planes was a large assortment of demolition type explosives. The plan was to make belly landings at the two airfields so the soldiers could spread out and blow up buildings, parked aircraft, and any other targets they could find. These specialized soldiers had gone through intensive infiltration and demolition training at Japan's premier intelligence and guerrilla tactics training center, the Nakano School. A potential suicide mission, the men were to attempt to make contact with troops of the 16th Division fighting southwest of the area when their work was complete.

The 350-mile flight to the Burauen airfields took approximately two hours. The aircraft flew at very low altitude to avoid encountering patrolling American fighters. At the expected time, Lieutenant Naka radioed that the detachment had reached its targets. That was the last anyone heard from them. Although the fate of the four planes and troops aboard them was unknown, Imperial General Headquarters was so convinced the mission had been a great success that they broadcast a public announcement praising the men involved.[8]

This plan using the demolition teams was a temporary measure because the Japanese knew the Americans eventually would be able to repair any damage they caused. What they needed was an assault powerful enough to drive the enemy out of all the airfields, not just the three around Burauen, but also Tacloban and Dulag. This more comprehensive plan combined paratroopers and infantry.

The major effort to gain control of the airfields was on December 6. Four days earlier, 16th Division commander General Makino assembled troops from his division and marched them toward the Buri airstrip, the northernmost of the three Burauen airfields. His men were to link with paratroopers flown in transports from Clark Field on Luzon. Additional infantry troops from the 26th Infantry Division advanced from the west. Bad weather delayed the airdrop, but faulty communications resulted in the infantry not being aware of this. Shortly after dawn on the sixth several hundred soldiers from the 16th Division attacked a campsite used by American and Australian engineers working on the nearby airstrip one mile north of Burauen. They killed a number of these noncombat soldiers and drove the others off.

In the early afternoon of December 6, the first wave of 365 delayed paratroopers from the 3rd Parachute Regiment led by Lieutenant Colonel Tsunehiro Shirai boarded twenty-six transports at Clark Field and joined fighter escorts headed toward Leyte. Four of the transports were brought down by ground fire, but the escorts were able to drive off American fighters as the transports flew at less than one thousand feet. Shortly after 6:30, the paratroopers began jumping into the darkness. As can be expected, most ended up scattered across the area.[9]

Despite much confusion, the paratroopers and the small number of infantry troops who reached the fields rampaged through them, inflicting considerable damage to the airfield buildings, parked aircraft, and equipment dumps. The American defenders were mostly noncombat service units driven out by the intense attack. The airfield remained occupied by Japanese infantry and parachute troops until American reinforcements arrived and forced them to withdraw into the nearby forest to wait for the second and third waves of paratroopers, which failed to arrive after the first drop.[10]

When Major General Joseph "Jumpin' Joe" Swing, commanding general of the 11th Airborne Division, learned of the attacks on the airfields, he ordered his combat troopers to counterattack. The 1st Battalion from the 187th Glider Infantry Regiment commanded by Colonel Harry B. Hildebrand arrived to begin driving the enemy off the airfields. By December 9 the few surviving remnants of Makino's 16th Division and the paratroopers fled through the jungles toward Ormoc on the west coast.[11]

ON DECEMBER 25, 1944, General MacArthur issued a statement claiming all organized Japanese resistance on Leyte had ended. Always anxious to speed operations up, the commander had gotten ahead of his two army commanders, making both unhappy. General Krueger estimated eight thousand enemy combat troops remained on the island. The actual number was closer to fifteen thousand. General Robert L. Eichelberger's Eighth Army received orders that evening to take over from Krueger's Sixth. MacArthur's dismissive comment that only mopping up operations was required angered Eichelberger; he knew better.

General Krueger had prepared plans for the invasions of both Luzon and Mindoro. The latter could be a stepping-stone to Luzon, offering the opportunity for several airfields from which land-based planes could attack. General Eichelberger took control of both X Corps and XXIV Corps and other selected units.

Writing after the war, Eichelberger was still bitter about this and proposed that in any future war the Army drop the expression "mopping up" from its vocabulary. It was not "a good enough phrase to die for." When he took command of Leyte, Eichelberger had eight divisions all engaged in combat. Adding to his problems of coordinating all these units was the fact that many of the Japanese troops who had withdrawn from Ormoc into the northeastern mountains suddenly came streaming down to support their comrades fighting the Americans. Unlike many of the troops the Eighth Army was battling, these men appeared well fed and equipped.[12]

Despite the continuing presence of strong units on Leyte, when word was received on December 18 from Fourteenth Area Army that American forces had landed on Mindoro, that sealed the fate of those units. With the Americans on Mindoro, there could be no more shipments of reinforcements or supplies to Leyte. General Yamashita informed General Suzuki that he should plan to make his forces on Leyte self-sufficient in terms of food supplies since none would be coming from Luzon. On December 21, Suzuki ordered a general retreat of all forces toward Palompon on the coast north of Ormoc Bay. Most remained there fighting scattered battles with American and Filipino patrols until the war ended.

CHAPTER TWELVE

LEAP TO MINDORO

In 1944, Mindoro, the seventh-largest of the Philippine islands, was one of the least geographically hospitable places in the archipelago. Roughly half the size of New Jersey, it resembles an egg standing on its end. Its population of slightly over one hundred thousand lived primarily along stretches of the coast on slender level plains where sugar cane fields flourished. Located in the west-central Philippines, Mindoro is 110 miles long and 58 miles wide. A rough, malaria-infested jungle covered its mountainous spine that stretches almost the entire length of the island with numerous rivers running to its narrow shorelines.

Mindoro had little strategic value to the Japanese, which accounts for why less than one thousand troops were stationed on the island. Fewer than half were actual combat troops from the 105th Division, while the others were air force engineers, Naval Air Service support troops, and roughly two hundred men who had survived ship sinkings off the coast. Shortly after the Americans landed, on December 13, 110 men from the 8th Division were sent from Luzon to join them.

American intelligence reports based on Ultra intercepts confirmed the island was lightly defended and that its primary value to the enemy was the airfields located in the southwestern and the northern portions of the island. Imperial Navy and Army aircraft staged through these airfields on their way to attack targets on Leyte.[1]

As far as MacArthur was concerned, Mindoro was a pathway to Luzon and Manila. The only way he could provide land-based fighter and bomber cover for an amphibious landing on Luzon was to have airfields closer to that island than the few available on Leyte. He expected General Yamashita to husband his resources for the defense of Luzon, which is exactly what the Japanese commander did.

Separating Mindoro from Luzon, MacArthur's ultimate objective, was the seven-mile-wide Verde Island Passage. The northern tip of Mindoro, known as Cape Calavite, was only ninety miles from Manila. Although Allied intelligence identified the northeast coast as having the most promising sites for airfields, the area posed two drawbacks: the constant heavy rain and fog made for dangerous flying weather, and the area was perilously close to what remained of Japanese land-based air units located on Luzon.

MacArthur's original plan for the liberation of the Philippines called for an amphibious landing on Mindoro on December 5, 1944. The fighting on Leyte dragged on longer than he expected, which the commander knew resulted from the lack of sufficient land-based air cover over the battlefields. Army engineers were unable to construct satisfactory airfields on Leyte due primarily to the terrain and weather conditions. The result was that thousands of Japanese reinforcements arrived at Leyte during the two months following the original landings. The reverse side of this was that the more Japanese soldiers killed on Leyte, the fewer there were to defend Luzon and Manila.[2]

During the planning for the invasion of Mindoro, code-named Love III, MacArthur's staff first identified the northeast region of the island as the likely place to land from a tactical standpoint, but this was soon discarded when the planners realized the invading forces would be subject to relentless attacks from enemy land-based aircraft on Luzon. So instead, they selected the port town of San Jose on the island's southwest coast near Mangarin Bay, the island's best anchorage and the location of a seaplane base. The plan called for gaining control of the sea routes through the Visayas and establishing airfields so General Kenney's aircraft could provide direct support of operations on Luzon. The invasion of Luzon was schedule for December 20.

At a November 30 meeting at Price House in Tacloban, MacArthur and Admiral Kinkaid argued over the date for the invasion. The admiral wanted to delay the invasion until the Army could provide better air support. He told MacArthur he was extremely reluctant to send his escort carriers into the Sulu Sea to provide air cover after their experience during the battle with Admiral Kurita's forces in Leyte Gulf and the kamikaze attacks that sank two escort carriers, two destroyers, and one destroyer escort, and damaged another half dozen of his Seventh Fleet ships. He dreaded having his escort carriers caught in the Sulu Sea by waves of kamikaze aircraft. For MacArthur, delaying the invasion of Mindoro meant delaying the invasion of Luzon, which was unacceptable.

The general stood his ground, even attempting to shame his admiral by offering to be aboard one of the ships leading the invasion convoy, but still Kinkaid fought back. Things suddenly changed when MacArthur received a message from Admiral Nimitz suggesting a short delay in the Mindoro invasion until Admiral Halsey's fleet carriers could complete their replenishment at Ulithi and return to support both the Mindoro and Luzon invasions. MacArthur agreed to reschedule the Mindoro invasion to December 15, and the Luzon invasion, which was to take place at Lingayen Gulf, until December 30. The Luzon invasion was further delayed until January 5 after General Kenney explained that his engineers needed more than fifteen days to prepare airfields on Mindoro.[3]

Adding further weight to the discussion of changing the date for the Lingayen landings, MacArthur's chief of staff, Lieutenant General Richard Sutherland, brought meteorological reports indicating that if the December 30 date held, Kinkaid's ships would have to approach the landing sites under a full moon. The ships would be clear targets to enemy pilots during night hours when they would normally count on being invisible.[4]

General Kenney was determined that land-based air support must be available for the Luzon landings. He was concerned that the escort carriers could not provide air cover for a prolonged period. If the enemy sent kamikaze attacks against them the thin-skinned baby carriers would be sunk or at the very least have to leave the area. MacArthur agreed and promised Kenney he would get the shipping required to move the equipment he needed to prepare landing sites on Mindoro for two heavy bombardment groups, a strafing group, and several fighter groups, along with the engineers to build the landing fields.[5]

On the evening of December 12, the Western Visayan Attack Force sailed from the east coast of Leyte heading south and west through the Surigao Strait toward the Mindanao Sea and then the Sulu Sea. Rear Admiral Arthur D. Struble commanded the force comprising thirty tank landing ships, thirty-one infantry landing craft, eight destroyer transports, twelve medium landing ships, seventeen minesweepers, and smaller specialized craft. Nineteen destroyers, one heavy cruiser, twenty-three PT boats, and three light cruisers, including the force flagship *Nashville*, closely escorted them. Following behind because of their slow speed was a Slow Tow Convoy consisting of an assortment of destroyers, destroyer escorts, tankers, and other vessels carrying fuel and materials required to construct a PT boat base at Mindoro. At a farther distance were six escort carriers each with twenty-four fighters and nine torpedo bombers on board, as well as three battleships, three light cruisers, and eighteen destroyers. On board the transports were the 19th Regimental Combat Team (RCT) of the 24th Infantry Division, one battalion from the 21st Infantry (also of the 24th Division), and the 503rd Parachute RCT for a total of nearly eighteen thousand combat troops. The parachutists were to fly in but there was no place on Leyte to accommodate their aircraft, so their assignment changed to the amphibious landing. In addition, the ships brought with them another ten thousand Australian and American air force personnel for airfield construction. The combat troops were under the overall command of Brigadier General William C. Dunkel.

As he had done so often in the past, MacArthur planned to accompany the convoy with the assault troops. Members of his staff dissuaded him from doing so, arguing that he would be isolated on board a ship sailing through enemy waters in radio silence without regular contact with his headquarters at an important time. Had he made the voyage, he likely would have been aboard the light cruiser *Nashville* that had served as his flagship so often in the past year.[6]

It was nearly 3 p.m. on December 13, when the Western Visayan Attack Force rounded the southern end of Negros and headed toward the Sulu Sea. Unknown to those aboard the armada, Japanese reconnaissance aircraft had been watching and reporting on their progress since nine that morning. They had not yet attacked the enemy ships as their intelligence officers awaited reports to determine where the Americans were going. Also, unknown to the men on the ships, three suicide pilots took to the air in "Vals" (dive-bombers) from an airfield on Cebu, accompanied by a seven-fighter escort—and were headed in their direction.[7]

At 2:57, a lookout aboard the *Nashville* reported a Val coming in at five thousand feet from the starboard side with bombs clearly visible attached to both wings. At first it appeared it be headed for another ship in the convoy, but then suddenly turned directly at the cruiser as antiaircraft guns fired relentlessly at the speeding plane. Apparently aiming for the ship's bridge, the plane's right wing hit a 40mm antiaircraft gun mount and smashed instead amidships. The aircraft's bombs exploded, as did the ammunition of several gun mounts as burning aviation fuel flowed in all directions. One sailor described the cruiser as "a vessel of death and destruction."[8]

The inferno aboard the *Nashville* cost the lives of 133 officers and men and wounded 190 others, including General Dunkel, whose injuries were described as "painful but not serious." Among the dead were Admiral Struble's chief of staff and General Dunkel's chief of staff. With the fires extinguished, Admiral Struble transferred his flag to the destroyer *Dashiell*. The convoy continued toward Mindoro while the *Nashville* began its long journey to Puget Sound Navy Yard for extensive repairs before rejoining the war. It was just luck that MacArthur had not joined the convoy, or he might have been wounded or killed in the attack. The *Nashville* was his favored ship; he thoroughly enjoyed standing on the same bridge where several of the dead and wounded officers were when the kamikaze struck.

The convoy arrived off the coast of Mindoro the following evening and assumed position for an early morning amphibious landing. At dawn on December 15, the convoy's destroyers prepared to shell the beaches as a prelude to the landings when the order not to fire quickly spread among the ships. The beaches were filling up with Filipino civilians running back and forth waving their arms, many carrying American flags. The minesweepers reported no enemy mines in the area as the various landing craft headed toward the beaches at 7 a.m.

First off were the LCIs (Landing Craft Infantry) that had been converted to fire rockets into the beach and the area behind. There was no enemy response, so the troops hit the beaches immediately. The 19th RCT was on the south side at White Beach, the men of the 503rd Parachute RCT were on the north end at Green and Blue Beaches. The 21st Infantry Regiment remained in reserve and engaged in some feint attacks at other locations to confound the enemy. Some confusion arose among the Americans on the beaches as they discovered they had all landed about four hundred yards south of their intended landing sites. Following some shuffling around that took an hour to sort out their proper locations, the first patrols moved inland.

The only Japanese troops near the landing beaches were one company from the 359th Independent Infantry Battalion and a few dozen men from the naval seaplane base at nearby Caminawit Point. When they realized the size of the invading force, they fled the area and headed for Bulalacao on the opposite coast. Two days later, they joined the small local garrison to establish a line of defense in the hills northwest of Bulalacao. They remained in place until driven out by combined American and Filipino forces on January 24.[9]

There was no sign of the enemy until Company E from the

503rd followed a narrow-gauge rail line toward the town of San Jose and a sugar mill. During the prewar years, the railroad transported sugar cane collected from the fields to the mill. All signs indicated the railway had not been used for several years. Groups of civilians appeared from their hiding places and pointed out where the Japanese garrison had lived. Although the soldiers were gone, their departure was rushed as they left behind their partially consumed breakfasts and many personal effects. Pushing right behind the combat troops were the aviation engineers with their tractors and bulldozers in a hurry to get to work. All along the invasion site, the men advanced and eventually established a perimeter seven miles inland and seventeen miles long, within which the engineers could lay out at least three airfields.[10]

Four soldiers of the 532nd Engineer Boat and Shore Regiment who were members of a railroad platoon accompanied the combat troops to inspect the condition of the rail line and the rolling stock. It was obvious from the state of the tracks and several rail cars they found that the Japanese had not used the line for several years. Inside the San Jose roundhouse were a few locomotives, but all were mysteriously missing parts. Filipinos who had worked on the railroad explained to the four that they had removed vital parts from the engines and buried them nearby to prevent the Japanese from using the line. Within ten hours, they had one engine running and the others well along.[11]

The army engineers, along with their construction equipment and supplies, pushed directly behind the invading combat troops who were about one hour behind schedule due to the confusion on the beach. American and Australian airfield construction crews realized the existing airfield at San Jose could not be expanded to meet Allied needs, so they immediately began building a new one three miles to the south, christened Hill Drome. Thanks to the efforts of the 1874th US Engineer Aviation Battalion and the Australian No. 3 Airdrome Construction Squadron, the field was able to receive a flight of fighter aircraft five days later. A second field, Ellmore Field, two miles to the northwest, reached completion on December 23.[12]

As the landing proceeded, aircraft from the Third Fleet attacked Japanese airfields on Luzon to suppress their opposition. Flights from the escort carriers that accompanied the invasion fleet flew air cover over the landing beaches and the ships still unloading. Although mostly successful in driving off or downing enemy planes, several kamikazes made it through the protective screen on that first day. The Japanese suicide pilots struck two Landing Ship Tanks (LST) and several other ships. Damage to most of the vessels was light other than the LSTs. One, LST-472, was quickly abandoned and sank, but the other, LST-738, was full of aviation fuel and oxygen bottles that needed to be saved. The kamikaze, identified as a Nakajima B5N torpedo bomber, known to the Allies as a "Kate," smashed into the LST and exploded. The explosion damaged the ship's firefighting equipment, making it impossible to extinguish the spreading flames. The commanding officer, Captain J. T. Barnett, ordered the ship abandoned while he destroyed the ship's radar equipment. A second explosion caused the destroyer *Moale*, which had pulled alongside to assist, to back away with a damaged bow. Barnett was the last to leave the ship and he along with the entire crew were rescued by the destroyer. While no lives were lost among the LST crew, the second blast resulted in the death of one man and a dozen injuries aboard the destroyer.[13]

UNABLE TO STOP the American advance on Mindoro with the few troops on the ground and General Yamashita's decision to send no

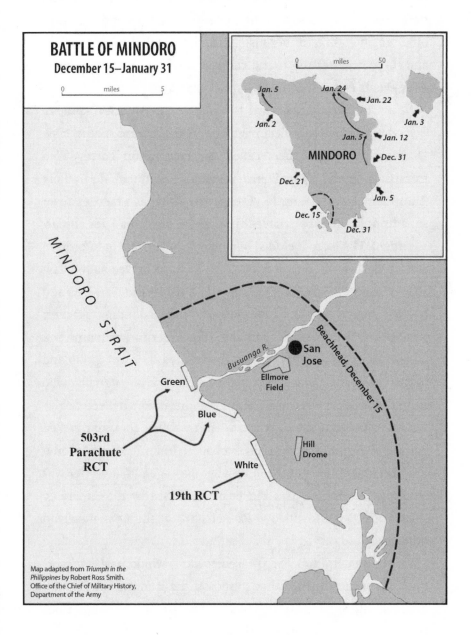

BATTLE OF MINDORO
December 15–January 31

0 miles 5

0 miles 50

Jan. 5
Jan. 24
Jan. 22
Jan. 2
Jan. 3
Jan. 5
Jan. 12
MINDORO
Dec. 31
Dec. 21
Jan. 5
Dec. 15
Dec. 31

MINDORO STRAIT

Beachhead December 15

Busuanga R.

San Jose

Ellmore Field

Green

Blue

503rd
Parachute
RCT

Hill
Drome

White

19th RCT

Map adapted from *Triumph in the
Philippines* by Robert Ross Smith.
Office of the Chief of Military History,
Department of the Army

additional reinforcements from Luzon to anywhere, the Japanese response focused in the air and on the sea. Every day following the landings, Japanese aircraft attacked the troops and the ships offshore, including numerous kamikazes. Dogfights over the bay and the portion of the island controlled by the Americans were daily events coupled with constant suicide attacks.

When the air attacks failed to dislodge the Americans, Japan turned to its partially decimated navy to accomplish the task. On December 24, a fleet called the Penetration Force sailed from Cam Ranh Bay in French Indochina commanded by Rear Admiral Masatome Kimura. A respected career as a fast destroyer squadron commander made Kimura the ideal man for the assignment. His force included one heavy cruiser, one light cruiser, and six destroyers, one of which, the *Kasumi*, served as his flagship. His orders were to sink any Allied ships near San Jose and to shell the airfields and other targets near the landing beaches. By the time he arrived off Mindoro, the American warships and larger landing ships had already completed their missions and begun their return to Leyte Gulf, leaving behind a few small cargo ships. It was expected the recently commissioned fleet carrier *Unryu*, carrying thirty Yokosuka MXY-7 Ohka rocket-propelled suicide planes intended for the kamikaze units at Manila, would join them. Unknown to Kimura when he sailed, that carrier was sunk on December 19 in the East China Sea by the American submarine *Redfish* with the loss of 1,238 of the 1,383 men and officers aboard it.[14]

As the Penetration Force raced toward Mindoro at 25 knots to attack whatever ships they found off the landing beaches and hopefully delay MacArthur's plans, two American submarines reported its position and speed. It was obvious they were heading for Mindoro. In the early evening of December 26, a US Navy

PB4Y "Liberator" four-engine patrol plane spotted the ships below him and radioed his report to the Seventh Fleet at Leyte Gulf. The enemy was approximately 180 miles from the Mindoro landing beaches. To ensure his report was understood, Lieutenant Paul F. Stevens landed his Liberator at Ellmore Field to personally report his sighting to the local commander.[15]

Shortly thereafter, eight pilots of a flight of B-25s searching for a reported fleet of enemy cargo ships were surprised to find not freighters but warships racing toward Mindoro. They turned back and reported their finding at Ellmore Field. On receiving Lieutenant Stevens's report, Admiral Kinkaid pulled together two heavy cruisers, two light cruisers, and eight destroyers commanded by Rear Admiral Theodore E. Chandler to form an attack group and sent them on their way. The only problem was they would not reach the Mindoro site until late the next day, well behind the time the Japanese were expected to arrive. With no sizeable warships in the vicinity, the entire defense of the Mindoro landing force rested on the 105 aircraft on the island. This was not going to be a pleasant experience since the Americans knew the Japanese had loaded up their destroyers with extra antiaircraft guns, and there were at least six of them in the enemy fleet. This was compounded by the fact there were few night fighters on the island.

The primary naval defense was eleven PT boats commanded by Lieutenant Commander N. Burt Davis. The PTs formed a line three miles from the beach and prepared to defend the Liberty ships and other noncombat ships in the area as well as the landing beaches. Before reaching the PT line, the enemy ships came under constant attack from the aircraft stationed on Mindoro. Also under air attack was a convoy of troop transports and cargo ships near Subic Bay, Luzon. With the impending arrival of the warships, General Dunkel assumed the troop transports were heading to the same landing beaches the Americans had used and the warships were their protection against attack.

General Dunkel prepared the army troops to defend against an enemy landing force as the aircraft on the island continued attacking both convoys. Davis ordered his boat commanders to ignore the warships if the troop ships approached the beaches and attack them and any landing craft they put in the water using their machine guns and torpedoes. They were to prevent enemy troops from making a counter landing at all costs. The assumption proved incorrect, as the convoy off Luzon was delivering reinforcements to Manila.[16]

The Penetration Force succeeded in pushing its way through the PT boat screen in the dark and shelled the shore and a few nearby ships for less than one hour, but their fire proved inaccurate as the gunners and their equipment came under continuous air attack. Every Japanese ship suffered some damage, some more than others, and by first light they withdrew beyond the reach of the Mindoro-based planes. The unlucky destroyer *Kiyoshimo* had the misfortune to run into a PT boat just arriving from a mission aiding guerrillas in north Mindoro. Following a brief gun battle, the destroyer, already wounded by two direct bomb hits from army bombers, exploded and sank when one torpedo fired from Lieutenant (jg) Harry E. Griffin's PT 223 smashed into its hull. The following day PT boats picked up five survivors from the enemy destroyer.[17]

THE AMERICAN war effort was severely hampered on December 18 when the Third Fleet, operating off the east coast of the Philippines, was struck by a massive typhoon that resulted in the sinking of three destroyers and various degrees of damage to seven additional ships. Included was the loss of 186 planes off the fleet's carriers. The deadly storm took the lives of eight hundred men of the fleet. Halsey had to withdraw from the area and sail to Ulithi for repairs and replenishment. It was fortunate the Mindoro airfields were able to fill at least part of the void created by the withdrawn aircrews.[18]

WITH AMERICAN forces firmly entrenched on Mindoro, General Yamashita decided the time had come to focus on the defense of Luzon. On December 25 he sent a message to Suzuki on Leyte pointing out that it was sixty days since the enemy landing and despite the heroic efforts of Suzuki's Thirty-Fifth Army, the superior forces of the Americans were making great headway. He instructed Suzuki to deploy his force to fight a holding action in areas of the island in which they could be self-sustaining. In other words, the imperial forces on Leyte would not be receiving any more reinforcements or supplies. They were on their own and should prepare to die for their "beloved country."[19]

As aircraft landing conditions improved on Mindoro, Fifth Air Force planes kept arriving, including twin-engine P-61 night fighters known as Black Widows, which were of extra value since the Japanese had demonstrated their skill and propensity for attacking at night. Not to be outdone, the Imperial Naval Air Service, anxious to stop the American expansion on Mindoro, flew in some fifty planes from Formosa. They focused on attacking convoys heading toward Mindoro, including a large number of kamikaze attacks. These attacks took a serious toll on the convoys, accounting for the sinking of several LSTs and at least three Liberty ships. The beaching of several other

Liberty ships prevented their sinking. Their lost cargoes slowed down airfield construction as many carried supplies and equipment requested by the aviation engineer units building the airfields.[20]

The year 1944 ended on Mindoro with a series of attacks on ships approaching or unloading at San Jose. On December 28 kamikazes attacked two Liberty ships, *John Burke* and *William Sharon*. They were part of a multiship convoy with supplies for Mindoro. The *John Burke* was carrying a full cargo of ammunition when a Val dive-bomber survived fierce antiaircraft fire from the ship's Naval Armed Guard to slam into the hull and explode at 10:20 a.m. Within seconds, a huge fireball and an immense smoke cloud erupted and the ship was gone. It disintegrated along with the sixty-nine men aboard. The explosion was so great that flying debris killed or wounded men on nearby ships and sank an army Freight and Supply ship, killing all aboard save one man. The *William Sharon* carried three thousand tons of ammunition, trucks, pontoon bridging, and other miscellaneous cargo when another Val crashed into its bridge and exploded. Despite the loss of fifteen men from the crew and Armed Guard, including its commanding officer, and a raging fire, it survived. After four unmerciful hours of firefighting by the crew of the destroyer *Wilson*, a tug towed it home for repairs. Two days later, as several ships unloaded, they along with their escorts came under kamikaze attack. The destroyer *Pringle* was hit near its bridge, killing eleven men and taking it out of the war for two months. A second destroyer, *Gansevoort*, received serious damage from another Val suicide plane. Towed to a nearby beach, its crew camped out on shore while they spent a month making enough repairs to have it towed to Ulithi for major repairs.[21]

THE AUSTRALIAN and American engineers soon had four airfields operational on Mindoro. General Kenney was able to move two night fighter squadrons, three day fighter squadrons, two medium-bomber groups, three reconnaissance squadrons, one photo recon squadron, and an air-sea rescue squadron to Mindoro by January 9. He now had the full complement of air cover he considered necessary for the invasion of Luzon. On January 1, General Krueger's Sixth Army relinquished control on both Leyte and Mindoro to General Eichelberger's Eighth Army in order to prepare for the invasion of Luzon. Major General Roscoe B. Woodruff and the 24th Infantry Division replaced General Dunkel.[22]

THE IMPERIAL Army had not given up on Mindoro despite General Yamashita's desire to focus all efforts on defending Luzon. For some ranking officers, Mindoro was too close to Luzon for their comfort. About the same time Admiral Kimura's Penetration Force attacked the American landing site near San Jose, a raiding party from the 8th Division assembled at Batangas on the southern coast of Luzon. The Japanese troops included men from the Gi-Go Airborne Raiding Unit, which was an infantry unit specially trained and equipped for airborne operations behind enemy lines. Forgoing an airborne assault, the plan called for transporting them aboard landing craft across the Verde Island Passage that runs between Luzon and Mindoro to land at Calapan on the northeast of Mindoro.

Their final destination was Pinamalayan along Mindoro's east coast. The troops were ordered to support a small garrison stationed there and to plan an assault on the American airfields near San Jose. They arrived on January 5, two days after a guerrilla force of about seventy fighters fought a bitter but unsuccessful battle to dislodge the garrison. They remained for only three days as a combined American and Filipino force moving up the island's coast drove them back to Calapan.[23]

GENERAL MACARTHUR wanted Mindoro for two primary purposes. Most importantly was the establishment of airfields from which the Army Air Forces could cover his troops landing on Luzon. MacArthur also wanted to use the island as a diversionary tactic to confuse the Imperial Army of his true intentions. MacArthur wanted the enemy to transfer troops into southern Luzon away from his planned invasion in the north. He did this in convincing ways, including increased reconnaissance flights over southern Luzon, having paratroopers dropped in the area, and increased bombing missions on Japanese sites along the southern coast. US Navy minesweepers cleared three bays along the Verde Island Passage—Balayan, Batangas, and Tayabas—as if preparing them for amphibious landings. Several times landing ships and cargo vessels approached these bays but withdrew when the coastal guns fired on them. They were all part of the deception to convince the enemy they were potential landings sites. In addition, MacArthur's headquarters instructed guerrilla forces to increase their attacks and sabotage operations against Japanese forces throughout southern Luzon.[24]

Several small but important military operations were conducted as part of the deception. The invasion and occupation of Marinduque Island had two goals: fool the enemy as to where the Americans were going to land on Luzon, and install a radar installation. This 368-square-mile, heart-shaped island is 12 miles off the southern coast of Luzon. In January, Company K of the 21st Infantry Regiment of the 24th Division, accompanied by a unit of Filipino guerrillas, traveled by PT boats from northern Mindoro to Marinduque, landing at the southern coast near the town of Buena Vista. The landing was unopposed as there were not many Japanese in the vicinity, most having been killed or captured by Filipinos, and the radar was installed.

Throughout January, General Woodruff, anxious to secure Mindoro, ordered a series of landings along the east, west, and northern coasts. The Americans attacked and annihilated enemy garrisons at little cost to themselves or the Filipino troops who routinely joined them. Small bands of guerrillas hunted down and killed stragglers who avoided the landing forces. Remaining Japanese scrambled as far as they could into the jungle-covered mountains where many faced their ultimate fate at the hands of mountain tribesmen. To survive, many Japanese soldiers turned to banditry, attacking small villages around the island for food. Rape and pillage became widespread for men fully aware they were abandoned by their nation. Patrols of Americans and Filipinos roamed the uncharted mountains and valleys, killing and on the rare occasion capturing enemy soldiers.

Some of the worst fighting on Mindoro took place at a large village in the northwest corner of the island. The Japanese had occupied Paluan since first landing there in March 1942. They took over two schoolhouses as their headquarters and built a lookout tower to keep an eye on the normally busy waterway nearby. They also installed a radio transmitter station with the aim of warning Luzon when they saw a flight of bombers heading that way. In October 1943, a mixed unit of American and Filipino guerrillas led by Major Lawrence Phillips constructed on nearby Mount Calavite their own radio transmitter to monitor and report on ship movements around Manila Bay. Phillips had been sent from Australia to establish a coast watching station, which is what he did. A spy informed the Japanese of the transmitter's existence and they raided the location in March 1944, killing Phillips and everyone with him. The Japanese had such high regard for Phillips that they buried him with full military honors. The major was posthumously awarded the Distinguished Service Cross for his work on Mindoro, and his service to his country was acknowledged with a personal condolence letter from MacArthur to his parents.

When American intelligence learned of the existence of the Japanese air raid warning station at Paluan, Company B of the 503rd Parachute RCT received orders to destroy it and kill the Japanese stationed there. An LCI took them to a location twenty miles south of Paluan. Once ashore they found a jungle trail heading toward the town. Along the trail, a Filipino stopped them and explained there were thirteen enemy soldiers farther up the trail looking for the landing party that had been spotted from the lookout tower. The paratroopers successfully executed a trap, killed the Japanese, and the men moved on.

Arriving at the town about 2 a.m., they learned from a local guerrilla that the men in the schools awoke at dawn and assembled into formations so they could bow toward the Emperor. Since they usually did this without arms, it seemed the ideal time to attack. Unfortunately, before the enemy troops fell out, an unrelated local guerrilla group attacked a nearby ammunition dump. Alerted by the firing, the men in the buildings secured themselves into trenches around the schools and prepared to defend their position. A firefight ensued throughout the day with little success in dislodging the Japanese from their log-fortified trenches. During the night, the dozen or so surviving Japanese slipped away toward the north. At daylight, a platoon led by Sergeant Jack Herzig pursued the fleeing enemy but found several had drowned trying to escape in a small boat while guerrillas killed the remainder. Five Americans lost their lives in the encounter that destroyed the air raid warning system, which likely saved the lives of dozens of American pilots.[25]

General MacArthur realized his desire to make Mindoro the home of a massive air power to cover his planned invasion of Luzon. By the middle of January a third airstrip for fighters and light bombers was complete and another for heavy bombers was under construction. General Krueger's Sixth Army, charged with taking Luzon, would have sufficient air cover to satisfy the commander.[26]

The invasion of Mindoro, followed by the deceptive overflights of southern Luzon, landings on several nearby islands, and a variety of naval activity along the coast by PT boats, convinced many in Manila that the Batangas area was the most likely place MacArthur's forces would come ashore. They considered Lingayen Gulf a secondary possibility. If, on the other hand, the Americans landed at Lingayen, then the southern coast of Batangas was a likely place for a secondary landing. MacArthur's tactics to confuse the Fourteenth Area Army were enough to cause General Yamashita a major headache. It made planning for the defense of Luzon a great deal more difficult.[27]

CHAPTER THIRTEEN

MacArthur Returns to Luzon

From Australia, General MacArthur told the world he planned to return. He was not merely relating to the Philippines, or even the island of Luzon, but to the city of Manila. The country's capital, the "Pearl of the Orient," had been MacArthur's home from 1935 until President Roosevelt ordered him to leave for Australia in 1942. It was in Manila his son Arthur was born. It was where he and his family had thrived among a people he loved. He knew the city's inhabitants had suffered at the cruel hands of the Japanese occupiers and he wanted to relieve their suffering as quickly as possible. From the time he arrived in Australia and fought the enemy across New Guinea, Manila was his main objective.

By the end of December 1944, MacArthur's forces were firmly entrenched on Mindoro. MacArthur kept busy reviewing the plans for the Luzon landings. His senior staff knew of his desire to declare the liberation of Manila on his sixty-fifth birthday, January 26, 1945. He was also gravely concerned about rescuing and liberating prisoners held by the enemy in the Manila area, both military and civilian.[1]

The invasion of Luzon was planned for Lingayen Gulf on the northwest coast of the island. The Japanese forces came ashore in 1941 at the same location where General Yamashita and his planners presumed MacArthur would. Yamashita expected it, but remained troubled over the increased activity along the southern coast, so he dispatched additional troops to that region.

For General Yamashita it was no longer a question of if the Americans would reach Luzon, but when. His planners estimated that a major enemy invasion would come sometime between January 10 and 20. More importantly, the question was where the landings would occur. Deciding the Americans would likely land at two locations, they selected Batangas in Luzon's southwest corner, and Lingayen Gulf.[2]

It was at Lingayen Gulf that General Homma's forces came ashore on December 22, 1941, and began the Japanese occupation of the Philippines. General MacArthur knew from his years in the islands that the beaches at Lingayen were the ideal location for the initial landings on Luzon, just as Homma had known it three years earlier. The wide mouth of the gulf would enable the invasion fleet clear access to the beaches along the shore. The American commander knew from his intelligence reports that the enemy expected him to land his forces there, but it was the best way to reach Manila and Manila Bay quickly. Manila's importance went beyond its role as the country's capital. Its dominance of Manila Bay made it the best port for putting the reinforcements and supplies ashore required to battle the several hundred thousand enemy troops north and east of Manila.

GENERAL YAMASHITA wrestled with developing a plan to deal with the Americans once they landed, since stopping the invasion at the beaches was out of the question. The American control of the air and the sea made defending the beaches impractical. He expected the enemy plan would be to push quickly south toward Manila just over one hundred miles away. He feared that a decisive battle fought in the central plains between the landing zone and Manila could destroy his forces, especially with the skies filled with American aircraft.

With the agreement of his superiors in Tokyo, Yamashita instructed his operations staff to develop a plan based on a protracted campaign to delay the enemy advance and wear down their forces. The goal had now shifted from defending Luzon to destroying or reducing enemy strength to impede attacks against other locations in the empire, especially Formosa and the Ryukyu Islands that stretch southwest from the Home Islands and include Okinawa.

Being among the more pragmatic of the top imperial generals, Yamashita realized when Leyte had all but fallen that there would be no decisive battle leading to victory. Yamashita had numerous problems as he prepared for MacArthur's invasion, including critical shortages of food, ammunition, and men. He had sent nearly thirty thousand men to Leyte, which he had done reluctantly and could now see was a waste of valuable manpower. Rice shipments that had in the past arrived on a regular basis from Indochina no longer made it through the American naval forces, and supplies promised from Japan were virtually nonexistent. American attack aircraft and submarines had made Manila Bay a death trap for any ship that attempted to bring in supplies. Yamashita recognized that with no support from Japan, he and his forces could only delay the enemy as long as possible while the planners in Japan devised a scheme that might save their country from destruction.[3]

Toward the end of November, he and his planners devised a defensive strategy that hopefully would meet their need to delay MacArthur. First, he had to abandon any thought of defeating the Americans on the beaches of Lingayen Gulf, the most obvious site of an amphibious landing. It was obvious because it offered an invading force two great advantages. One was that the terrain throughout the region was ideal for the maneuvering of armored division tanks and the artillery forces. Another was the one-hundred-mile clear run from the gulf across Luzon's Central Plains to Manila, MacArthur's primary target.

Staving off the attack on the beaches or even the Central Plains of Luzon would be futile, with Japanese defenders subjected to constant bombardment by Allied aircraft with little means of defense since the imperial air forces were reduced to little more than suicide planes. Finally, Manila would be left undefended as an open city, just as MacArthur had done in 1942 when he withdrew his forces to Bataan. The city was home to over one million people to feed when there was already a shortage of provisions for his troops. Compounding this, most of the structures in Manila were wood and therefore highly flammable. His already diminished troops could not be spared from battle to fight urban fires.[4]

Yamashita's best hope was to fight a static defense from positions that Japan's enemy would find extremely costly to attack or impregnable. This location could only mean the mountainous regions of Luzon. He divided his 260,000 men into three separate groups, each assigned to defend a specific area. The largest of these was Shobu Group, containing 150,000 men whose job was to occupy the mountains of north Luzon and delay MacArthur's forces as long as possible. General Yamashita himself retained direct control of the Shobu Group. Major General Rikichi Tsukada commanded the 30,000 troops of the Kembu Group, charged with defending the huge airfield complex at Clark Field northwest of Manila and the Bataan Peninsula. Tsukada had earlier served as the chief of intelligence in north China, and then commanded a special forces unit before this assignment.

The remaining 80,000 troops became the Shimbu Group with orders to evacuate all supplies from Manila for use by the other groups and occupy the mountains east of Manila. This group, commanded by Lieutenant General Shizuo Yokoyama, would control the reservoirs and dams that supplied Manila with most of its water. Yokoyama, formerly commander of the 8th Division, was also responsible for ordering the evacuation from the city of the 17,000 naval personnel under the command of Rear Admiral Sanji Iwabuchi. In November 1942, Iwabuchi had been disgraced over the loss of a battleship he commanded off Guadalcanal and assigned to desk duty. A shortage of experienced ranking officers resulted in his transfer to command of the 31st Naval Special Base Force in Manila. This included several battalions of combat-trained naval troops responsible for the defense of various naval facilities. The admiral refused to obey Yokoyama's instructions to leave Manila even though the order originated with Yamashita, who was Iwabuchi's legal superior officer. Instead, he decided to obey his navy superior Vice Admiral Denshichi Okochi's orders to defend the city as long as he could. Okochi's instructions included the destruction of all naval supplies and facilities so they did not fall into the hands of the Americans. That decision was to come at a terrible cost to both the American and Japanese troops, but especially to the one million civilians living in the capital.

In late December, Yamashita decided to transfer his head-quarters out of Manila to the summer resort city of Baguio, twenty-five miles northeast of Lingayen Gulf and five thousand feet up in the pine forest mountains. Admiral Okochi, who had ordered Iwabuchi to fight for Manila to the death, ironically soon moved his headquarters to the relative safety of Baguio as well.

Until the previous month, Manila had been a confusion of military headquarters. The result was that Yamashita, charged with the defense of the Philippines, had control of only half the forces in and around Manila. The senior of these headquarters was the Southern Expeditionary Army Group commanded by Field Marshal Count Hisaichi Terauchi. It was responsible for all Imperial Army forces throughout the entire southern Pacific and Asian region. It had moved to Manila from Singapore in May 1944. Now, on November 17, 1944, with Manila facing the threat of a successful enemy invasion, Terauchi moved his headquarters to Saigon in French Indochina. In addition to Yamashita's Fourteenth Area Army, Terauchi's command included Lieutenant General Tominaga's Fourth Air Army and Major General Masazumi Inada's 3rd Maritime Transport Command. Both these generals resisted most of Yamashita's attempts to conduct the defense of the Philippines and were thorns in his side. It must have given him some satisfaction when Inada took his headquarters to Saigon, leaving the service troops of the command in Manila for Yamashita. The Fourth Air Army came under Yamashita's command on January 1, 1945.[5]

In addition to the four army headquarters, there were three naval headquarters located in Manila not under Yamashita's control. The most important of these was the 31st Naval Special Base Force commanded by Admiral Iwabuchi. Before evacuating his headquarters, Admiral Okochi assigned an additional four thousand combat troops to Iwabuchi's original thirteen-thousand-man force and christened it the Manila Naval Defense Force (MNDF).

With this increased force, Iwabuchi was to defend not only the capital city, but also the Cavite Naval Base and Nichols Field south of Manila that served as a base for the Japanese Naval Air Service fighters. The MNDF was also to mine Manila Bay and conduct small-boat suicide missions when required. Finally, they were to carry out Okochi's orders to destroy all naval facilities in the Manila area that might be useful to the enemy.[6]

Iwabuchi divided the city and surrounding area into three sectors, assigning roughly five thousand men to each sector's defense. His men immediately went to work fortifying strongholds in each sector and constructing barricades on various streets and at major intersections. They stripped weapons from vessels in the harbor and from damaged aircraft in nearby airfields and converted them for use by the city's defenders. Demolition charges were placed on or near many of the 101 bridges in the city, 39 of which were ultimately destroyed.[7]

Underground manufacturing facilities converted artillery shells, bombs, and other forms of explosives to mines that were placed around the city. Iwabuchi's objectives were to kill as many Americans as possible and cripple MacArthur's fighting strength; delay the use of the Manila port by the enemy; and destroy the city's ability to function as the center of government and commercial production. This was explained in an order he issued on February 3, 1945, in which Japanese troops were instructed to "destroy the factories, warehouses, and other installations" not required to fight the American and Filipino forces.[8]

Manila had been the supply hub for both the Japanese Army and Navy. As Yamashita prepared his forces to defend Luzon from the isolated strongholds, the city contained nearly seventy thousand metric tons of supplies. With his troops already on reduced rations, he faced the dilemma of how to move these supplies to where they would be needed. To exacerbate the situation, the road network on Luzon, once considered among the best in Asia, had suffered from American bombing attacks and guerrilla sabotage. There was also a shortage of vehicles to carry the supplies and fuel to keep the trucks running. By the time the invasion took place, Yamashita had been able to move only four thousand metric tons to locations where his forces could use them.[9]

Ironically, both the American and Japanese commanders were of one mind concerning the fate of the capital city. Yamashita intended to abandon Manila and leave the starving population to MacArthur to care for, while MacArthur expected the Japanese to declare Manila an open city as he had done. Both men were shocked by the destruction wrought on the city and its population by Iwabuchi's naval troops.[10]

Yamashita had also faced blowback from the naval and air force commanders when he ordered all Japanese women and children in Luzon to board a troop ship and return to Japan. Admiral Iwabuchi and General Tominaga refused to send home the large number of young girls working at their headquarters. Tokyo also opposed this humanitarian gesture but for different reasons. The country's leaders felt the arrival of women and children from Luzon in the Home Islands would reveal to the general population the true state of affairs in the Philippines, and reveal their propaganda that the war there was going well as a lie.[11]

Yamashita also had to deal with the fate of 8,300 prisoners interned at several locations around Luzon. This number included 1,300 American POWs. Civilians composed the rest of this population. He ordered that once the enemy landed on Luzon these prisoners be handed over to them, using a representative of a neutral nation. Yamashita chose to ignore opposition by

Field Marshal Terauchi's Saigon headquarters to the freeing of prisoners, whom Yamashita would be unable to feed; Terauchi demanded he hold the prisoners unless there was an emergency. Yamashita replied that when the Americans landed that would be the emergency.[12]

Despite his expectation that MacArthur would land at least the bulk of his forces at Lingayen Gulf, the Japanese commander realized the foolishness of attempting to defend the area against the overwhelming naval and air power of the Americans. But the gulf did have one important use for Yamashita: it could be the reception point for supplies Field Marshal Terauchi had promised to send. Terauchi had, in fact, ordered ten thousand drums of gasoline and ten thousand tons of rice for the defenders. And the resupply convoy was on its way.[13]

Adding to Yamashita's problems were reports arriving from Lamon Bay, a large bay on the eastern shore of Luzon roughly one hundred miles southeast of Manila. American submarines were said to be delivering weapons along the bay coast for use by guerrilla forces assembling in the mountains between the bay and the capital city. Japanese planners considered the possibility that MacArthur intended to land forces at Lamon Bay, as it had served as a secondary landing site for imperial troops in December 1941, resulting in the encirclement of Manila. It was not until the American invasion fleet approached Lingayen Gulf and Allied bombers began to focus their attacks on the region between Lingayen and Manila that the Japanese were resolute that the invasion would be at Lingayen Gulf.[14]

Yamashita and most of his staff left the Manila area on January 4. He visited briefly with General Yokoyama of the Shimbu Group, reminding him that he was to fight a protracted battle to slow the enemy's progress, and not to purposefully seek glory in his own death or those of his men, as this would not slow down the American advance.[15]

ON THAT SAME day, General MacArthur boarded the cruiser *Boise* in Leyte Gulf for the trip to Lingayen Gulf. A party comprising staff members from his Tacloban headquarters accompanied him. He made it clear he expected to establish his SWPA headquarters on Luzon just as soon as his forces secured the beachhead.[16]

The advance force heading toward Lingayen Gulf was under the command of Rear Admiral Jesse Oldendorf. It contained six battleships—including his flagship *California*—six cruisers, thirty-three destroyers, twelve escort carriers, six destroyer escorts, ten destroyer transports, two fleet tugs, one seaplane tender, eleven LCI gunboats, and seventy other warships including thirty minesweepers.[17]

All forces planning to move or currently moving toward Lingayen Gulf were under Oldendorf's command just as they had been for the invasion at Leyte Gulf. Admiral Kinkaid was to take over once his amphibious forces arrived at Lingayen Gulf.

Two days earlier, on January 2, the first echelon of what grew to over 160 ships departed Leyte Gulf at noon. These were the slow-moving minesweepers, hydrographic vessels, and other service and support ships whose responsibility was to locate and clear any obstacles from the waters off the landing zones in Lingayen Gulf. Commander Wayne R. Loud led them from his flagship, the Clemson-class destroyer *Hovey*, which had been converted to a high-speed minesweeper. The following morning as they rounded Negros and entered the Sulu Sea, several enemy aircraft that were likely Val dive-bombers flown by kamikaze pilots attacked the ships. Two of the aircraft, each with a massive bomb strapped below, zeroed in on the fleet oiler *Cowanesque*. The ship's antiaircraft and machine guns shredded both planes before they could reach their target. One was close enough that its violent explosion sprayed fuel and fragments over the ship's deck. Among the debris that landed on the oiler was an unexploded bomb that could have caused not only considerable damage but also increased fatalities. The crew raced to extinguish the fire and pushed the bomb overboard. Two members of the ship's crew died in the attack and two others received injuries. With the damage quickly repaired, the oiler continued on its mission.[18]

Despite their best efforts, the Japanese were having a difficult time attacking Oldendorf's massive war fleet. He had divided the fleet into two sections, each built around a group of escort carriers that worked tirelessly keeping dozens of fighters in the sky above them as combat air patrol to fend off the enemy aircraft. The attacking planes included 120 from various Luzon airfields. Unable to penetrate the Allied air cover, Japanese pilots were forced to fly time- and fuel-consuming circuitous routes in order to approach the fleet from the west.

Shortly after 5 p.m. on January 4, seventeen miles off the entrance to Mindoro Strait, a "Betty" twin-engine Mitsubishi medium bomber that had escaped detection by ship radar and the dozens of lookouts on the escort carrier *Ommaney Bay* raced toward the ship's island. It ricocheted off the island and smashed onto the flight deck. One of the Betty's two bombs penetrated to the hangar deck and exploded, as the second did the same in the forward engine room. Fully fueled planes parked in the hangar deck soon created a nightmare series of explosions and fuel fires like monstrous Molotov cocktails. A ruptured water main reduced water pressure for firefighting, while power and communications throughout most of the ship were lost. Overheated

.50-caliber machine-gun bullets firing off in every direction further hampered the crew's efforts to save their ship.

Thick, oily, black smoke poured into the evening sky as escort ships sped to the carrier's assistance. Several destroyers approached alongside, but the intense heat and exploding ammunition, including torpedo warheads, forced them back. The best they could do was to lower whaleboats to pluck survivors from the sea. At ten minutes to six, Captain Howard Leyland Young issued the abandon ship order, but by then most of the surviving crew members had already escaped the flames and explosions. The carrier was finally sunk by torpedoes from the destroyer *Burns*. Ninety-five sailors died in the attack, including two from a nearby destroyer.[19]

Aboard the cruiser *Boise*, which had been unsuccessfully attacked by an enemy submarine, General MacArthur realized that the attacks on Luzon airfields by land-based planes of the Allied air forces were having less than the desired effect on the enemy suicide formations. Late on the fourth, the same day *Ommaney Bay* sank, he requested Admiral Halsey, who had been launching his Third Fleet air units against enemy airfields on Formosa, to target Japanese airfields on Luzon north of Clark Field.[20]

The following day, January 5, while Halsey's fleet was recalibrating its plans and the Allied airfields on Mindoro were temporarily closed due to extremely wet weather conditions, the Japanese launched a series of kamikaze attacks on the Allied fleet now sailing north off the west coast of the Bataan Peninsula, heading unmistakably for Lingayen Gulf. Previously these attacks had been hit or miss, but the large armada sailing along the coast demanded action that was more concentrated.

With the bulk of land-based and fast carrier aircraft unavailable that morning, the combat air patrols from Oldendorf's escort carriers were the main line of defense as kamikaze planes and their fighter escorts swept in on the ships. Of the aircraft attacking that evening, which seemed to be the favored time for suicide attacks, only two survived. Five of the kamikazes managed to break through the American patrol planes and the fierce antiaircraft fire from the ships. One smashed into Rear Admiral Theodore E. Chandler's flagship, the heavy cruiser *Louisville*. The direct hit on the main battery killed one man and injured seventeen others including the ship's commander, Captain Rex LeGrande Hicks. A second heavy cruiser, HMAS *Australia*, suffered only slight damage but lost twenty-five crewmen killed and another thirty wounded from the exploding bomb hanging from a suicide plane. Both ships managed to continue their mission.[21]

MacArthur watched the action around his ship from an antiaircraft battery near the *Boise*'s quarterdeck. As his staff drifted away to attend to other duties, the commander remained at the rail as if glued to the spot. In a way, he was, for he was searching the eastern horizon for a glimpse at a familiar sight on Corregidor and Bataan.[22]

As the American fleet continued its passage and began to enter Lingayen Gulf, Japanese suicide missions increased, ultimately sinking five ships and damaging sixteen others. The *Boise*, with MacArthur aboard, was targeted but survived a near miss by an enemy fighter pilot determined to die for his emperor. Another narrow escape was the surprise surfacing of a Japanese midget submarine that fired two torpedoes at the *Boise*. The cruiser managed to avoid being struck. The enemy craft paid for its failed attempt when a nearby destroyer rammed it and sent it and its crew to the bottom.[23]

A Zero carrying a 500-pound bomb, and already in flames from antiaircraft fire, raced at the battleship *New Mexico* from its stern. The burning plane crashed into the ship's navigation bridge. The explosion knocked out two antiaircraft guns and killed thirty men, including the battleship's commander, Captain Robert Walton Fleming, who was said to have asked a crew member who came to his aid if the ship was all right. After being told it was, the captain died. Also among the dead was Lieutenant General Herbert Lumsden of the British Army. Lumsden, who had fought in the First World War and commanded an armored corps against Rommel in North Africa, was appointed Winston Churchill's personal representative to MacArthur's headquarters in November 1943. Lumsden and MacArthur had become close friends during that time. MacArthur wrote a personal message to the British prime minister informing him of Lumsden's death and praising his service to the Allied cause. He closed with the comment that his sorrow over Lumsden's death was "inexpressible." The highest-ranking British officer to die in combat during the war, he was buried at sea.[24]

At 8 a.m. on the morning of January 8, 1945, US Navy bombardment ships began firing at targets along Luzon's Lingayen Gulf coast, including the town of Lingayen. Ten minutes later a reconnaissance floatplane that had taken off from one of Admiral Oldendorf's battleships reported seeing the population forming into a parade, intending to march the town streets flying United States and Filipino flags. A destroyer that was close to the shore quickly confirmed the report. Leaflets were swiftly printed and dropped over the town warning people to leave the area to avoid the shelling from the warships. The population shortly gave up the idea of a welcoming parade for the Americans and headed to safety.[25]

Among the hundreds of ships participating in MacArthur's return to the Philippines was a small group of roughly twenty-five transports watched over by fifteen destroyers and destroyer escorts and three escort aircraft carriers. After a harrowing three-day trip from Leyte Gulf during which the ships were at general quarters almost continuously, the group entered Lingayen Gulf at dawn on January 9 and quickly began lowering their assault boats and filling them with the men of the US Sixth Army.[26]

Within hours 68,000 troops landed, followed over the next few days by an additional 136,000 men. The landing site was twenty miles wide stretching from the town of San Fabian on their left to Lingayen on their right. The invasion was composed of two corps. The command structure was similar to that at Leyte; in overall command was General Walter Krueger. Major General Innes Swift's I Corps with its 6th and 43rd Infantry Divisions were on the left, while Major General Oscar Griswold's XIV Corps made up of the 37th and 40th Infantry Divisions headed toward Lingayen on the right. Held in reserve was the 25th Infantry Division of Major General Charles L. Mullins, which went ashore on January 11.

By the end of that first day, the Americans controlled a seventeen-mile-wide beachhead that was in many places four miles deep. The men could see that moving farther inland was going to be tougher than conquering the beach. Ahead of them were swamps, rice paddies, and large fishponds. It made ideal territory from which the Japanese could resist the landings, but they found little if any signs of enemy troops.[27]

Despite intelligence reports that large formations of Japanese troops would make the landings highly dangerous, the troops who landed that day were surprised by how little opposition they faced. The landings cost the lives of less than 120 Americans from both the limited enemy fire and accidents. Their commander was not surprised by the enemy reception, for he fully expected that an experienced combat leader like Yamashita would not risk his forces on the beaches where MacArthur's ships and planes could devastate them, but pull farther inland to more easily defensible locations.

WHAT THE Americans did not know was that General Yamashita had realized that the size of MacArthur's invasion forces, coupled with his command of the sea and the air, except for the few kamikazes that still existed, made it impossible for his forces to defend the Lingayen Gulf beaches even if he wanted to. Better that he allow them to come ashore and draw them into a costly and time-consuming battle in the mountains. This was also true for the Central Plains region leading toward Manila, where the American strength in tanks and other mobile forces would work to their benefit. This was the kind of thinking that led to Yamashita being one of the empire's best combat commanders. He did not want to waste his men's lives rushing into battle screaming "Banzai" and getting mowed down by a technologically superior enemy.

Yamashita was still settling in at his new mountain headquarters when word arrived that an American convoy of approximately eighty ships had passed through the Surigao Strait southwest of Leyte. This was followed by reports of enemy landing craft assembling throughout the region and an increase in American submarine activity along the Luzon west coast. The following day came reports of a massive enemy warship fleet trailing the original convoy. This fleet contained at least a dozen escort carriers, battleships, and cruisers.

Yamashita ordered the 19th and 23rd Divisions to the gulf coast to meet and unload the several ships sent by Field Marshal Terauchi containing rice and fuel. Recently arrived from Korea, the 23rd Division had suffered heavy losses when American ships attacked the convoy in which it sailed. Unfortunately for these men, they arrived at the beaches just in time to witness MacArthur's invasion fleet enter Lingayen Gulf. Yamashita's promised resupply of rice and fuel never materialized because American warships sank the convoy. His chief of staff later remarked that they were expecting rice but all they got was the American Army instead.[28]

The troops landing on the beaches encountered only occasional enemy resistance as the soldiers of the 19th and 23rd Divisions withdrew into the interior in an attempt to preserve their lives. The only serious defensive action taken by members of the 23rd Division on the first day was some mortar fire and artillery shelling near San Fabian from positions on a ridgeline back from the coast.[29]

On the other end of the invasion beach near the town of Lingayen, there was virtually no enemy opposition to the Americans. It seems that during the Japanese invasion in 1941 the area around Lingayen was rejected as a landing site for imperial troops because it was believed the marshlands would prevent a rapid movement of troops to the capital city of Manila. Based on that expectation, Japanese planners refused to believe that MacArthur would land thousands of his troops in the area who they expected would also head toward Manila. But that is exactly what he did.[30]

FOUR HOURS after the landings began, MacArthur and a small entourage boarded a landing craft and headed toward the beach. Admiral Kinkaid reports that Seabees had used a bulldozer to construct a sandy pier of sorts that would enable the general to land on dry land. As MacArthur's boat approached the pier *Life* photographer Carl Mydans, the only still photographer who had been aboard the *Boise*, jumped from the landing craft to be able to photograph MacArthur landing on Luzon. To his surprise, the boat actually turned away from the pier and headed toward the nearby beach. The general, probably recalling the worldwide attention his unintentional wet landing at Leyte had received, decided to wade ashore again, as he had done dozens of times in New Guinea. Mydans bolted along the beach and succeeded in getting one of his most famous shots of the Allied commander wading through knee-deep surf to reach the beach.

MacArthur later described the landing beaches as "a scene of immense activity." That activity consisted of primarily American troops and vehicles busily unloading cargo and moving it inland. Arriving on the beach, MacArthur was greeted by a cheering crowd of Filipinos who had waited years for his return. Many had maintained faith in the man they worshipped as almost god-like. Now he was here and they could touch him and greet him with his Filipino title of Field Marshal. As was his custom at such times, he strolled around the beachhead, stopping to chat with officers and men and getting firsthand knowledge of what was happening. He visited several unit headquarters and commandeered a jeep to travel to nearby Dagupan where he planned to establish his own headquarters. The trip ended at a bridge that had recently been blown by the retreating Japanese.[31]

To everyone's surprise, there were hardly any Japanese to be found. Lieutenant Stanley Frankel of the 37th Division reported a somewhat typical experience. Once ashore, Frankel began furiously digging a foxhole when he suddenly heard voices calling "Veectorie! Veectorie!" Looking around he discovered a dozen Filipinos celebrating the American arrival. When he asked where the Japanese were, they told him, "All gone, two days ago, running to Manila."[32]

General MacArthur was not surprised by the absence of enemy defenses. On the trip in from the *Boise* to the beach, he had expressed as much when he told the men accompanying him that they would not be seeing or hearing any Japanese on that day.[33]

Meanwhile, life for those aboard the American fleet in the gulf was considerably more fraught with danger. Kamikaze planes and small surface vessels, including canoes, loaded with explosives harassed the invaders almost nightly. As the sun set over the gulf, the American ships lay down a great smokescreen to hide themselves from the eyes of the enemy seeking glory in their own deaths. A naval officer who served aboard one of the hundreds of ships that sailed to Lingayen Gulf described the experience of the thousands of men there: "If the enemy can't see you, he can't hit you. At least, that was our fervent hope."[34]

Shortly after midnight, as all eyes were on the dark skies watching for suicide planes, a new weapon of desperation appeared. From the southwest corner of the gulf, the Japanese launched seventy plywood boats, each manned by two or three soldiers. The eighteen-foot-long boats each carried one or two 260-pound depth charges as well as several hand grenades and a light machine gun. Their objective was to silently pull alongside an enemy ship, drop a depth charge overboard and race away. This was an entirely new weapon and caught lookouts aboard the ships by surprise until the radar aboard the Fletcher-class destroyer *Philip* picked up one of the boats approaching. Spotlights quickly flashed on and revealed the boat, which was targeted by .45-caliber submachine guns and a 20mm cannon. The Japanese increased speed and went directly for the *Philip*, hoping to crash into its port side amidships. When the boat got about twenty yards from its target, the shells caused it to explode and sink.[35]

After the war, Japanese sources reported that "nearly all" the suicide boats had been lost on that first night. They did manage to damage several landing craft, causing one to be abandoned. The most serious damage occurred to the armed transport *War Hawk*. At 4:10 a.m. the ship sat at anchor after having disembarked a portion of the troops it carried and was waiting for the dawn when an enemy bomb-loaded motorboat slammed into its port side. The resulting explosion blew a twenty-five-foot hole in it and started flooding an engine room. Sixty-one men perished in the explosion. As work crews struggled in the oppressive heat belowdecks to repair the damage, dawn broke and enemy planes attacked. The ship's gunners fought them off and allowed the vessel to disembark the troops still aboard as well as the mechanized equipment it carried. With enough power restored, it made a painfully slow trek back to Leyte Gulf for additional repairs.[36] The *War Hawk* received a Combat Action Ribbon for the events of January 10, 1945, in Lingayen Gulf.

Little serious fighting happened during the first day ashore. By the end of the day, MacArthur was back aboard the *Boise.* Moving inland through the waterlogged terrain forced the troops to avoid cross-country travel and stick to roads. But the numerous blown bridges created their own headaches; engineers had to repair them quickly in order to keep the men moving.

Despite the difficulties caused by the terrain, troops from General Oscar Griswold's XIV Corps' 40th and 37th Divisions went ashore on the right side of the invasion and by nightfall occupied three important targets, the towns of Lingayen and Dagupan, and the airfield near the former. On the left side of the invasion force, the 43rd and 6th Divisions of Major General Innis Swift's I Corps quickly moved inland. Troops from the

43rd took the town of San Fabian and halted only after running into strong defenses from enemy forces in the hills beyond. Here Japanese forces put up the only serious fighting of the day using well-positioned artillery and mortars.

Word of the successful landings at Lingayen Gulf rapidly spread across the globe. Typical of the reporting was this headline from the January 10, 1945, *New York Daily News*: "YANKS LAND ON LUZON, M'Arthur Ashore With Men; 4 Lingayen Beaches Seized."

MACARTHUR AND his party went ashore again on the morning of January 10. By now, the number of Americans at Lingayen Gulf landing beaches was approaching two hundred thousand. Speaking to various intelligence officers of the four divisions participating in the invasion, he found an almost universal apprehension that the enemy had pulled back from the beaches in order to lure the Sixth Army into a trap. The general disagreed. All along, he expected Yamashita to avoid defending the landing beaches and wait until his own troops were better situated in the mountains to put up a fight. Supporting this view was a message MacArthur had received just days before the landings from Lieutenant Colonel Russell Volckmann, who commanded over eight thousand guerrillas in northern Luzon. Volckmann's agents had been keeping a close watch on the Lingayen Gulf landing zones for several weeks and informed MacArthur there would be "no opposition on the beaches."[37]

When the Sixth Army was able to transfer arms to his guerrilla force, Volckmann's well-organized army grew to nearly twenty thousand. They blew up bridges and supply depots, destroyed Japanese communications equipment, and ambushed enemy patrols. MacArthur later wrote that Volckmann's forces accomplished the purpose of "practically a front-line division."[38]

Because the rapid advances of various units were creating gaps in their lines, the units held in reserve began to move ashore.

While MacArthur spent the next two days aboard the *Boise* planning his new headquarters ashore, General Krueger's forces pushed their front line to thirty miles wide and fifteen miles deep in most places. Of paramount importance, the XIV Corps had turned control of the Lingayen airfield over to General Kenney's Fifth Air Force, which brought in several fighter units on the thirteenth. Speed was of the essence in opening the airfield to American planes. Admiral Halsey's carriers had been providing air support along with the escort carriers of the invasion force, but Halsey planned to withdraw in a few days to move on to attacking Okinawa. Most of the land-based aircraft were making trips from Mindoro, but to be more effective they had to move to Luzon to provide close air support to the ground forces.

Despite some difficulties in getting the airfield equipment ashore in rough surf, especially the steel matting used for landing runways, the man in charge of the work, chief engineer Brigadier General Leif Sverdrup, rushed ashore with the first landing parties and headed toward the airfield. Responsible for airfield construction, Sverdrup was against the clock for several reasons, including the planned withdrawal of the navy aircraft that had to be replaced immediately. He had also promised Generals MacArthur and Kenney that he would have Lingayen airfield operational in seven days after the landing. He even bet Kenney a bottle of scotch that his men could accomplish the task.

Arriving at the airstrip, totally devoid of enemy soldiers, Sverdrup spotted a company of American tanks heading directly for the nice hard open ground he intended for aircraft landings.

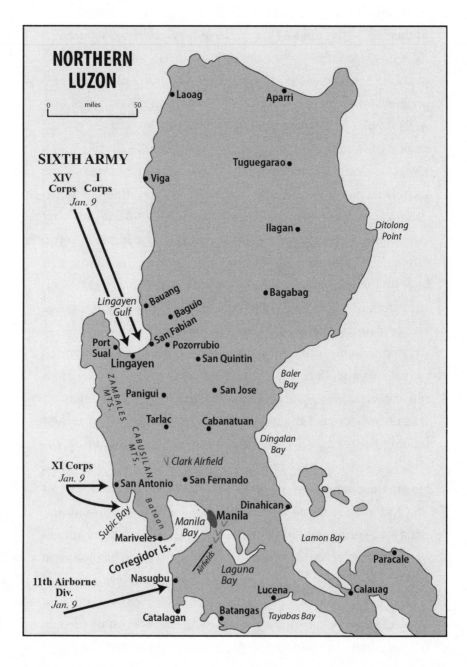

NORTHERN LUZON

0   miles   50

SIXTH ARMY

XIV   I
Corps Corps
Jan. 9

Laoag

Aparri

Tuguegarao

Viga

Ilagan

Ditolong Point

Bagabag

Lingayen Gulf

Bauang

Baguio

San Fabian

Port Sual

Pozorrubio

Lingayen

San Quintin

Baler Bay

ZAMBALES MTS.

Panigui

San Jose

CABUSILAN MTS.

Tarlac

Cabanatuan

Dingalan Bay

XI Corps
Jan. 9

V *Clark Airfield*

San Antonio

San Fernando

Dinahican

Subic Bay

Bataan

Manila

Manila Bay

Mariveles

Lamon Bay

Corregidor Is.

Airfields

Paracale

11th Airborne Div.
Jan. 9

Nasugbu

Laguna Bay

Lucena

Calauag

Catalagan

Batangas

Tayabas Bay

He realized the treaded vehicles would tear up the surface and cost him several days to repair the damage. He leaped from his jeep, pulled his .45 from its holster, and waved his arms wildly at the tanks. When the tank commander opened his hatch and demanded to know what was going on, the angry engineer told him his tanks could not cross the field because it was needed for a landing strip and if they insisted on doing so, he, the general, would open fire with his handgun. The tanker, perhaps thinking the man was out of his mind if he thought a .45 would stop a tank, decided to take a different route to his destination.[39]

General MacArthur had a hearty laugh when he heard about the confrontation on the airfield. Because of the speed with which Sverdrup had prepared the field for fighters and bombers and perhaps also his standoff with the tankers, MacArthur promoted him and awarded him the Distinguished Service Cross. MacArthur pinned the medal on personally, and then did something rather unusual: he gave his chief engineer a set of 14-karat gold castle insignias for his uniform lapels, the emblem of the Engineer Corps. The commanding general explained that the pins were a gift from his father, a Civil War Medal of Honor recipient, upon his graduation from West Point into the Engineer Corps in 1903. He had worn them until he transferred to the infantry, but had always carried them with him the rest of his life. Calling Sverdrup an "engineering soldier at his best," he made him promise the pins would never end up in a museum. Sverdrup kept his promise. In 1975, a year before his death, he presented the castles, along with the explanation of their significance, to the then current chief of engineers, Lieutenant General William C. Gribble. When he retired, Gribble passed them on to his successor, and they are worn today on the uniform of the current chief of engineers of the US Army.

General Sverdrup won his bottle of scotch from General Kenney when the first Fifth Air Force P-38 fighters landed on the airfield on January 15. The following day B-24 bombers joined them. It was just in time, for Admiral Halsey had to pull his carriers out on the seventeenth to prepare to attack Okinawa. With the Japanese air force virtually nonexistent on Luzon, General Kenney sent thirty B-24s and fifty-three P-38s from Lingayen to attack an enemy airfield on Formosa on January 17. Four days earlier, Kenney had declared that enemy air units in the entire Philippines were no longer an offensive force to be reckoned with.[40]

AS THE AMERICAN forces advanced, General Yamashita remained inside a cave he had dug into a mountainside at his headquarters in Baguio, the former summer capital of the Philippines government where officials went to escape the heat of Manila during the hottest months. Now it and a nearby mine were filling up with badly wounded and dying soldiers. Men could be heard asking nurses to put them out of their misery. Not only was the Japanese commander tied to the ground with no air force, but also his forces were severely impeded in their movements by the American bombing of rail yards and bridges, and the destruction of half the locomotives in the country. Vehicles attempting to transport troops were subject to constant attack from American aircraft as soon as they became visible. The sky over Luzon, once the domain of the Imperial Air Force, now belonged exclusively to their enemy. The man once called the Tiger of Malaya was reduced to issuing an order to his troops explaining that their duty was to not just die with honor, but to do all they could to slow the American advance for a day or even a half a day.[41]

ON JANUARY 13, General MacArthur moved permanently from the *Boise* to a set of school buildings in the coastal town of Dagupan to serve as his new headquarters. This was to be a temporary headquarters as his plan was to move to Manila as quickly as possible, to General Krueger's consternation. Unlike the Price House in Tacloban, enemy aircraft would not target it. The general tried taking walks around town for exercise and chatting with local inhabitants. However, each time he did he found he was soon leading a parade of admirers who wanted to touch him or kiss his hand. He soon had to revert to taking a jeep and driver anywhere he went at speeds that kept the crowds as bay. Later that day General Krueger went ashore to establish his own headquarters.

THE KAMIKAZE menace had all but abated by then but would be revived vigorously at Okinawa. The few naval aircraft Admiral Fukudome still had on Luzon flew off to Formosa. The admiral transferred to Singapore where he spent the remaining months of the war as commander of the Thirteenth Air Fleet composed of mostly training aircraft. General Tominaga, commander of the Fourth Air Army, who in opposing Yamashita's plan to evacuate Manila spoke of fighting for the city to the death with his men, proved somewhat cowardly by taking one of his few remaining aircraft and flying to Formosa without asking Yamashita's permission. Yamashita was furious when he learned of the air force commander's abandonment of his post despite Yamashita's orders and demanded he be court-martialed. Fortunately, for Tominaga, he had friends in high positions who protected him from Yamashita's rage.[42]

Air force ground crews and pilots with no aircraft were absorbed into army infantry units unless they were located in Manila, in which case Admiral Onishi's suicidal naval forces took control of them.

General Yamashita's defense plan precluded any meaningful resistance of the beach landing zones due to the American monopoly of air and sea power. The Imperial Army was going to have to fight without that type of support. As a result, in mid-December a plan for a protracted defense was developed that would be a long-term delaying action and would cost the Americans time and lives. This was disrupted by a combination of heavy air attacks and significantly increased guerrilla attacks just prior to and during the landings. These greatly impeded the movement of troops and supplies, especially food and ammunition to units stationed around the northern sections of Luzon.

On January 17, MacArthur visited Krueger's Sixth Army headquarters. His mission was to bully Krueger into speeding up the advance toward Manila. MacArthur remained convinced that Yamashita was not going to defend Manila, just as he himself had not in 1941. He was of course correct. The Fourteenth Area Army commander had ordered all troops out of the city when the Americans approached. Unfortunately, Admiral Onishi, who was not in Yamashita's chain of command, had other ideas. He and General Tominaga decided to fight to the death, except that Tominaga changed his mind, leaving his troops behind and flying to Formosa. General Krueger, ever the cautious Prussian, was concerned about exposing the XXIV Corps flanks if they moved too fast. He understood his commander's drive to capture both Clark Field and Manila, but he was concerned about falling victim to enemy attacks without sufficient flank guards. He was waiting for reinforcements to arrive.

When persuasion failed to convince Krueger to speed up his forces, MacArthur told an aide, "Walter's pretty stubborn. Maybe I'll have to try something else." He actually had two "something elses" to try. First was to embarrass Krueger by moving his own headquarters from the school in Dagupan to a sugar mill facility called San Miguel some fifty miles closer to Manila than Krueger's Army headquarters. This apparently did have the desired results, but MacArthur was not finished pushing Krueger.

When the Sixth Army withdrew from Leyte and prepared for the Luzon landings, the fighting there was taken over by Lieutenant General Robert Eichelberger's Eighth Army. A history of bad blood existed between Krueger and Eichelberger. It began when MacArthur brought Krueger to SWPA to command the newly formed Sixth Army, which MacArthur disguised as a task force called Alamo Force, in order to retain direct command of it. Krueger had never commanded troops in combat before arriving in Brisbane on February 8, 1943, but had demonstrated strong leadership and strategic thinking while training troops sent to Europe. Eichelberger had already proven himself in the fighting around Buna when he salvaged a losing campaign. Krueger was given command of the Sixth Army, something Eichelberger thought should have gone to him. Despite this disappointment and a failed attempt to gain a transfer out of SWPA, Eichelberger continued to perform brilliantly throughout the remainder of the New Guinea campaign, and he was now doing the same on Leyte.

MacArthur's plan following the landings at Lingayen Gulf was to launch an Eighth Army landing at the southern end of Luzon at Nasugbu Bay fifty-five miles southwest of Manila near the Verde Island Passage. This was to serve as a diversion to draw as many Japanese troops from the defense of the Manila region as possible. Planning for this landing had gone through several variations. But now MacArthur wanted General Joseph Swing's 11th Airborne Division to forgo an amphibious landing and instead parachute into Nichols Field located on the southern end of Manila and widely believed lightly defended, especially since virtually all enemy aircraft were destroyed or flown to Formosa.

The original plan called for landing two Glider Infantry Regiments, the 187th and 188th from 11th Airborne Division, on the beaches at Nasugbu Bay. The 511th Parachute Infantry Regiment would then drop on Tagaytay Ridge less than forty miles from Manila along Route 17 to trap retreating Japanese and to secure the highway for use by the Americans. The commanding general sent his chief of staff, Sutherland, and air force chief Kenney to meet with Eichelberger and explain that MacArthur wanted him to "capture Manila if possible." The two even implied that if the 11th got into Manila before troops from Krueger's Sixth Army he might be awarded with a fourth star. Eichelberger decided against the change in plans. He would land his forces at Nasugbu Bay on January 31 as planned.[43]

When the 11th Airborne finally reached Nichols Field, control of the division was passed from Eichelberger's Eighth Army to Krueger's Sixth Army as part of Griswold's XIV Corps.

As additional troops, supplies, and equipment poured ashore at Lingayen Gulf, General Krueger continued to worry about the lack of strong enemy resistance to the landings. Following Krueger's lead, General Griswold pushed the troops of his XIV Corps gradually south, ever mindful of exposing his flanks, especially his left flank, to a strong enemy attack from the large Japanese forces in the eastern mountains. Yamashita avoided such attacks since it would require his attacking units to cross the open farmland to reach the Americans, exposing them to enemy aircraft.

Frustrated with what he considered Krueger's slow pace, MacArthur constantly harassed his army commander, trying every trick up his sleeve to get the results he desired. He even hinted at the possibility of Krueger earning a fourth star. In the midst of fighting a huge war, MacArthur and the Sixth Army commander were engaged in what historian Walter Borneman called "a contest of wills."[44]

Krueger was also getting pressure from General Kenney, who was anxious to move his air units from Mindoro to Clark Field, which was northwest of Manila. In response, Krueger requested that Kenney's aircraft stop bombing bridges and roadways as the destruction was doing little against the enemy, but compounding the repair work of the engineers who were running out of bridging material.

XIV Corps had two primary objectives after landing at Lingayen Gulf: the city of Manila and the airfields that composed the twelve-square-mile Clark Field complex located fifty miles northwest of the capital. Because of either pressure from MacArthur and/or Kenney, or the speed at which several of the corps units had moved south since the landings, Krueger finally decided his flanks were safe enough to order Griswold to attack Clark Field. He sent the order in the evening of January 21.

Griswold had to deal with concerns about advancing on Clark Field, primarily that his own supply units were having difficulty keeping up with the speed of his combat troops. In addition, there was a lack of clear intelligence of what his men would face once they approached enemy defenses at Clark Field. SWPA intelligence reported there were approximately 130,000 Japanese troops on Luzon but they were unlikely to mount a strong defense once the Americans had landed and began moving south. We now know that estimate grossly understated how many Japanese soldiers remained on the island even after sending tens of thousands to fight and die on Leyte. Krueger's own intelligence officer, Colonel Horton V. White, told Krueger that based on his own research using guerrilla informers reporting the arrival of reinforcements from other locations in the empire, Yamashita had fifty thousand troops who were prepared to attack Griswold's left flank. Clouding the issue further, patrol units sent out from I Corps in the region reported little or no contact with the enemy.[45]

Yamashita recognized the importance of the Clark Field airstrips to the Americans, but there was little he could do to halt Griswold's rapid advance. On January 23, the US 40th Division, commanded by Major General Rapp Brush, reached the first airstrip in the northeastern section of Clark Field. The 37th Division joined them the following day. The Americans formed a line along the eastern perimeter of Clark, facing west toward the foothills of the Zambales Mountains where the bulk of Major General Rikichi Tsukada's Kembu Group were prepared to deny the airfields to the enemy. Tsukada was ordered "to check an anticipated penetration of the Clark Field sector, facilitate the operations of the air forces as far as possible, and as a last resort hinder the enemy utilization of the airfields by operating from the strongpoint west of Clark Field."[46]

This was a tall order for a force of thirty thousand men containing only eight thousand troops from two actual combat units. There also were seven thousand noncombat troops from army service units that included five airfield construction battalions. Rear Admiral Ushie Sugimoto had fifteen thousand sailors who were mostly ground support forces of the now planeless 26th

Air Flotilla. Sugimoto reported to Tsukada. These forces were not well equipped when it came to heavy armament. They had a limited number of field artillery pieces and anti-tank guns as well as two battalions of naval 120mm antiaircraft guns that had been converted to function as ground support weapons to defend the approaches to the airstrips. An abundance of machine guns and cannons removed from the large number of damaged aircraft spread around Clark Field were mostly located in the mountains and hills west and northwest of the airfields. The mountainous terrain worked to the benefit of the Japanese, whose guns were able to rain death and destruction on the advancing American infantry.

The Japanese also had less than two dozen Type 97 Chi-Ha Kai medium tanks and Type 2 Ho-Ro self-propelled guns. Despite the size of the Kembu Group, it was lightly armed and relied on too many soldiers and sailors with little or no combat experience, including labor gangs from Okinawa, Formosa, and Korea. Despite the stronger than expected resistance, the XIV Corps forces inched their way westward over the coming days.

Meanwhile, as the battle for Clark Field pushed Tsukada's defenses westward, on January 29 MacArthur landed thirty thousand fresh troops behind the enemy along the west coast of Luzon in Zambales Province. This was the XI Corps commanded by Major General Charles P. Hall consisting of the 38th Infantry Division transported from Leyte and the 34th Regimental Combat Team of the 24th Division from Mindoro aboard ships of the Seventh Fleet. This landing had two goals: to prevent the enemy forces in the region west of Clark Field from withdrawing to the Bataan Peninsula as the Americans had done following the Japanese invasion of the Philippines, and engaging in a prolonged and costly defense; and to add the corps' weight to the drive toward Manila. It also aided in cutting off the Kembu Group's communications with Yamashita's headquarters in Baguio. General Akira Muto, Yamashita's chief of staff, later reported that they had lost all contact with the Kembu Group in mid-January and lost track of Tsukada's activities until after the surrender.[47]

Shortly after arriving off the landing beaches near the towns of San Antonio and San Felipe, the fleet received instructions to withhold all pre-landing shore bombardment unless the landing forces received enemy fire. The local guerrilla organization had reported no enemy troops in the area. The landings went off with little trouble and no resistance.

By the end of the day, January 29, troops from the 38th Division arrived at one of their objectives, the prewar airfield at San Marcelino, to find that guerrillas had already taken control of it. Grande Island, which commands the entrance to Subic Bay thirty-five miles north of Manila Bay, was their second target. The island and Fort Wint located on it were also occupied that day. Within a week, Allied forces controlled the road leading to the Bataan Peninsula, effectively preventing Japanese troops from retreating there.

Fighting was going on across a broad front. I Corps was heavily engaged with forces Yamashita had assigned to the mountains north and northeast of the Luzon Central Plain leading to the Japanese stronghold at Baguio, while the XIV Corps continued hammering away at the units defending Clark Field.

On January 30, Krueger's headquarters issued Field Order No. 46, the plan for the drive against Manila.

CHAPTER FOURTEEN

THE LIBERATION OF MANILA

The liberation of Manila, which began on February 3, 1945, resulted in the capital's terrible destruction and horrifying loss of life—all due to Admiral Iwabuchi's decision to stand and fight to the last man. Using his available naval and army forces, Iwabuchi set about turning a large city of mostly wooden structures into a combination fortress and tinderbox. He had age-old palm trees cut down along boulevards and stretched across the roadways to block or at least slow down the invading enemy. He had artillery pieces, including antiaircraft guns, removed from the Imperial Navy ships sitting uselessly in Manila Bay and positioned at strategic locations throughout the city, including residential sections. Operational weapons were stripped from the hundreds of severely damaged aircraft at local airfields and some were placed inside buildings and bunkers throughout Manila and the remainder were mounted on trucks for hit-and-run attacks. Because General Yamashita had no time to move most of the large quantities of guns and ammunition in military stores around the city, Iwabuchi's forces had a virtually unlimited supply with which to fight.

The landings on January 31 at Nasugbu by the 11th Airborne further assured Iwabuchi that the major assault on the city would come from the south. As a result he had his forces construct a strong line of defenses facing south called the Genko Line.

His formidable defense ran from near Manila Bay through Nichols Field, a former US Army Air Corps facility, across the Manila Polo Club and ended at Fort McKinley, a former US Army installation. For the attacking Americans, it was roughly six thousand yards of pure hell containing every imaginable form of defense, including concrete pillboxes with interlocking fields of fire, two- and three-story brick buildings with antiaircraft guns, shore artillery pieces, and 5- and 6-inch naval guns. Manning the Genko Line were over five thousand infantry and naval troops. Called the Southern Force, its commander was naval Captain Takesue Furuse.[1]

The defense of the city was based on an order that called for every man to fight to the death: "In the all-out suicide attack every man will attack until he achieves a glorious death. Not even one man must become a prisoner. During the attack, friends of the wounded will make them commit suicide."[2]

East of the city, General Yokoyama had reorganized his forces to provide for fifty-four thousand men in the mountainous terrain overlooking much of Manila's water supply reservoirs. His orders from Yamashita were to remove all food and ammunition from the city as quickly as possible and ship everything north to the new headquarters. He was not to attempt a defense of the city, but instead withdraw to the east and destroy all bridges behind him. This was to include all naval forces in the city. Technically Admiral Iwabuchi should have included his forces, now numbering over sixteen thousand men, in that withdrawal. Instead, at several conferences the admiral made clear his intention to follow orders from his naval superior, Admiral Okochi, and destroy all naval port and harbor facilities in the city. Concerned over friction, and to avoid actual fighting between Imperial Army and Navy troops, Yokoyama conceded. He even gave Iwabuchi control over several thousand army troops still in the city.

Disregarding the orders of General Yamashita, Iwabuchi ordered his forces to defend Manila to the last man and destroy enemy strength in doing so. He remained convinced the larger American force would be coming from the south and that the troops who invaded Lingayen Gulf were moving too slow to be of immediate concern.

IWABUCHI WAS surprised by the sudden rapid move south resulting from General Krueger's Field Order No. 46. Under General Griswold's command, XIV Corps led the way to the capital in two columns. Major General Robert Beightler's 37th Division was on the right and the recently arrived 1st Cavalry Division commanded by Major General Verne Mudge on the left. Coming from Nasugbu in the south was Major General Joseph Swing's 11th Airborne.

Two thousand guerrillas joined the Airborne from a group known as the Hunter's ROTC. One of the most active and effective guerrilla groups in the Philippines, they were commanded by Lieutenant Colonel Emmanuel V. de Ocampo, who remains a great hero to the Filipino people. Three hundred reserve officers and cadets from the Philippine Military Academy originally comprised the Hunter's but it had grown since its founding in January 1942. One of their first operations had been to raid a

Japanese arsenal in Manila and steal 130 rifles. From then on, they became a deadly thorn in the enemy's flesh with numerous raids and the collection of intelligence passed on to the Allied forces. The Airborne and guerrilla force fought their way through fierce Japanese resistance over sixty miles right up to the general post office headquarters on the Pasig River in Manila.

Having earlier learned of the Japanese massacre of over one hundred American POWs on the island of Palawan, and the successful raid on the POW camp at Cabanatuan by elements of the 6th Rangers, MacArthur rushed to General Mudge's head-quarters on January 30. He told Mudge about the massacre and his concern for the prisoners held in camps and prisons through-out Manila and the surrounding area. MacArthur told him about the nearly four thousand prisoners held at Santo Tomas University in the city. "Go to Manila. Go around the Nips, bounce off the Nips, but go to Manila. Free the internees at Santo Tomas."[3]

By the following day, Mudge organized a flying column of eight hundred men, all volunteers, who rushed south in trucks, jeeps, and light tanks. For the next three days, they fought their way through enemy blockades and right up to the gates of the university. When the tanks smashed through the front gate, the Japanese fled into a nearby building but eventually negotiated a peaceful handover. Over four thousand prisoners, some in miser-able condition, emerged from the university. The 37th Division arrived the following day at Old Bilibid Prison and took command of the facility with its five hundred civilians and eight hundred American soldiers.[4]

Ever since the landings, MacArthur had spent an inordinate amount of time for a commander at the front lines. Just as he had done on New Guinea, he defied enemy snipers and machine-gun fire to stop and briefly talk with combat troops and their officers while they were engaged with the enemy. He was constantly being driven to see firsthand what was happening and not simply rely on reports. Now he was almost at his goal of the last three years—his former home, Manila. Anxious to see the situation of the survivors he felt he had abandoned when the president ordered him to escape from Corregidor and make his way to Australia, he attempted to rush down Route 5 in two jeeps to catch up with the flying column from 1st Cavalry. He was able to get in among the main body of the division when the tanks, trucks, half-tracks, and jeeps came to a halt.

MacArthur's driver made his way to the front of the convoy to find a wide deep ravine across the highway. After the flying column had taken the enemy guards on the bridge by surprise and raced across, the Japanese troops had blown the bridge, halting all advances along the highway. Here he found a major who appeared to be in charge. MacArthur asked him how long they would have to wait to get across on a replacement bridge. The major, startled by MacArthur's presence, responded that it would be at least one full day before the engineers could place a new bridge across the gap. A badly disappointed MacArthur thanked him and told his driver to return to headquarters.

The following morning the two-jeep unit, with MacArthur as usual sitting in the front passenger seat and two aides in the rear, barreled down Route 3, the route taken earlier by the 37th Division. This time they made it into the city and headed for Bilibid Prison, where MacArthur, obviously moved by the experience, walked through what now amounted to hospital wards and held outstretched boney hands or touched a man on the shoulder who was unable to lift his arm, and in each case he whispered a message of encouragement. The place was filthy and the men were starving; their captors treated them as less than human.

Overwhelmed by the pitiful condition of the former prisoners and by their joyous welcome to him, during which several women kissed him and the men clapped their hands and thanked him for returning, MacArthur quietly told his aide, "This has been a bit too emotional for me. I want to get out and I want to go forward until I am stopped by fire, and I don't mean sniper fire." The aide took it to mean he wanted to get back to fighting the vicious, inhuman enemy who had treated all these people so badly.[5]

As MacArthur continued to tour the war-torn city in which gunfire erupted from virtually every building and around every corner, he was shocked by the wanton destruction. He had hoped that Yamashita, as a professional experienced soldier, would recognize the city had no real military value and would withdraw his forces into the mountains and declare Manila an open city. General Griswold noted in his diary, "MacArthur has visions of saving this beautiful city intact. He does not realize as I do, that the skies burn red every night as [the Japanese] systematically sack the city."[6]

MacArthur did not know that Yamashita's order to withdraw would have left the city intact. At one point, he even ordered General Yokoyama to use troops from the Shimbu Group to assist Admiral Iwabuchi in withdrawing his naval troops. But by then the city was under attack from American forces and guerrilla units from all sides, and his attempt to do so met with bloody resistance from the Americans on February 14 and 15. For the remainder of his life, Yamashita was adamant that Admiral Iwabuchi's defense of Manila was "entirely contrary to my plans for Manila."[7]

A large part of the defense within the city relied on the heavy artillery removed from nearby aircraft and vessels—as well as the crews that manned them. American soldiers were surprised at how little rifle fire there was; instead the naval cannons and shore artillery pieces were firing on them. From the beginning, General MacArthur had banned any aircraft bombing of the city. His concern was that his air forces would be killing thousands of innocent Filipinos. When Krueger pressed him, MacArthur's response was that it was "unthinkable" to bomb a city full of allied civilians.[8]

MacArthur had also limited the use of artillery, banning the heaviest weapons until his generals complained that their shells could not penetrate several of the buildings used by the enemy as strong points. The city was prone to earthquakes, so many of the more recent structures were built to withstand the tremors, which made them also resistant to penetration by 105mm shells, the most common weapon the Americans used at the time. MacArthur's requirement when using heavy weapons was that the gunners had a clear view of the enemy and did not fire at buildings unless Japanese were obviously inside.

The civilians paid the heaviest price for the liberation of Manila. Although most were starving from lack of food, American troops found buildings filled with huge amounts of food supplies that could feed hundreds of civilians but were reserved for the exclusive use of the Japanese.[9]

No one expected the Japanese to fight a house-to-house battle for Manila. In fact, General Eichelberger wrote to his wife on February 14 that the Japanese were not expected to make such a stand, but would probably withdraw to the east and declare Manila an open city. He learned quickly how wrong he was.[10]

Guerrilla agents had reported seeing several thousand soldiers departing the city and heading east into the hills, but what they did not see were the nearly twenty thousand rabid troops who had stayed behind and been ordered to fight to the death. Advancing house-to-house, the liberating forces were often forced to destroy buildings in order to kill or drive the Japanese into the open. Every building left standing and every home in the city had to be cleared by the American infantrymen. Inside most, they found the mutilated bodies of civilians subjected to inhumane tortures at the hands of bayonet-bearing troops and sword-swinging officers. Thousands of female Filipinos, from infants to the very elderly, were raped, often repeatedly. Recovery units attempted to count the dead civilians, but soon gave up as in some places the bodies had been torched by the Japanese and left to burn.

Important buildings such as the Post Office, City Hall, and the iconic Manila Hotel where the MacArthur family had once resided were reduced to rubble. Even then, the surviving enemy continued firing from under the ruins until fuel was poured over them and flamethrowers set them ablaze, in some way retribution for the thousands of civilians they had burned to death. Gradually the defenders died by the dozens, then the hundreds, and then the thousands.

As the Americans and Filipinos tightened their stranglehold on the city, the focus increasingly became an imposing stone citadel near the harbor. The Americans referred to it as the Walled City; Filipinos called it Intramuros. Covering 160 acres along the banks of the Pasig River that bisects Manila, its walls, built in the late sixteenth century, are as much as forty feet thick at the base and run to as much as twenty-two feet high. To the Americans looking at this city within a city, it resembled a great old medieval fortress. It may have looked old, but it was armed with formidable weapons for its defense.

On February 16, General Griswold broadcast a message in Japanese addressed to the enemy commander inside the walls. It was known he had about four thousand troops with him, and some unknown thousands of civilians being held there. The message told the Japanese commander that his situation was hopeless and his defeat was inevitable. Griswold gave him the opportunity for what he called an "honorable surrender." There was no reply. Griswold noted this in his diary, writing, "It is to be a fight to the death."[11]

What the American general did not know at the time was that on the previous day Admiral Iwabuchi broadcast his own message to his troops, telling the world that his troops were glad for the opportunity to serve in the battle for Manila and they were determined to make a last stand there.[12]

The day following Griswold's broadcast, he ordered the 37th Division to begin reducing the walls to rubble. Soon 140 guns of various sizes began pounding the thick walls of the fortress city. American artillery that had earlier been moved in place bombarded the walls on the northern and northeastern sides of the Intramuros where the walls were suspected to be most vulnerable. Over the next five days they pumped eight thousand shells into the wall, punching holes large enough for infantry and dismounted cavalry to get in once the order was given. Self-propelled 105mm guns, 76mm tank destroyers, tanks firing 75mm shells, and 240mm howitzers conducted the assault on the ancient walls.

As THE WALLS of the Intramuros were pummeled into a dust that blocked out the sun, troops from the 38th Division, led by Major General Henry L. C. Jones, and Colonel Aubrey S. "Red" Newman's 34th Regimental Combat Team of the 24th Division that made up the XI Corps, spread out from their landing beaches. As the corps, commanded by Major General Charles P.

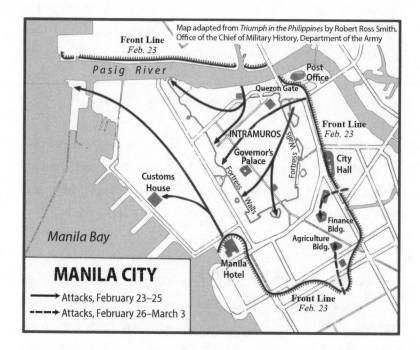

Map adapted from *Triumph in the Philippines* by Robert Ross Smith. Office of the Chief of Military History, Department of the Army

MANILA CITY

→ Attacks, February 23–25
--→ Attacks, February 26–March 3

Hall, secured its landing along the coast of Zambales Province, Filipinos waving American flags and crying "Liberty!" greeted them. Originally scheduled to land at the provincial capital of Vigan along the Luzon west coast one hundred miles north of Lingayen Gulf, it was decided the enemy forces stationed along that portion of the coast were not a threat to the landing beaches at Lingayen Gulf. Instead, the ships transporting the corps were rerouted to the Zambales coast south of Lingayen Gulf. This placed thirty thousand Americans to the rear of the Kembu Group battling the XIV Corps for control of Clark Field.

The corps successfully sealed off the entrances to the Bataan Peninsula to prevent retreating Kembu Group troops from attempting to duplicate MacArthur's earlier defense of Bataan and engage in a prolonged defense that would be both costly and time consuming for the Americans. US planners were unaware that

General Yamashita had decided not to mount a defense of Bataan or even Manila Bay for the same reasons he opted not to fight over Manila: he did not have enough experienced combat troops. Many of his best troops had been killed or stranded on Leyte, and the geography required spreading his forces over too great an area. Estimates of the number of Bataan defenders varied widely. Some American intelligence officers thought it as high as 8,000 troops but were never as low as the 2,800 men Colonel Sanonebu Nagayoshi had at his command, called the Nagayoshi Detachment. His command comprised most of the 39th Infantry Regiment of the 10th Division, two provisional infantry companies, a battery of mixed artillery consisting of 37mm and 105mm cannons, and heavy mortars. He also had a large amount of heavy and light machine guns and a platoon of light tanks. The heavier guns and tanks were situated so they could stay in the protection of the many caves dotting the mountains, pull out when they needed to fire, and quickly withdraw to the safety of their caves. They were for the most part partially invisible to American aircraft searching for them.[13]

Filipino troops from the Western Luzon Guerrilla Forces organized and commanded by Captain Ramon Magsaysay joined the Americans and moved to occupy the east coast of the peninsula. The goal was to secure the entire Manila Bay so US naval ships could bring in supplies and reinforcements. The landing sites at Lingayen Gulf and Nasugbu Bay where the 11th Airborne had landed were overworked and backed up.

General Krueger recognized the need to expedite access of Manila Bay for Allied shipping. At a meeting with MacArthur on February 1, he asked if a plan existed to make full use of the bay. The general told him Krueger's troops had to capture the east coast of the Bataan Peninsula as early as possible, followed by the capture of Corregidor Island at the entrance to the bay. Then once Bataan and Corregidor were seized, the south shore of the bay could be cleared. These were tall orders, but they had to be done if the main enemy forces under Yamashita were to be defeated.[14]

The Allied troops encountered only light resistance as they moved deeper into the Bataan Peninsula. They drove south with the goal of securing the entire region down to Mariveles opposite the final target, Corregidor. The first stubborn defense they met was in the Zambales Mountains just below the border between Bataan and Zambales Provinces. This extremely rugged terrain required the single road through the area to climb several miles and cut back on itself in a horseshoe curve then slip through a narrow canyon. The Americans called it Zig Zag Pass, and it offered the defending force innumerable ideal positions from which to fire down on the invaders.

On February 1, the first to enter Colonel Nagayoshi's carefully planned defenses was the 152nd Regiment of the 38th Division. The intense, deadly machine-gun fire stopped them dead in their tracks. Everywhere they looked the enemy was firing down on them and they had very little ability to hide. One of the soldiers later described the enemy positions: "Each hilltop was a fortress."[15]

Over the next two days, all advances came to a halt as the Allied forces found it impossible to break through the Japanese defenses. At one point, it was decided to attempt a pincer movement by sending troops around in a wide arc and attack the enemy from two directions. So the 149th Regiment from the 38th Division walked for five days through the mountain jungle where no vehicles could pass. Along the way food and other supplies were parachuted in from cargo planes. With some luck, they found a local indigenous tribe that hated the Japanese and offered to guide the Americans through the area. Arriving behind the Japanese, they launched their attack. Despite a counterattack by the light tanks, the pincer worked and with the aid of the Fifth Air Force, the Japanese at Zig Zag Pass were finally defeated on February 15.[16]

The fighting at Zig Zag Pass cost the American and Filipino forces 250 killed and over 1,100 injured. The Japanese paid a high price for the defense of Zig Zag Pass, which in the scheme of things accomplished very little. A body count found nearly 2,400 dead Japanese while 25 surrendered. Another approximately 300 men, including Colonel Nagayoshi, retreated south in hopes of linking up with other imperial units.[17]

Nagayoshi led his dwindling force into the jungle slopes of Mount Natib in the central part of the peninsula. They spent their time unsuccessfully attempting to make contact with Japanese units, searching for food, and avoiding American troops and Filipino guerrillas, until finally surrendering to an American military police force in September 1945. By then the Nagayoshi Detachment consisted of less than 250 emaciated men and their commander.

As most of the troops now in Bataan Peninsula began the slow march south and mopped up enemy units left stranded, the 151st Regimental Combat Team of the 38th Division boarded ships at nearby Olongapo for a much more relaxed trip down Subic Bay to the southern end of the peninsula. They landed at Mariveles Harbor on February 15 against light opposition. Once ashore the regiment split with half the men proceeding north along the east coast the other half north along the west coast. Following some mopping up operations against disheartened Japanese soldiers and marines, Bataan was declared secure once again on February 21, 1945.

WHILE THE FIGHTING at Zig Zag Pass was underway, General Griswold decided to throw the full weight of his corps against the Japanese resistance around Clark Field and nearby Fort Stotsenburg. The 37th and 40th Divisions had overwhelmed the enemy with coordinated tank and infantry attacks that captured both locales on January 29. The Kembu Group fought a ferocious defense of the Clark Field area, but ultimately withdrew into the nearby mountains. They left behind a huge amount of supplies, including over two hundred new aircraft engines, hundreds of radio communications equipment, several months' food supplies, and over forty artillery pieces of various sizes. On January 30, General Krueger arrived at General Griswold's request to witness the raising of the United States flag over Clark Field once again.

AMERICAN AND Filipino troops lay in wait around the Intramuros during the night of February 22/23. At 7:30 a.m. on the twenty-third, the artillery barrage blasted away, sending many of the Japanese inside into a dazed confusion. Angered at their apparent inability to strike back, many of them took their frustrations out on civilians within the wall, killing and raping on a massive scale. The Japanese soldiers, marines, and sailors who took part in the slaughter of tens of thousands of defenseless civilians were following orders from their superiors. A February 13 order claimed there were several thousand Filipino guerrillas at large in the city, including women and children. "All people," it said, found within the battle area except Japanese military and civilians and members of Special Construction Units (usually Formosan or Korean) "will be put to death." It did not seem to matter if those civilians were discovered sneaking around a military facility or sitting at the dining room table. They all had to die in the most painful and horrendous manner as payback for the coming Japanese defeat.[18]

A follow-up order described the manner in which Filipinos were to be killed. They were to be gathered together and killed with the expenditure of the least amount of ammunition and manpower. Bayonets and swords were the favored weapons of death used by the Japanese. Bodies as well as still-living victims were driven into buildings scheduled to be burned down and set aflame, which is the way thousands were slaughtered.[*] So many incinerated bodies were found after the battle that they could not be counted. An alternative was to throw bodies into the river.[19]

At 8:30 a.m., the American guns fired shells that released a thick red smoke and ceased the heavy bombardment. This was the signal for the infantry assault to begin. As troops poured through the openings in the Intramuros wall created by the artillery, or through preexisting gates, members of the 3rd Battalion of the 129th Regiment boarded assault boats on the opposite bank of

---

[*] The most controversial war crimes trial of the postwar period concerned Yamashita's responsibility in the Manila slaughter of civilians. A military tribunal tried the general and sentenced him to death. American defense lawyers charged that he faced execution for acts committed by the naval forces in Manila that were not under his control. MacArthur's critics claimed the trial was MacArthur's revenge for what the Japanese had done to the Filipino people. Yamashita's attorneys appealed to the United States Supreme Court, but the Court refused to intervene, although two associate justices voiced their opposition to the trial. Justice Frank Murphy wrote it represented the "spirit of revenge and retribution." Justice Wiley Rutledge claimed the trial was not done "in the tradition of the common law and the constitution." In an article written years later for the *Filipino Reporter*, Jim McInerney claimed both Rutledge and Murphy called the execution "legalized lynching." Yamashita's conviction, and execution by hanging at Los Banos prison on February 23, 1946, was not based on anything he personally had done, but by acts committed by troops under his command. This reasoning survives today as the Yamashita Standard. Command accountability has become part of the Geneva Convention.

the Pasig River and made for the opening in the wall that backed up onto the river. At 8:35, the battalion hit the beach and found to their surprise no enemy resistance. By 8:45, the amphibious assault troops linked up with members of 145th Regiment who had entered through two gates along the east wall unopposed.

Then things got dicey as the Japanese began releasing nearly three thousand hostages from a nearby church and hotel. Predominantly women and children, along with a few priests, were released to create confusion among the Allies and oblige responsibility for the care of these people to them. Very few males were released. For the most part, the Japanese had slaughtered the men and piled their bodies up in nearby basements.

Allied troops gradually drove the enemy back, trapping many in basements and lower levels of buildings where fuel and flame-throwers were used to kill them. Everyone knew the enemy was not going to surrender, so it was always a fight to the death. The Japanese goal was to kill as many civilians and enemy troops as possible and destroy as many bridges and buildings as they could on their path to self-destruction. Even Admiral Iwabuchi gave up the ghost on February 26 when he along with members of his staff took their own lives rather than face capture. The coward most responsible for the destruction in Manila spent his last hours hiding in the earthquake-proof agriculture building just outside the Intramuros walls.[20]

While enemy forces still held out at several locations around the city, General MacArthur decided it was time to give the Filipino people back their country and to fulfill his promise to former president Manuel Quezon. MacArthur's friend, Quezon had died after a long battle with tuberculosis in New York on August 1, 1944. MacArthur had earlier on Leyte declared Tacloban the temporary capital, but now he was in the actual national capital.

By some miracle the presidential palace, the Malacanan Palace, had survived virtually untouched amid a city of almost total destruction. Its stained-glass windows and hanging tapestries and even crystal chandeliers remained intact. The general had previously told the War Department that he wanted to avoid any "imperialist policy" that might be introduced "under the guise of military operations or necessities." He wanted the Filipino people to experience the freedoms and liberties they had under the Commonwealth Government prior to the Japanese occupation.[21]

It is also quite possible he was recalling the attempt by Secretary of the Interior Harold Ickes, a relentless critic of MacArthur, to oppose establishing Filipino rule and instead assume for himself the role of High Commissioner of the Philippines. MacArthur had won the support of Secretary of War Henry Stimson in stopping Ickes. Quickly turning over civilian control to the Commonwealth Government would further obstruct Icke's plans.[22]

Under a bright morning sun on Tuesday, February 27, a large crowd of American and Filipino soldiers and a throng of Filipino civilians gathered expectantly around the entrance to the palace. At 8 a.m., General MacArthur left his temporary headquarters at the San Miguel sugar mill and was driven into Manila. The car halted outside the steps leading into the palace and the general stepped out. The troops snapped to attention and smartly saluted as he entered the building and strode along the red-carpeted hall toward the state reception room where President Osmena, along with members of his cabinet and other government officials, waited. Several of his senior officers, including General Kenney and General Krueger, accompanied MacArthur. In a scene reminiscent of the first American commander in chief turning over control to the civilian members of the Continental Congress, MacArthur was relinquishing what he could easily have had as the man to whom all the troops, American and Filipino, gave their loyalty: control of the nation. He had arrived in this ruined and burned-out city to restore the civilian government that had existed prior to the Japanese invasion and occupation.

At 11 a.m., MacArthur stepped to the microphone and spoke briefly, retelling the series of events that had led them all to this moment. He included the fact he had in 1942 declared Manila an open city with the hope the invaders would abide by the rules of warfare and spare "its churches, monuments, and cultural centers...the violence of military ravage." The enemy, he said, had not done so and by his actions "wantonly fixed the future pattern of his own doom."

In closing, MacArthur told the Filipinos, "On behalf of my government, I now solemnly declare, Mr. President, the full powers and responsibilities under the constitution restored to the Commonwealth whose seat is here reestablished as provided by law. Your capital city, cruelly punished though it be..." At this point, his voice broke and his eyes filled with tears. A few minutes later, he completed his remarks and stepped aside for President Osmena.[23]

PRIOR TO RETURNING the government to civilian control, Mac-Arthur had headed for Bataan. Most of the fighting there had been completed except for small, scattered groups of enemy with nowhere to go. The 151st Regiment was at the tip of Bataan working its way up through the jungle, killing enemy troops along the way. Additional forces landed along the Manila Bay shore and trapped many Japanese. MacArthur wanted, predictably, to see all this firsthand.

In the predawn hours of February 16, MacArthur and a party

of officers accompanied by several jeep loads of men armed with automatic rifles, set out on the road along the Bataan east coast. It was the same cobblestone road the American and Filipino prisoners had taken north during the infamous Death March. The commanding general was lost in thought for much of the trip as he revisited the sites of his 1942 defeat. It is also likely he was attempting to get as close to the southern tip of the peninsula as possible and perhaps get a look at the paratroopers who were to drop on Corregidor. When many of the same troopers who were about to drop on Corregidor dropped on New Guinea's Nadzab Airfield on September 5, 1943, MacArthur had visited with the men at the airfield waiting to board their C-47s and then followed their flight in his B-17 so he could watch the drop from above. This time the paratroopers were coming from Mindoro, so he did not have the opportunity to visit but he in all likelihood wanted to watch as they floated down from their aircraft.

Twenty miles down the coast they passed through Pilar and the countryside changed from farmland to ever-thickening woods and jungle. They drove through the site of a very recent battle with dead men from both sides on the ground and some burning vehicles. Surprised to see the commanding general so close to the front, a captain told MacArthur that Japanese troops in considerable numbers were just ahead. Urged to turn back, he learned that two American scouts were just ahead, which was all he needed to give the order to continue.

A half-mile farther, they encountered the two American soldiers. The scouts were on either side of the road slowly making their way south listening for sounds of the enemy when MacArthur's jeep pulled up. The general asked them if there were any Americans farther down the road. They responded "None of our men ahead of here sir! No sir!" To the surprise of the two scouts,

MacArthur gave the order to proceed. Twenty minutes later, now well behind the enemy lines, they came upon a recently deserted campsite used by Japanese soldiers. The still-burning fire heating a pot of steaming rice sat uneaten among other signs of a hasty retreat. They surmised that the enemy must have heard their vehicles approaching and, thinking it was a large American force, withdrew.

Continuing south, they crossed open fields and periodically drove through dark thick jungles with climbing vines and hanging leaves blocking out the sun. They passed another deserted campsite and a small ammunition dump and came to a halt at a deep stream with a blown bridge. They could find no way across. MacArthur's "personal patrol" was now some five miles ahead of the Sixth Army front line, deep in enemy territory. The American troops heading north from Mariveles were still eight or ten miles away. MacArthur was obviously disappointed since the location they were at afforded him no clear view of Corregidor and he was thus unable to see the paratroopers when they floated down.

As they searched for a way across the stream, a P-38 overflew them. They watched the plane circle back around and come in lower to give the pilot a better look at the large clearing near the stream in which several military vehicles and men were waiting. The plane circled again and came in low and slow. Realizing the pilot must have mistaken them for the enemy, several of them began waving their arms wildly while others sought the only nearby cover behind a vehicle or a fallen log. MacArthur, frustrated by the stream, paid little attention to the aircraft as he sulked around with his hands in his pockets as the plane suddenly departed. The Fifth Air Force P-38 pilot had radioed his base that he sighted what he believed was a Japanese motor column and wanted permission to strafe and bomb them. The request went to General Chase who found on further investigation that MacArthur and a group of senior officers and others were out there in Bataan somewhere. Thinking this might be them, he refused the pilot's request. One can only guess the result had the pilot received the go-ahead.[24] But MacArthur's attention was on Corregidor and the paratroopers landing there.

CORREGIDOR, KNOWN AS "The Rock," held a special place in MacArthur's heart. It was his last home in the Philippines, from which President Roosevelt had ordered him to leave for Australia. It is located right at the entrance to Manila Bay just seven miles southeast of Mariveles at the southern tip of Bataan. The island served as a guardian and warning outpost for Manila since the mid-sixteenth century, protecting against Chinese and Dutch pirates, as well as the Spanish Navy, the Royal Navy, and the United States Navy under Commodore Dewey, then finally in 1942 against the forces of Imperial Japan.

The island is tadpole-shaped and barely over four miles long and slightly over one mile at its widest point. It totals just over 2,200 acres. To be successful in re-taking The Rock, American paratroopers would have to land on the island's highest and most prominent aspect, which at 589 feet is known as "Topside."

Dug in on Corregidor were about six thousand Japanese of the Manila Bay Entrance Force under the command of naval Captain Akira Itagaki—most of them just waiting for their turn to die for their emperor. It was a mixed bag of troops, including men from a naval base force normally assigned to guard naval facilities, a provisional battalion of army infantrymen, men assigned to suicide boats called "Shinyo," two companies of antiaircraft artillery, and four companies of fortress artillery. They were under

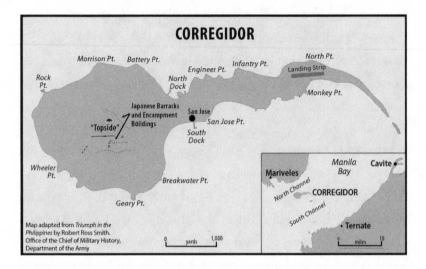

the overall command of Admiral Iwabuchi and knew of his fight-to-the death command. Warned of the possibility of an enemy parachute attack, Itagaki conducted a personal survey of Topside, which he had calculated as the only logical place for jumpers to land. But after his survey, he decided that, based on the condition of the terrain there, his concern was misplaced. Therefore, he focused most of his defensive efforts on repelling an amphibious landing and placed only minimal efforts to defend against an airborne attack.[25]

Even before the assault on Manila, General Kenney discussed the island with MacArthur. Intelligence reports led them to believe the garrison had provisions to last a long time and so could withstand an extended siege. There was a large assortment of artillery, and they were well stocked with ammunition of all sizes. Notwithstanding all that, the island dominated the entrance to Manila Bay and as long as it was in enemy hands, the resupply ships could not safely bring supplies or reinforcements to Manila Harbor. With work racing ahead on repairing the runways at Clark Field, heavy bombers and other aircraft would soon be arriving. The airplane fuel situation was becoming critical as the landing beaches at Lingayen were overloaded. Kenney was already flying in gasoline from Mindoro, but even that would not meet the needs as additional planes arrived. He needed tanker ships full of fuel to keep the pressure on the enemy, especially as forces began moving north against the main body of Yamashita's army.

Kenney sought and received MacArthur's approval to begin to "slug the place to death." He wanted to use heavy bombs against what he knew was a strong rock fortress and then follow up with paratroopers to kill whatever Japanese survived the bombing. This plan was not without great risks.[26]

MacArthur approved Kenney's proposal but wanted to reinforce the paratroopers with an amphibious landing. He recalled that the Japanese lost half their amphibious force assaulting the island in 1942, and knew infantry was required as well as back up by paratroopers. Although he was unsure about his intelligence unit's estimate of about eight hundred to nine hundred enemy soldiers on Corregidor, MacArthur expected that Kenney would be able to land two thousand paratroopers with minimum resistance, at least during the first few minutes. Several members of MacArthur's staff were skeptical of the paratroopers being able to land on Topside. And any Japanese stationed at Topside would be able to dominate all the possible amphibious landing sites below, including what is known as Bottom Side. From the higher ground, a great many troops might be killed before they even got a few feet inland. Despite its shortcomings as a paratroop landing site, it offered the ability to surprise the defenders who were unlikely to expect enemy soldiers falling from the sky on their rather small target.

Beginning on January 23, bombers, dive-bombers, and fighters from the Army's Fifth Air Force and Thirteenth Air Force, as well as from a US Marine wing stationed near Lingayen, pounded Corregidor with over four thousand tons of bombs and hundreds of thousands of rounds of ammunition. Added to this was the use of "liquid fire," or napalm. This was a mixture most often of gasoline and a gelling agent, developed in 1942 by chemist Louis Fieser of the United States Chemical Warfare Service, and began its use as a key tactical weapon against Japanese fortifications such as bunkers and tunnels.

While the bombardment of Corregidor was underway, the 3rd Battalion, 34th Regiment of the 24th Infantry Division (now under Major General Roscoe B. Woodruff) withdrew from the Zig Zag Pass area and moved south toward Mariveles Harbor. The men were headed toward their fourth amphibious assault of the war, having hit the beaches at Hollandia on New Guinea, then Leyte, and then along the Luzon west coast. At Mariveles, they were met by the twenty-five LCMs (Landing Craft Mechanized) of the 592nd Engineer Boat and Shore Regiment that would take them across the seven-mile stretch of open water to Corregidor.

The paratroopers were waiting on Mindoro for the orders to mount up and head to Corregidor. They were members of the 503rd Parachute Regimental Combat Team. Their commander, Colonel George M. Jones, had overflown the island to survey for landing sites on February 6 while seated in the Plexiglas nose of a B-25 bomber. He returned with the recommendation that his men use a small airfield located on the tail of the tadpole for their drop. General Krueger rejected that because it would place the paratroopers at sea level and what he wanted was to have them on Topside dominating the region below. So instead, Krueger selected a small nine-hole golf course and a former parade ground, neither of which the Japanese had made use of since occupying Corregidor, as drop zones. They were small, but would have to do.[27]

On February 13, five naval cruisers and nine destroyers of Rear Admiral Russell S. Berkey's Task Group 77.3 began shelling the island and minesweepers began sweeping the waters around what could be the proposed landing beaches. Return fire from Japanese artillery on Corregidor was extensive, sinking one minesweeper and damaging two destroyers. The wood-hulled minesweeper *YMS 48* was set ablaze as enemy fire from Corregidor proved lethally accurate. The destroyer *Fletcher* came alongside the burning wreck to rescue its crew. An armor-piercing shell that set its ammunition storage area ablaze had earlier hit the destroyer. As crewmen fought the spreading fire in a losing battle, twenty-five-year-old Watertender Second Class Elmer C. Bigelow from Hebron, Illinois, armed with two fire extinguishers and disregarding life-preserving and breathing equipment, entered the burning area and extinguished the flames. It was agreed he had saved the ship from total destruction. The following day Bigelow died, probably from inhaling the toxic fumes of the fire. He was awarded the Congressional Medal of Honor for his selfless act, and a new destroyer was named in his honor. An additional seven members of the crew died and three were wounded in the action.

A second destroyer, *Hopewell,* also came to the rescue of the minesweeper's surviving crew, most of whom were now in the surrounding water as the vessel burned to its waterline. With the enemy gunners having the range of this small gathering, the

Hopewell received three hits from the Corregidor gunners and was forced to withdraw with seven dead and twelve wounded sailors.[28]

By midday on the fifteenth, additional warships arrived to increase the pounding on the enemy guns that were for the most part in the protective custody of various caves and concrete enclosures on the hillside. The added firepower was provided by three cruisers, *Minneapolis, Portland,* and HMAS *Shropshire,* and six destroyers commanded by Commodore H. B. Farncomb of the Royal Australian Navy. The augmented force spent most of that day forcing the enemy to remain underground as smoke from their exploding shells smothered the island.[29]

That evening at the airstrips on Mindoro where the 503rd paratroopers prepared for the next day's drop, Colonel Jones assembled his men for a movie. This film was unlike those the men were used to being entertained with that featured Hollywood stars. This was a captured Japanese film made following the surrender of the American and Filipino forces on Corregidor in 1942. It showed Japanese soldiers beating and otherwise mistreating POWs and stomping on American flags.

On February 16, the troopers of the 3rd Battalion were awakened at 5:30 a.m. and fed a breakfast of soggy pancakes or dehydrated eggs and coffee. After their meal, they were trucked to the waiting Douglas C-47 Skytrains a half hour away. Each of the fifty trucks bore a chalked number corresponding to the chalked number on one of the planes of the 317th Troop Carrier Group commanded by Lieutenant Colonel John Lackey. Each plane had one jump door and held twenty-four paratroopers. After donning all their equipment, including their main chute and reserve chutes totaling eighty pounds, they boarded their assigned planes. The first plane to lift off was at 7 a.m., piloted by Colonel Lackey with Colonel Jones seated in the cockpit. Jones had been designated Rock

Force commander, ultimately commanding both the paratroopers and the infantry preparing to set out from Mariveles Harbor. Fifteen minutes later the planes were in formation and heading northwest toward Corregidor, seventy-five minutes away.[30]

A few minutes after the C-47s took flight, fourteen destroyers and eight cruisers of Task Force 78 resumed their shelling of Corregidor targets. To the amazement of the men aboard the ships, there was no return fire from the Japanese guns on Corregidor. The enemy had withdrawn deep into the many tunnels and caves on the island. At 7:45, thirty-six air force Consolidated B-24 Liberator heavy bombers hit selected areas of the island with 500-pound fragmentation bombs, followed by North American B-25 Mitchell medium bombers and Douglas A-20 Havoc medium bombers. Unfortunately one thing all this shelling and bombing accomplished was to spread more building debris and broken trees on locations such as Topside where the paratroopers were supposed to land, increasing their physical danger on hitting the ground.[31]

At roughly 8:30, Captain Itagaki learned that American troops had boarded landing craft at Mariveles and looked to be heading toward the beach on Corregidor's south shore. Occupying an observation post, the captain and his armed escort were so intent on watching the approaching assault force that they missed entirely that about two dozen paratroopers had landed around them. In the ensuing gunfight, the paratroopers killed Itagaki and his entire escort. The imperial forces were now leaderless, a situation made even worse by the fact the morning shelling and bombing had destroyed the island's central communications center. Now each small or large group of imperial soldiers and marines were fighting independently of each other.[32]

At various points around the island, the first one thousand para-
troops who had landed uninjured that day soon hunted down the
enemy and were joined by the assault troops and spent the next
few days hunting down enemy units and using flame throwers
and phosphorous grenades to drive them out of their underground hiding places or kill them where they hid. A worry for
most planners of parachute drops, including the troops drifting to
earth, is wind. Although not strong, the wind across Topside was
powerful enough to send many troopers landing elsewhere on the
island, plus several dozen splashed down in the nearby sea and
were rescued by one of a dozen PT boats patrolling the area.

As the paratroopers filled the sky, the twenty-five LCMs of
the 592nd Engineer Boat and Shore Regiment pushed their way
through the choppy waters between Mariveles and a location on
Corregidor called Black Beach. Five destroyers escorted them. On
board the LCMs were troops from the 24th Division's 3rd Battalion that had been waiting at Mariveles, commanded by Lieutenant
Colonel Edward M. Postlethwait. These were experienced troops
who had made assault landings in New Guinea at Hollandia and
Biak, and subsequently on Red Beach at Leyte. They came ashore
in five waves and included several Sherman tanks, two of which
were disabled by mines planted along the shore.[33]

Most of the fighting between the paratroopers, infantrymen,
and the Japanese soldiers and marines took place in small, scattered groups owing to the surprise parachute drop combined with
the assault landing, and the lack of organized resistance with the
Japanese commander dead and the radio center destroyed. Where
there were large numbers of Japanese there were also officers to
entice them, even the reluctant, to commit suicide in banzai attacks such as the one on February 18 outside of the Battery Smith
armory, when five hundred screaming marines emerged in the

middle of the night in an attempt to break through American and Filipino lines. When they finally retreated, they left about 250 of their comrades dead on the ground. This kind of fight continued for several more days.

One concern in the back of many of the American minds was the belief that the enemy had stored a huge amount of ammunition and explosive weapons in the tunnels and might as a last resort commit suicide and kill many of the invaders by setting them ablaze. This is just what happened during the night of February 21/22 when a deafening explosion rocked the island and sent huge tongues of flame out several tunnel entrances. It caused a landslide that buried six men from the 34th Infantry alive. Several more explosions shook the island over the next few days as the suicidal enemy set off more large-scale explosions. One of the worst of these took place on February 26 when a massive explosion inside a deep arsenal blew rocks and debris onto the deck of a destroyer two thousand yards at sea and caused a landslide that killed 50 paratroopers and injured 150 others. An unknown number of Japanese inside the arsenal perished into bloody dust.[34]

Two days later, Colonel Jones and General Hall declared Corregidor secure, although there were still random Japanese hiding in deep holes, but they presented no serious problem as American and Filipino troops sealed up cave openings and dropped grenades into many. About twenty of these enemy survivors finally emerged and surrendered in January 1946, bringing the total of prisoners to thirty-nine. The battle for Corregidor had cost the lives of 38 members of the 34th Infantry assault force, along with 153 wounded; it left 169 dead parachutists, and 531 wounded or injured during the jumps. Of the "800" imperial troops that American intelligence reports initially claimed were on the island, between 6,000 and 6,700 died. Many of their bodies were uncountable because they were either buried deep in sealed caves following explosions, blown to pieces, or carried away by the sea when they jumped or were blown into the water. Several dozen were machine-gunned attempting to swim to Bataan when they fired on potential rescuers.

General MacArthur was anxious to return to Corregidor, the site of his embarrassing defeat, as soon as possible. After arranging to borrow four PT boats from the Navy, he organized his return. Four was the proper number, for MacArthur, his wife and son, and selected officers escaped from Corregidor in the same number of PT boats on March 11, 1942. It was obviously a very emotional and symbolic trip for him and the members of the old Bataan Gang who joined him at Manila Harbor for the brief voyage across Manila Bay on March 2. In addition to the commanding general, aboard the boats were Brigadier General William F. Marquat, who had visited the island a few days earlier to look things over, and Generals Willoughby, Sutherland, Marshall, and Casey. Not part of the 1942 group, but important to MacArthur and included, were Generals Kenney and Krueger, Filipino General Carlos Romulo, and recently promoted Vice Admiral Daniel Barbey.[35]

Just after 8 a.m., MacArthur and his entourage boarded the PT boats at Manila's Dock 2. Later, describing the thirty-mile trip, the general commented that they had been forced to leave Corregidor in the darkness of night but were now returning in bright sunlight. He wore a newly starched uniform, his trademark Ray-Ban sunglasses, and the famous crumpled Filipino field marshal hat with the tarnished gold braid on its brim.

The commanding officer of *PT-373*, Lieutenant Belton A. Copp, greeted the commanding general. It was obvious to all that

MacArthur had selected this particular boat for his return trip to Corregidor. It was his way of recognizing the bravery of Copp and his crew for having been the first American surface craft to enter Manila Bay and reconnoiter the area around Mariveles Harbor on February 7, 1945, prior to the 34th Infantry landing there on its way to Corregidor. Copp received the Silver Star for the hazardous mission. MacArthur shook hands with Copp and remarked on the boat number, explaining that he had departed Corregidor on *PT-41*.[36]

He spent the brief trip sitting on a deck chair in the bow staring straight ahead at the island he had last called home before leaving for Australia. As the island came into view, they all got their first glimpse of the immense wreckage the bombings and explosions had caused. It was a depressing sight: piles of rubble with bodies of enemy soldiers scattered among them. At one point, he turned to General Kenney and remarked, "Corregidor is living proof that the day of the fixed fortress is over."[37]

At 10 a.m., MacArthur's boat docked at the North Dock at San Jose Beach. They were greeted by Colonel Jones, who had managed to round up some operational jeeps to give his visitors a tour of the island. Jones had earlier received a shipment that included new uniforms for many of his men; unfortunately, they were destroyed in an accidental fire, so the visitors stood out in sharp contrast in their clean and pressed uniforms while Jones and his paratroopers wore the dirty uniforms and grimy boots they had fought in. For the next hour, they toured the island with MacArthur, anxious to see locations that had served him during his time there. At several spots, he dismounted and walked inside a tunnel or around a shattered building as if there was no possibility of enemy snipers in the area, making the paratroopers who knew better very nervous as they held their submachine guns ready to react.[38]

The party arrived at Topside at 11 a.m. Jones had done a masterful job of using bulldozers to clear away enough rock and rubble to gather an honor guard composed of paratroopers and soldiers from the 34th Infantry for the ceremony. When all were assembled, the troops drew to attention and Jones turned to his commanding general, saluted, and announced in a strong clear voice, "Sir, I present you Fortress Corregidor."

MacArthur returned the salute and, in a voice loud enough for all 336 men of the honor guard to hear, called the capture of Corregidor one of the "most brilliant operations in military history." He then announced that he had cited the entire Rock Force with a Presidential Unit Citation for their bravery and fortitude, and presented Jones with the Distinguished Service Cross as their commander. He then looked up at the badly bent and shell-scarred ship's mast that had served all this time as a flagpole and still stood in the center of the parade ground. MacArthur commented on the survival of the makeshift flagpole, and instructed Jones, "Have your troops hoist the colors to its peak, and let no enemy ever haul them down."[39]

The entire group saluted as two buglers played "To the Colors." The flag was slowly raised up the pole as it snapped in the brisk wind that swept across the parade ground. MacArthur and his party bid Jones and his troops farewell and boarded the PT boats for the return trip to Manila.

BY NOW, THE Walled City was virtually destroyed and the streets around it littered with stone, rubble, and thousands of bodies, mostly Filipino civilians who had been slaughtered by the Japanese, although there were some losses to the American artillery. The last Japanese holdouts in the city had been three government buildings, Legislature, Agriculture, and Finance. These buildings were among those constructed to withstand earthquakes so they proved especially resistant to most American shelling. The final building in which Japanese troops remained actively fighting was the Finance building. Artillery shells had decimated the other two, and still the enemy fired from under the rubble, until gasoline-fueled fires and flamethrowers eventually wiped them out.

The five-story, trapezoidal Finance headquarters was built around an internal courtyard. As they had with the other two government structures, Legislature and Agriculture, the Japanese had converted it into a powerful fortress with sandbagged gun positions and barricaded windows and doors. Expertly sited machine-gun emplacements covered all approaches to the building and were able to fire down stairwells and corridors should enemy troops get inside the structure. The roughly two hundred marines in the building represented the remnants of Admiral Iwabuchi's troops and were committed to fight to the death. There was some discussion among the Americans of laying siege to the building and attempting to starve the enemy out, but they soon realized the Japanese had stockpiled huge amounts of food, provisions, and ammunition in the building and could hold out for a long time. There was also the danger their presence created to the surrounding area with their numerous machine guns and snipers throughout the building. They would be killing people in the nearby park and streets for weeks if not months, so there was little to be done except drive them out and kill them.

The day before MacArthur's journey to Corregidor, troops from the 37th Infantry Division broadcast a message to the enemy marines inside the Finance building. It was similar to the message broadcast to the Japanese in the other buildings. They could surrender in an honorable manner, be blown to bits by the artillery facing the building, or commit suicide. Their cause was now hopeless, they were told, and if they surrendered, they would not be humiliated or disgraced. They were given thirty minutes to decide whether their lives would end now or they would live to serve Japan when the war was over. With less than two minutes left, a single Japanese came out, stumbling among the rubble at the building entrance. In a brief period, twenty-two enemy marines came forward to surrender. Then until dusk closed in, American artillery, anti-tank guns, tanks themselves, and any weapon that stood a chance of penetrating the well-built structure fired. The firing resumed on the morning of March 2 at 8 a.m. and halted at 10 a.m. as the 148th Infantry Regiment prepared to assault the building. During the lull, three additional Japanese emerged from the building holding a white flag.

Those left in the building could not resist the opportunity to fire on the American troops who had welcomed the surrender party. As a result, the infantry canceled the planned assault on the building and the heavy guns resumed pounding what was left of it. Finally, the infantry went in to locate and wipe out small pockets of the roughly seventy-five fighters in the building. At 8:30 p.m. on March 3, General Griswold reported to General Krueger the elimination of all organized resistance in Manila. The Sixth Army commander passed this information on to General MacArthur the following day.[40]

GENERAL MACARTHUR'S critics, of whom there was never a shortage, questioned his decision to capture Manila. In doing so, they overlook his belief, which was accurate, that General Yamashita would not mount a defense of the city. What neither of the commanding generals realized was that an irrational and fanatical admiral would do what they did not want to happen: destroy Manila and kill as many inhabitants as possible before committing suicide. MacArthur refused to allow the air force to bomb the city, and delayed as long as possible the use of heavy artillery against Japanese strongholds.

Manila suffered more destruction than any other Allied city in the war other than Warsaw. Also lost were irreplaceable historical and cultural treasures as well as truly handsome architectural structures that had served as government and university build-ings, museums and libraries, churches and monasteries. What had previously been called the "Pearl of the Orient" was now to be remembered as one of the worst tragedies of a hugely tragic war.

Although the total number of civilians who perished from Japanese brutality and American artillery may never be accurately counted, we do know that it exceeds one hundred thousand people. Between sixteen thousand and twenty thousand Japanese troops also died, as well as slightly over one thousand Americans with another nearly six thousand wounded.

Finally, what would have happened if the Americans had by-passed Manila? As Filipino guerrilla leader and national hero Lieutenant Colonel Emmanuel V. de Ocampo said years later, "An even higher proportion of civilians would have been massacred." Had MacArthur ordered his forces not to attack Manila, Ocampo claimed the guerrillas would have gone in without them. For sure, the POWs and other internees would have been slaughtered as a matter of routine, and the Japanese marines and soldiers in the city would have spent their time abusing the people as they had been doing. Left to themselves, the Japanese would have killed most if not all the civilians in Manila. Fighting the Americans distracted them periodically from their bloodlust.[41]

CHAPTER FIFTEEN

THE WAR MOVES SOUTH

As the fighting continued elsewhere on Luzon, General Mac-Arthur shifted his focus to the southern islands of the Philippine Archipelago. These included Mindanao, the second-largest of the Philippine islands and the one originally selected for MacArthur's initial invasion; Panay, Cebu, Negros, Bohol, a group of small islands that reach almost to Borneo known as the Sulu Archipelago, and the island of Palawan.

MacArthur's strategists identified Palawan, the westernmost of the Philippine Islands, as the most important in the southern region. Control of Palawan would enable General Kenney to use airfields on the island for his land-based aircraft. From there, American dive-bombers and medium bombers would have free range over the South China Sea. When combined with naval and air units based on the islands of the Sulu Archipelago, the American forces could sever the enemy's supply route between the Dutch East Indies and the Home Islands. Long-range bombers flying from newly built airfields on Sulu islands would be able to attack Japanese oil facilities on Borneo, starving the enemy of his vital supply of oil.

Palawan's significance to MacArthur was more personal. The island brought to mind the plight of POWs and civilians interned in Japanese camps and their fate as the enemy faced defeat. In February, he had learned of a massacre of American POWs at a compound on the island. The emaciated prisoners were subjected to savage Japanese torture and abuse. Forced to exist on limited rations, the men struggled to survive each day. The 150 Americans spent every day crushing coral by hand and pouring cement for a new airfield. Constant beatings without provocation were routine.

Earlier, on December 14, Japanese patrol planes reported a large enemy fleet in the area. Japanese officers on the island mistakenly interpreted the sighting as an expected invasion of Palawan; the ships were actually going to Mindoro. Work on an airfield by American POWs was halted and the men were ordered to return to camp. The POWs were corralled into three air raid shelters. Each primitive shelter was 150 feet long and only four feet high, forcing the prisoners to crawl on hands and knees. There was a narrow entrance on each end and each shelter had a covering of logs and dirt. Although it was soon obvious the fleet was simply passing by, Lieutenant Yoshikazu Sato ordered his men to pour gasoline over the shelters and set them ablaze. As burning men fled the shelters screaming, they ran directly into deadly machine-gun fire. The Japanese soldiers then clubbed the survivors to death with axe handles.

A handful of men managed to swim across a nearby bay where local inhabitants cared for them. When they had recovered their strength, the survivors were transferred to a local guerrilla unit that was able to arrange transport to Leyte where they told their story to American officials.

MacArthur had been horrified when he learned what had happened to the POWs on Palawan and had immediately ordered plans developed to free detainees at several prisoner compounds identified by Filipino guerrilla leaders. At that time he ordered Major General Verne Mudge to expedite men under his command to free the prisoners at Santo Tomas University. On February 3 two columns from the 1st Cavalry raced far ahead of their own lines, entered Manila, and, following a brisk gunfight, liberated 3,700 American and other civilians held since 1942. The following day men from the 37th Division overcame Japanese guards at the Bilibid Prison and set eight hundred POWs and five hundred civilians free. On February 24, a force made up of troopers from the 11th Airborne joined with a large contingent of Filipino guerrillas to attack the prison camp at Los Banos, some thirty miles southeast of Manila and well behind Japanese lines. Following a firefight that killed two Americans soldiers and all 250 Japanese guards, they set free over 2,100 inmates and evacuated them to American lines.

Even as the fighting for Luzon raged, General MacArthur ordered Eighth Army commander Lieutenant General Robert L. Eichelberger to prepare his forces, many of whom were supporting the Sixth Army on Luzon, for the liberation of the southern Philippine islands. In addition to the strategic importance of several of these islands to closing the South China Sea routes, MacArthur had two reasons for avoiding delaying the movement south. He was concerned over the fate of prisoners at locations the Allies were not aware of, and the treatment the local civilian populations were subjected to as the Japanese forces faced ultimate defeat and humiliation. It was also extremely important to honor his pledge to return to the Philippines and liberate the people from the Japanese. In his mind, this meant all the people

LUZON
●Manila

MINDORO

Mindoro Strait

Calamian Islands

Sibuyan Sea

MASBATE

SAMAR

Visayan Sea

PANAY

●Tacloban
●Ormoc

Iloilo●
Bacolod●

Cebu

●CEBU

LEYTE

DINAGAT

●Puerta Princessa

NEGROS

Dumagueto●

BOHOL

Butuan●

PALAWAN

Sulu Sea

Dipolog●

Cagayan●

●Waloe

●Malaybalay

BALABAC

Zamboanga
Peninsula

Malabang●

●Maramag

Illana
Bay

Parang●

●Kibawe

Davao●

SOUTHERN
PHILIPPINES

Zamboanga●

Moro
Gulf

Digos●

Davao
Gulf

0   miles   100

Jolo●

Sulu Archipelago

MINDANAO

Celebes Sea

on the entire islands, even if it meant ignoring the fact he had no instructions from the Joint Chiefs in Washington to do so. MacArthur also envisioned extending the reach of his air force, and stationing aircraft near Puerto Princesa to allow American patrol planes access into the South China Sea to hamper Japanese sea-lanes along the Chinese coast.[1]

The Joint Chiefs had not only not issued orders for the capture of the southern Philippines, General Marshall is said to have told his British counterparts at the Yalta Conference in February 1945 that no American troops would be sent to the southern islands to drive the Japanese out. Various Filipino guerrilla forces and units of the newly re-formed Army of the Philippine Commonwealth would accomplish that fighting.[2]

Months prior to the conference, MacArthur had already decided that once the Sixth Army was on the road to success on Luzon, he would assign Eichelberger's Eighth Army the job of liberating the islands of the south, especially Palawan and Mindanao. Mac-Arthur had not overlooked the islands of the Dutch East Indies. These he assigned to the Australian forces. The official navy history of the war could not explain how and when MacArthur assumed the authority to proceed into the southern islands since he "had no specific directive for anything subsequent to Luzon." The history called it "somewhat of a mystery."[3]

When Washington finally got around to giving MacArthur orders to engage the enemy south of Luzon and Leyte in April, it was already in full motion. Taking it upon himself as theater commander, MacArthur had his forces invade the Palawan port of Tawi Tawi, which served as a major base for the Imperial Navy's Southwest Area Fleet; Mindanao's Zamboanga Peninsula; and the islands of Basilan, Negros, Panay, Guimaras, and Cebu, where more than thirty thousand Japanese troops were stationed.

MacArthur had been informed by the Joint Chiefs that he had to be prepared to host twenty-two divisions to be shipped from the United States and Europe after the German defeat. They were to take part in the invasion of mainland Japan, so he was especially anxious to control the two large port cities of Cebu City (on Cebu) and Iloilo City on Panay for use as staging areas.[4]

Eichelberger's Eighth Army consisted of the Americal Division, the 41st Infantry Division, and the 164th Infantry Regiment. As their targets were all islands, a strong naval presence was required to both transport troops and supplies and provide cover for the landing forces. Establishing the many beachheads needed would be Admiral Barbey's 7th Amphibious Force, which made fourteen major and twenty-four minor amphibious assaults against southern Philippines islands.[5]

The liberation of the southern Philippines began on February 28, 1945, against the long narrow island of Palawan, covered in mostly jungle-filled mountains. Palawan was a primitive place with no railroad and very few usable roads. It was an important target since its old Spanish naval base could be converted for use by the US Navy. General Kenney's engineers could readily renovate the poorly constructed Japanese airfields on the island. From those airfields, the air force could support the future planned invasions of the Dutch East Indies and Borneo.[6]

One problem with Palawan was that there were few beaches to serve as suitable landing sites that were not clogged with coral reefs and mangrove swamps, so it became time-consuming getting men and supplies on land. The responsibility for getting combat troops, vehicles, and other material ashore fell to the Army's 2nd Engineer Special Brigade. Developed by the Army Corps of Engineers to facilitate especially shore-to-shore amphibious landings, these soldiers were recruited from occupations that required familiarity with the sea. This meant actual boat builders, small boat operators, professional fishermen, and marine engineers. Known as the "Seahorse Soldiers" because of their uniform shoulder patch picturing a red seahorse, they had supported dozens of amphibious landings in New Guinea before moving to the Philippines.[7]

At 8:20 a.m. on the twenty-eighth, 5,700 combat troops and 2,300 service troops comprising Brigadier General Harold H. Haney's 186th Regimental Combat Team of the 41st Infantry Division under Major General Jens Doe disembarked from amphibious ships commanded by Rear Admiral William Fechteler near Palawan's principal city, Puerto Princesa. General Eichelberger observed the landings from a B-17 circling overhead. The landings followed two days of air force bombing and naval shelling from four destroyers and three light cruisers of Rear Admiral Ralph S. Riggs's Cruiser Division 12.[8]

This was preceded on February 10 by the arrival on Palawan of two US Navy PT boats near the mouth of the Babuyan River. They were from Motor Torpedo Boat Squadron 25 stationed on Mindoro. Lieutenant Edward J. Pope in *PT-134*, nicknamed "Eight Ball" by its crew, commanded the boats. News of the approach of two American boats spread fast and a large gathering of local people was on hand to cheer their arrival. Once ashore, Pope was met by Major Pablo Muyco, commander of the well-organized Palawan Special Battalion and several other leaders of the Palawan guerrilla forces. The PSB operated two coast watcher stations, aided POWs escaping from a nearby internment camp, and rescued downed American pilots. Pope's mission was to gather intelligence concerning the number of Japanese soldiers on the island and especially around the city of Puerto Princesa. Muyco estimated there were 1,285 enemy troops in or near the capital. After a reconnaissance of the limited potential landing sites, Pope and his men returned to Mindoro, taking three PSB volunteers with them to help guide the assault troops.[9]

There was only minor resistance to the February 28 landings. Any Japanese still in the area had likely served as camp guards during the massacre of the American prisoners on December 14. Now these soldiers had withdrawn into the thick jungles toward the center of the island well before the assault forces arrived. General Eichelberger confirmed the absence of enemy troops as the Americans went ashore when his B-17 flew over Puerto Princesa and the airfield at treetop level and saw "little immediate enemy reaction."[10]

Despite some difficulty in finding locations to unload the larger vessels, such as LSTs, the landings went well and the troops spread out and headed to their objectives at a few minutes before eight thirty that morning. Searches of Puerto Princesa discovered the enemy had not prepared defensive positions in and around the town, and no enemy soldiers were discovered. What was found though were the remnants of the detention camp in which the 150 American POWs were held and forced to work on building two nearby airstrips. Temporary markers were positioned at locations that appeared to have been used as burial sites by the Japanese. Following the liberation of the island, it became the job of Major Charles Simms and the 601st Quartermaster Company to exhume the burned remains of the Americans. Many of the skulls of the men had bullet holes in them or showed signs of being crushed by a large object such as a rifle butt. The remains, mostly bones, were given a military funeral on the island. They remained there for several years until removed to Jefferson National Cemetery at St. Louis, Missouri, in February 1952 and buried in a mass grave. A diary belonging to a Japanese sergeant major stationed at the camp and found by American soldiers described the murder of the men: "They truly died a pitiful death."[11]

By noon, soldiers of the 186th Infantry Regiment occupied both airstrips and waited for the engineers to arrive and begin preparing both for American aircraft. Some of the men began to feel uneasy about the fact they had not seen one enemy soldier, even as they fanned out and formed a defensive perimeter around the airfields and the town. It was not until March 3 that troopers for the 186th encountered Japanese willing to fight. This was ten miles northwest of Puerto Princesa where several enemy units had dug in among the jungle-covered hills. Americans and Filipinos spent most of the following month hunting down and killing or capturing scattered groups of Japanese who had lost all semblance of a unified military force. By April 21, most of the 186th pulled out and were replaced by men from the 386th Infantry. During their time on Palawan, the 186th suffered the deaths of ten men and had forty-five wounded. Japanese losses were close to nine hundred dead along with twenty taken prisoner.[12]

PROBLEMS WITH BEING able to compact the soil on the two runways on Palawan hampered their use in support of the March 10 invasion of the Zamboanga Peninsula on Mindanao. Instead, the air force turned to help from a local guerrilla force called the 105th Division commanded by Colonel Hipolito Garma. The guerrillas held the prewar Dipolog airstrip and had used it to ferry in supplies to the guerrilla army led by Colonel Wendell Fertig, an Army Reserve officer who left Corregidor prior to its fall and organized a force that at times controlled great portions of Mindanao.

The rest of the division landed on the Zamboanga Peninsula on March 10. Here they ran into stronger resistance than on

Palawan with an enemy of nearly nine thousand troops on the peninsula manning well-prepared defensive positions such as pillboxes. In all, Lieutenant General Suzuki's Thirty-Fifth Army had slightly over one hundred thousand men on the southern islands. Handicapped by the need to spread his forces across most of the islands, Suzuki could not predict where the Americans would land next.

As had happened during previous amphibious landings, the Japanese commander on the peninsula, Lieutenant General To-kichi Hojo, had only a scattering of units assigned to the beaches. Instead, he pulled most of his 8,900 troops, which included the 54th Independent Mixed Brigade as well as naval troops and soldiers from several other army units, back about three miles from the shore. Making use of the high ground around Zamboanga City, they fought the Americans to a standstill about 145 miles southwest of the Dipolog airfield until a squadron from the US Marines' Air Group 12 flew support for the infantry and the beachhead.

For the next two weeks, the 162nd and 163rd Infantry Regiments of the 41st Division fought a determined enemy who had stockpiled supplies for a long siege in an extremely difficult terrain. With few actual roads, the battles for Mindanao required bulldozers to open passages through the dense and mostly unexplored jungle for the infantry and limited the availability of tanks to participate. The front line was approximately five miles long and was heavily mined with long stretches of barbed wire and many booby traps. General Hojo had planned well for his assignment of slowing the American advance.

By March 31, General Hojo realized he could no longer hold his positions and ordered a withdrawal up the coast but met stiff opposition from a guerrilla army of the 105th Division led by Captain Donald J. LeCouvre. They were forced to scatter into small groups, most of which were hunted down by patrolling Americans and Filipinos. Of the 8,900 men Hojo commanded, roughly 6,400 died either in combat or from starvation or disease.[13]

THE EIGHTH ARMY engaged in combat in both the perilous jungles of the southwest Pacific and urban fighting in several cities. Thousands of local guerrillas fought alongside the invading forces. They were instrumental in the speedy success of the Eighth Army and the establishment of numerous airfields from which to attack Japanese shipping. Over the coming weeks, American and Filipino forces battled various Japanese-defended southern islands, including the main portion of Mindanao, Negros, and Panay.

Although General Eichelberger informed MacArthur that organized resistance had ended by June 30, thousands of Japanese soldiers remained in small groups scattered in the thick jungles and mountain hideaways determined to fight to the death—or just try to survive. When the emperor surrendered, over 22,000 came forward to give up the fight. The campaign for the southern Philippines had cost 2,100 American lives, and wounded 7,000.

The war in the Southern Philippines committed 100,000 Japanese soldiers and sailors against 40,000 American troops and 60,000 Filipino guerrillas. The horrific fighting began on February 27, 1945, and ended for the most part on July 4, 1945. Traditional southwest Pacific jungle warfare raged through jagged mountains and crocodile-infested rivers and swamps; street-by-street urban warfare decimated several large cities. Because of the lack of modern roads, especially on Mindanao, the Army relied on the vast river network for transportation. This resulted in the introduction of riverine warfare, something widely used twenty years later in Vietnam.

CHAPTER SIXTEEN

FINAL DEFEAT

Victory in the capital city of Manila was not the end of the campaign to liberate Luzon. In some respects, it was the beginning. Thirty thousand Japanese troops of the Shimbu Group were deployed south and east of Manila with another 20,000 in reserve and flank protection. To the capital's west was the Kembu Group, with 35,000 men deployed throughout the Zambales Mountains north of Bataan and down to its tip at Corregidor. Yamashita remained in the mountains of northern Luzon with over 150,000 men composing the Shobu Group.

Yamashita knew his cause was lost. The best he and his army could hope for was to delay MacArthur's advance and make it costly enough to force a negotiation with the Tokyo government and minimize the shame of losing the war. Yamashita's reputation as a great military leader was earned, in part, when he forced General Percival to surrender at Singapore. He had confidently boasted he would bring MacArthur to his knees in the same way in the Philippines. With resignation, the "Tiger of Malaya" left his last post in Manchuria with the expectation the Philippines would be his Waterloo.

To achieve his tactic of delaying an American victory, Yamashita looked to the mountainous areas of Luzon, well aware of the difficulty an attacking force encountered as it struggled up dangerous mountains with deep crevices and tree-clogged surfaces. It would be useless to defend against the Americans in open country where enemy airpower dominated the skies, but a well dug-in army, spread along miles of mountainous strongholds, could hold out at least until their supplies were exhausted—and he had plenty of hardware and ammunition. Perhaps, Yamashita hoped, that would be long enough for negotiations to begin.

As the fighting in Manila wound down, General Krueger sent troops east against the Shimbu Group and others west against the Kembu Group. All the while, Yamashita and his men waited in the northern mountains for their last chance at valor.

The Kembu Group commander, Lieutenant General Rikichi Tsukada, had been charged by Yamashita to deny their enemy the most vital landing field in the entire Philippines, Clark Field. His thirty thousand troops had salvaged heavy weapons from wrecked aircraft and entrenched themselves in nearly impregnable positions around the runways in an attempt to stave off the Americans. When the first of General Krueger's men from the 145th Regiment reached the edge of the runways on January 26, they were reinforced by troops from the 37th Division. Pummeled by Allied air support, the Japanese had gradually withdrawn west of the field. Later the XI Corps of Major General Charles Hall landed along the west coast of Luzon, behind the Japanese. Realizing his remaining men had lost most of their heavy weapons and were about to be trapped by the enemy, General Tsukada had ordered them to disperse into the nearby Zambales Mountains in small groups where they remained until the final surrender.

East of Manila, the Shimbu Group under General Yokoyama faced a major offensive by the 43rd and 6th Infantry Divisions, the 1st Cavalry Division, and the 112th Cavalry Regimental Combat Team that began on February 20. Three Japanese reserve battalions launched a counterattack against the American line on March 12, but ran straight into another attack by the 6th Division led by Major General Edwin Patrick that decimated the Japanese battalions. The following month, Patrick became one of only three American division commanding officers to die in combat during the war.

Despite its best efforts, the Shimbu Group was relentlessly pushed back toward the Sierra Madre Mountains. Unable to transport the huge amount of supplies the group's units had removed from Manila, the food dwindled to the point where some Japanese resorted to eating tree bark and digging around in long abandoned Filipino gardens. By the last week in May, Yokoyama ordered a general withdrawal of all forces still under his command. Within weeks, as the Americans kept the pressure on them, the remaining thirteen thousand troops still able to walk broke up into small groups focused on trying to locate food. The over ten thousand guerrilla fighters who infiltrated the mountains and ambushed the starving Japanese increased their struggle. By the time they surrendered, slightly over six thousand survivors remained from the original fifty thousand who had withdrawn from Manila.

MacArthur then turned his attention north toward the largest and best-equipped Japanese force on Luzon, or the entire Philippines for that matter. The Shobu Group comprised 150,000 troops under the direct command of General Yamashita. The

Japanese commander knew victory was beyond his reach, so he adopted a defense strategy of delay.

Yamashita took full advantage of the terrain of northern Luzon. To his east rose the rugged Sierra Madre Mountains like a fortress wall with peaks reaching to six thousand feet and no roads connecting the central valley to the eastern shore. It was virtually impenetrable for invaders.

To Yamashita's west were the Ilocos Mountains and Cordillera Central, the highest mountain range in the entire Philippines. These parallel mountain ranges running north and south offered limited access to the Americans. In the center of the region controlled by the Japanese was the Cagayan Valley, the major rice-producing area for the entire island. Under Yamashita's orders, Japanese troops spent almost as much time and effort gathering food in the valley and nearby areas as they did fighting off attacks by Filipino guerrilla and army units. After stripping the country-side of rice and other staples, and rounding up as many water buffalo as they could find, the army began moving north. A single division remained behind in Baguio to delay the American forces advancing on the now-abandoned headquarters, which they did for five days. Ten thousand soldiers managed to evacuate the area and move to Yamashita's new headquarters in the tiny village of Bambang.[1]

With the mountains protecting his flanks and the valley a source of food, Yamashita estimated he could hold out for many months. He had with him some of the best units left in the Imperial Army, including the 23rd and 19th Divisions, as well as portions of three other divisions, including the 2nd Tank Division.

Logic dictated that the Americans and their Filipino allies, who were consolidating their hold on the capital region, would attack from the south, so Yamashita established a strong forward defense line along his southern perimeter. The tankers were a favorite target of American pilots as they anchored the defense line around the town of San Jose. During one week of relentless air attacks, they lost 108 of their 200 functioning tanks.

As the Japanese defense line had contracted under pressure from Allied forces, the Imperial General Headquarters in Tokyo demonstrated how far removed it was from the reality of Luzon. In late January, it had ordered the evacuation of as many key personnel as possible to the Home Islands. Submarines were to remove pilots, engineers, and other technicians before they fell into enemy hands or died. The first and only such mission involved three submarines leaving the submarine base at Takao on Formosa on February 10, heading for the Aparri coast at the very northern tip of Luzon. Although troops from the 103rd Division garrisoned the coast, the entire area was subject to hostilities from the five-thousand-man guerrilla and commonwealth army commanded by Lieutenant Donald Blackburn. Their presence was sure to hinder any attempt to evacuate the so-called key personnel. As if the situation could not be worse for Japan, two of the submarines sank in route to their proposed landing site at Batuliano thirty miles east of the town of Aparri. One did succeed in taking a small number of evacuees aboard and returning them to Formosa. No further attempted evacuations took place.[2]

While operations continued in central and southern Luzon, General Krueger ordered the I Corps under Major General Innis Swift to begin pushing north against the Shobu Group. He sent the 33rd Infantry Division commanded by Major General Percy W. Clarkson toward the former Philippine summer capital at Baguio. Joined by the 37th Division and the 66th Infantry Regiment of the Philippine Commonwealth Army, they struggled against fanatical resistance from imperial soldiers who, knowing there was no escape, wanted to take as many of their enemies with them as possible. On April 26, Baguio, which had been serving as Yamashita's headquarters until recently, fell. Among the prisoners freed that day was major General Manuel Roxas, who had served as MacArthur's liaison with the Philippine government prior to his evacuation. Roxas would serve as the first president of the newly independent Philippines until his death in 1948.

Over the following weeks additional American and Filipino soldiers as well as thousands of organized guerrilla bands poured into the region, slowly pushing Yamashita's forces back into the Cordillera Central Mountains. A key element in the fighting against the Shobu Group were the forces commanded by Colonel Russell W. Volckmann, who was praised by MacArthur for his contributions to the victory. When the Sixth Army landed at Lingayen Gulf, Volckmann had approximately eight thousand mostly Filipino troops under his command. His primary problem pre-invasion was that only about two thousand were actually armed. Soon after landing, the Americans started sending arms to Volckmann by small boats and then by C-47 aircraft that could land or parachute supplies to them in areas Volckmann controlled. His army soon grew to between eighteen thousand and twenty thousand troops, divided into five infantry regiments and even an artillery battalion that used mostly captured Japanese field artillery pieces. Volckmann's forces played a decisive role right up through the surrender of the Shobu Group.[3]

General Yamashita withdrew further and further into the mountains as the enemy pushed his troops back. When, at last, he reached what would serve as his final headquarters, Mount Prog, some 9,600 feet high, he settled into a long-deserted native village and waited for the end. He still had enough ammunition to continue fighting for weeks and possibly months. Their problem was food. There was none except for a scarce amount of rice that was doled out in spoonfuls along with whatever wild vegetables they could find.[4]

With great humiliation, Yamashita surrendered his forces on September 2, 1945, two weeks after the emperor had broadcast a radio message ending the war and the very same day imperial representatives aboard the USS *Missouri* signed the surrender documents in Tokyo Bay where MacArthur oversaw that ceremony, accompanied by dozens of representatives from the victorious Allied powers. Much to the surprise of the American intelligence officers, Yamashita still had over sixty thousand troops under arms when he surrendered—over forty thousand more than American intelligence had estimated.

Epilogue

The fighting on Luzon resulted in 8,310 Americans killed and 29,560 wounded. Of the 275,685 Japanese troops on the island at the time of MacArthur's invasion, 205,535 perished in combat or from other causes, 9,050 became prisoners of war prior to Yamashita's surrender, and 61,100 joined his capitulation.

Along with his soldiers, Yamashita surrendered one of his most prized possessions, his personal sword. Produced in the late 1600s, the blade was fitted with a new handle shortly after 1900. MacArthur donated the weapon to the museum at West Point.

Acknowledgments

This book could not have been written without the assistance of a great many people. Perhaps too many to actually list here, but I will try. As with my earlier book on MacArthur, I am deeply indebted to James W. Zobel, archivist at the MacArthur Memorial in Norfolk, Virginia, for sharing his vast knowledge and for providing the photographs in this volume. Also, I must express my appreciation to my three readers, Alexandra Duffy, Michele Del Monte, and Kathleen Duffy. They each did a fine job of reviewing the manuscript and offering comments and advice that improved the work.

To my agent, Deborah Grosvenor, a special thanks for her always excellent input and for selecting a fine home for this book, and to Robert Pigeon, an editor of great patience and understanding. Finally, a thank-you to all those who contributed in numerous ways to the final book.

NOTES

When I read a book, I generally use two bookmarks: one for the last page I've read, and one for the page housing the corresponding source notes. I do this because I often want to know more about a person, a quote, or an incident mentioned by the author, but not discussed in-depth in the book I am reading. Examining the author's cited source enables me to dig deeper into questions and events that interest me, such as what was said before or after the quoted passage, how did others respond to the incident, and what was the background of the person mentioned. That information may not be appropriate for inclusion in the present work but may be interesting and often results in my purchasing another book. This becomes difficult when the sources identified are located in an archive not easily accessed. Because of this, I have endeavored as often as possible to select sources that are accessible to readers who wish to learn more about the events about which I have written.

PROLOGUE

1   Duus, Myers, and Peattie, xii.
2   James, 489.

CHAPTER ONE: DECISIVE BATTLE AND GUERRILLA WARFARE

1   Woodward, 20.
2   Kenney, 1951, 157.
3   Pu Yi, 200.
4   Duus, Myers, and Peattie, xiii.
5   Shin and Sneider, 241.
6   Ibid., 242.
7   Snyder, 112.
8   Ito, 7.
9   Keegan, 272.
10 Prados, 1995, 126; Behr, 174–175.
11 Prados, 1995, 126.
12 Ugaki, 365.
13 Morton, 500; Hogan, 66.
14 Hogan, 66.
15 MacArthur, 202.
16 Hatch, 78.
17 Whitney, 128–129.
18 Ibid. 130.
19 James, 507–508.
20 Ingham, 28.

CHAPTER TWO: FDR SETTLES THE GREAT DEBATE

1   Pogue, 443.
2   Fleming, 2001, 390–407.
3   Persico, 389.
4   Morison, vol. 12, 8.
5   Buell, 467.
6   King and Whitehill, 566–568.
7   Halsey and Bryan, 195.
8   Buell, 466.
9   Ibid., 469.
10 Borneman, 2016, 394.
11 Duffy, 347.
12 Rhoades, 256.
13 Persico, 389.
14 E. B. Potter, 316.
15 Leahy, 249.

16   Perry, xi, 269.
17   Leahy, 250.
18   Persico, 390.
19   E. B. Potter, 217.
20   Hunt, 332; E. B. Potter, 315.
21   Pogue, 452.
22   Larrabee, 347; Pogue, 452.
23   Adams, 253.
24   E. B. Potter, 317–318.
25   Hunt, 335.
26   Manchester, 369.
27   Leahy, 251.
28   E. B. Potter, 319.
29   Rhoades, 260.
30   FDR Presidential Library, PPC.
31   Pogue, 452.
32   FDR Presidential Library, MSF.
33   Buell, 469.
34   Black, 978; FDR Presidential Library, PPF.
35   James, 535.
36   E. B. Potter, 321.
37   Buell, 469.
38   E. B. Potter, 322.

CHAPTER THREE: "BULL" HALSEY CHANGES THE PLANS

1   Willoughby and Chamberlin, 236.
2   Borneman, 2016, 409.
3   Adams, 258; King and Whitehill, 569.
4   Adams, 258.
5   Falk, 42.
6   Drea, 160; Vego, 2006, 61; Cannon, 50.
7   Reel, 18–19; Falk, 55; Cannon, 50–51.
8   Toland, 535.
9   Kenney, 1949, 421–422; Cannon, 42.
10   Halsey, *Memoir*, 463; Cannon, 42.
11   Falk, 51.
12   Halsey and Bryan, 198.
13   Sommerville, 258; Cannon, 42–43.
14   Halsey and Bryan, 199.
15   Falk, 52–53.
16   Albert Rosenfeld, "A Message that Shortened the War," *American Legion Magazine*, March 1960, 12–13, and 48.
17   Halsey, *Memoir*, 464.
18   Ibid.
19   Hughes, 338–339.

20   E. B. Potter, 323.
21   Kenney, 1949, 431–432.
22   Pogue, 453–454.
23   Herman, 519.
24   Marshall, 170.
25   State of the Union address, January 6, 1945.

CHAPTER FOUR: PASSAGE TO LEYTE

1   Rhoades, 290.
2   Morison, vol. 12, 17–18.
3   James, 550; Day, 230.
4   Borneman, 2016, 426.
5   Willmott, 65.
6   Perry, 285.
7   Bowd, 7.
8   Perret, 417.
9   Cannon, 35.
10   Hoyt, 1989, 112; Willmott, 308.
11   Prados, 2016, 161.
12   Barbey, 241.
13   Vego, 2006, 185.
14   Cannon, 40–41.
15   Willmott, 308–309; Morison, vol. 12, 81–83.
16   Dunn, 243.
17   Perret, 417.
18   Kenney, 1949, 445–446.
19   Whitney, 154.
20   MacArthur, 214.
21   Egeberg, 65–66.
22   MacArthur, 217–218; FDR Presidential Library, PSF.
23   MacArthur, 215.

CHAPTER FIVE: "IN THE DRAGON'S JAWS"

1   *Reports*, vol. 2, 322–323.
2   Morison, vol, 12, 68; Wilmott, 64.
3   United States Strategic Bombing Survey (USSBS), Interrogation of Japanese Officials, Nav #75, Nov. 1945, Admiral Soemu Toyoda, 317.
4   Vego, 2006, 65; Koyanagi, 119.
5   Wells, 9–10.
6   Herbig, 260–300; Holt, 462–471.
7   Perras, 181–182.
8   Bradley, 192–198.
9   Cannon, 42–43; Sommerville, 258; Spector, 424.

10 Cannon, 43.

11 Willmott, 89, 339n3.

12 Morison, vol. 12, 90.

13 Ibid.

14 Hughes, 347.

15 Prados, 1995, 608; Sommerville, 263.

16 Prados, 1995, 608; Ugaki, 469.

17 Vego, 2009, 156.

18 Connaughton, 179.

19 USSBS, Interrogation of Japanese Officials, Nav #64, Nov. 1945, Rear Admiral Toshitane Takata, 263; O'Brien, 376, 404.

20 Prados, 2016, 126–127.

21 Thomas, Evan, 161.

22 Prados, 1995, 609.

23 Fukudome, 103–104.

24 Spector, 424.

25 Ugaki, 469.

26 Sherman, 5.

27 Fukudome, 105.

28 OSRD, 248.

29 Price, 224–225.

30 Mooney, 525.

31 Falk, 59.

32 Davison, 9.

33 USS Franklin (CV-13), War Damage Report No. 56, 3–4; Davison, 9.

34 USS Canberra (CA70), War Damage Report No. 54, 12–13.

35 Halsey and Bryan, 201.

36 Ibid., 206.

37 Bartholomew and Milwee, 163; Early, 9.

38 Halsey and Bryan, 206.

39 Willmott, 60; Prados, 1995, 609.

40 USS Houston (CL81), War Damage Report No. 53, 6–7.

41 Fukudome, 108.

42 USSBS, Interrogation of Japanese Officials, Navy #115, Dec. 1945, Vice Admiral Shigeru Fukudome, 501.

43 Falk, 60.

44 Boyne, 262.

45 Hughes, 348–349; Cannon, 44.

46 Prados, 2016, 148.

47 Woodward, 18.

48 Fukudome, 110.

49 Halsey and Bryan, 207–208.

50 N. Miller, 457.

CHAPTER SIX: THE "SPECIAL ATTACK CORPS"

1   Toland, 568.
2   Kennedy, 119.
3   Sears, 125–126.
4   Pineau, 3–8.
5   Kennedy, 125–126; Rielly, 2010, 46.

CHAPTER SEVEN: THE RANGERS AND THE FROGMEN GO IN FIRST

1   Morison, vol. 12, 118–119.
2   Nicholson, 160.
3   Cannon, 54–55.
4   Black, 240.
5   Morison, vol. 12, 120–121.
6   Prados, 2016, 160; "U.S. Bombers Open Attack on Mindoro," *Lewiston (Maine) Evening Journal*, January 2, 1945.
7   Morison, vol. 12, 121.
8   Black 244–247; Morison, vol. 12, 121n.
9   Prefer, 37–39; Fane and Moore, 149–156.

CHAPTER EIGHT: "A-DAY" AT LEYTE, OCTOBER 20, 1944

1   Whitney, 155.
2   Cannon, 60–61.
3   Ingham, 148–153.
4   AP, "School Ma'am Led Guerrillas on Leyte," *Lewiston (Maine) Daily Sun*, November 3, 1944.
5   Prefer, 46.
6   D. Miller, 185.
7   Harries, 434.
8   Prefer, 30.
9   Bix, 481.
10 Harries, 160.
11 Falk, 70–71.
12 Toland, 538–539.
13 Falk, 94.
14 Cannon, 70–72; Valtin, 44.
15 Morison, vol. 12, 154.
16 Manchester, 386.
17 Dunn, 6.
18 Borneman, 2016, 428.
19 Valtin, 32–33.
20 Herman, 538.
21 Rhoades, 298.

22   MacArthur, 216–217.
23   DM to FDR, October 20, 1944, FDR Presidential Library, PSF.
24   FDR to DM, October 20, 1944, FDR Presidential Library, PSF.
25   The American Presidency Project, http://www.ucsb.edu/ws/.
26   Falk, 94.
27   Cannon, 99–102.
28   Morison, vol. 12, 145–146.
29   Breuer, 55.
30   Herman, 541.
31   Cannon, 124.
32   Zaloga, 45.
33   Gill, 510–511; Morison, vol. 12, 148.
34   Kenney, 1949, 450; Rhoades, 301.
35   Kenney, 1951, 166.
36   Kenney, 1949, 452.
37   Dunn, 245.
38   Hopkins, 265.
39   McCallus, 56–58.
40   Manchester, 390.
41   Kenney, 1949, 464.
42   Falk, 103.
43   Cannon, 153–157.
44   Perret, 427.

CHAPTER NINE: THE RAGING SEA

1   Cutler, 89.
2   Koyanagi, 120.
3   Morison, vol. 12, 162.
4   Borneman, 2016, 433.
5   Vego, 2006, 227; Cutler, 85; Morison, vol. 12, 161–162.
6   Cutler, 89.
7   Ito, 100–101; Toland, 547; Willmott, 86.
8   Stewart, 38.
9   Koyanagi, 122.
10   Ugaki, 487–488.
11   Cutler, 94–110; Morison, vol. 12, 169–174; Stewart, 38–44. Willmott, 101–
     104; http:/ / warfarehistorynetwork.com.
12   Whitney, 162.
13   Borneman, 2016, 433–434.
14   Willmott, 107.
15   Dull, 316.
16   Stewart, 56–61.
17   Prados, 2016, 201–202; Stewart, 47–49; Cutler, 118–119.
18   Ito, 103.
19   Ugaki, 489.

20   Morison, vol. 12, 187.
21   Cutler, 140–141.
22   Dull, 319–322.
23   Ito, 105–108.
24   Thomas, Evan, 222.
25   Koyanagi, 124; Prados, 2016, 213.
26   Spector, 432.
27   Morison, vol. 12, 192; Woodward, 66–67.
28   Emerson, 80–84.
29   Taussig, 111.
30   Halsey and Bryan, 217.
31   Prados, 2016, 223.
32   Morison, vol. 12, 57–58.
33   Halsey, *Proceedings*, 481.
34   Reynolds, 267.
35   Halsey and Bryan, 217.
36   Halsey, *Proceedings*, 483.
37   Ito, 125–126.
38   Reynolds, 22.
39   Ito, 127.
40   Koyanagi, 125.
41   Spector, 438.
42   Thomas, 300–301.
43   Koyanagi, 129.
44   Prados, 2016, 333.

CHAPTER TEN: BATTLING ACROSS LEYTE

1   *Reports*, vol. 2, 369.
2   Cannon, 99.
3   Kenney, 1949, 459.
4   Prados, 2016, 330–333; Dull, 330–331.
5   Kenney, 1951, 170.
6   MacArthur, 173.
7   Herman, 546.
8   Manchester, 146; MacArthur, 99.
9   US Merchant Marine, http://www.usmm.org; US Navy Armed Guard, www.armed-guard.com.
10   Dod, 579.
11   Kenney, 1949, 464.
12   Hoyt, 1992, 138–139.
13   Sears, 154.
14   Bruning, 436.
15   McGowan, 244; Kenney, 1949, 467.
16   Morison, vol. 12, 340–341.
17   Hughes, 376–377.

18   James, 367.
19   Drea, 168.
20   Falk, 222; J. D. Potter, 112.
21   James, 370.
22   Holzimmer, 197.
23   Falk, 239–240.

CHAPTER ELEVEN: BREAKING THE YAMASHITA LINE

1   Prefer, 134–162.
2   Prefer, 129–130.
3   77th Division Operations Report Leyte, 16.
4   Salecker, 191.
5   Cannon, 295.
6   Flanagan, 1948, 34.
7   *Reports*, vol. 2, 424.
8   Rottman and Takizawa, 44–45.
9   Toland, 595.
10   *Reports*, vol. 2, 426–427.
11   Prefer, 224–233.
12   Eichelberger and MacKaye, 182.

CHAPTER TWELVE: LEAP TO MINDORO

1   Drea, 187–188.
2   James, 603–604.
3   Borneman, 2016, 446–448; James, 606.
4   Smith, 22–23.
5   Kenney, 1949, 478–479.
6   Perret, 438.
7   Smith, 46.
8   Bustin, 133–134.
9   *Reports*, vol. 2, 444.
10   Abbott, 6.
11   Casey, 513.
12   Smith, 48–49.
13   Rielly, 2010, 147–148.
14   Prados, 1995, 695; Morison, vol. 13, 37.
15   Morison, vol. 13, 38.
16   Ibid.
17   Dull, 332; Bulkley, 357–359.
18   James, 608.
19   J. D. Potter, 122; Toland, 603.
20   Smith, 49–51.
21   Rielly, 2010, 152–153.

22 Smith, 52.
23 *Reports*, vol. 2, 449.
24 *Reports*, vol. 1, 252; Whitney, 180.
25 O'Donnell. 167–172.
26 Morison, vol. 13, 50.
27 *Reports*, vol. 1, 252n22; vol. 2, 450n47.

CHAPTER THIRTEEN: MACARTHUR RETURNS TO LUZON

1   Murray and Millett, 495.
2   *Reports*, vol. 2, 450.
3   Cannon, 370.
4   J. D. Potter, 127.
5   Smith, 92–93.
6   Sandler, 468–469.
7   Scott, 95–99.
8   *Japanese Defense of Cities*, 1.
9   Smith, 92.
10 Wahlman, 70.
11 J. D. Potter, 129.
12 Scott, 53.
13 J. D. Potter, 130.
14 *Reports*, vol. 2, 460–462.
15 J. D. Potter, 130.
16 James, 616.
17 Morison, vol. 13, 98.
18 Ibid.
19 Sears, 258.
20 Smith. 59.
21 Barbey, 297.
22 MacArthur, 240.
23 Barbey, 297; Herman, 566.
24 James, 619; Taylor and Melzer, 98–99.
25 Smith, 68.
26 Marsden, 91–95.
27 Herman, 568.
28 J. D. Potter, 130.
29 *Reports*, vol. 2, 467.
30 Ibid., 467fn4.
31 James, 621.
32 Astor, 256.
33 Egeberg. 105.
34 Marsden, 95.
35 Cox, H-040-3 (online).
36 Morison, vol. 13, 140.
37 Volckmann, 181.

38   MacArthur, 241.
39   Egeberg, 106.
40   Griffith., 216; Kenney, 1949, 512.
41   J. D. Potter, 131.
42   Ibid., 133.
43   Perret, 443–444.
44   Borneman, 2016, 462; Perret, 442.
45   Smith, 168; Holzimmer, 218.
46   *Reports*, vol. 2, 483.
47   *Reports*, vol. 1, 267n46.

CHAPTER FOURTEEN: THE LIBERATION OF MANILA

1   Scott, 95.
2   Wahlman, 78.
3   James, 632.
4   James, 632–633; Perret, 446–447.
5   Egeberg, 139.
6   Hastings, 232.
7   Reel, 23–24.
8   Scott, 394.
9   Wahlman, 79.
10   Luvaas, 216–218.
11   Scott, 394.
12   Badsey, 238.
13   Smith, 311–312.
14   Ibid. 309.
15   Mann, 1163.
16   "A Veteran's Story," *The Citizens*, November 10, 2019, https://www
      .rockdalenewtoncitizen.com/features/a-veteran-s-story.
17   Smith, 330.
18   Eaton, 8.
19   Thomas, Elbert, 14–15.
20   Wahlman, 86.
21   MacArthur, 251.
22   Willoughby and Chamberlin, 269.
23   Scott, 410–411; Whitney, 192–193.
24   Egeberg, 144–151; Smith, 334.
25   Devlin, 32.
26   Kenney, 1949, 521.
27   Devlin, 36–37.
28   Ibid., 40–43.
29   Morison, vol. 13, 201.
30   Devlin, 44–46; Flanagan, 1988, 190–191.
31   Devlin, 49; Morison, vol. 13, 203.
32   Smith, 345; Astor, 403.

33   Devlin, 67.
34   Herman, 598.
35   *Reports*, vol. 1, 280n69; Scott, 412.
36   Barbey, 308.
37   Kenney, 1949, 521.
38   Scott, 413.
39   MacArthur, 250.
40   Smith, 305; Scott, 419.
41   Connaughton, 108.

CHAPTER FIFTEEN: THE WAR MOVES SOUTH

1   Morison, vol. 13, 217–218.
2   James, 737.
3   Morison, vol. 13, 214.
4   James, 738.
5   Barbey, 310.
6   Eichelberger and MacKaye, 205.
7   Casey, 7.
8   Eichelberger and MacKaye, 205; Morison, vol. 13, 218.
9   Moore, 260–261; Ponce de Leon, 126–127.
10   Eichelberger and MacKaye, 203.
11   Wilbanks, 160; Ponce de Leon, 147.
12   Smith, 589–591.
13   Ibid. 596–597.

CHAPTER SIXTEEN: FINAL DEFEAT

1   J. D. Potter, 142.
2   *Reports*, vol. 2, 504.
3   Smith, 465–466.
4   J. D. Potter, 147.

BIBLIOGRAPHY

Abbott, Don. *Remembering Mindoro.* http://corregidor.org/heritage
_battalion/abbott/mindoro.html.

Adams, Henry H. *Witness to Power: The Life of Fleet Admiral William D. Leahy.* Annapolis, MD: Naval Institute Press, 1985.

Astor, Gerald. *Crises in the Pacific.* New York: Donald I. Fine Books, 1996.

Badsey, Stephen, ed. *The Hutchinson Atlas of World War II Battle Plans.* New York: Routledge, 2000.

Barbey, Daniel E. *MacArthur's Amphibious Navy.* Annapolis, MD: Naval Institute Press, 1969.

Bartholomew, Charles A., and William I. Milwee. *Mud, Muscle, and Miracles: Marine Salvage in the United States Navy.* Washington, DC: US Navy, 2010.

Behr, Edward. *Hirohito: The Man Behind the Myth.* New York: Villard Books, 1989.

Bix, Herbert P. *Hirohito and the Making of Modern Japan.* New York: HarperCollins, 2000.

Black, Robert W. *Rangers in World War II.* New York: Ballantine Books, 1992.

Borneman, Walter R. *The Admirals: Nimitz, Halsey, Leahy, and King—The Five-Star Admirals Who Won the War at Sea.* New York: Little, Brown, 2012.

————. *MacArthur at War: World War II in the Pacific.* New York: Little, Brown, 2016.

Bowd, Reuben R. E. *The Basis for Victory: The Allied Geographical Section 1942–1946.* Canberra: Australian National University, 2005.

Boyne, Walter J. *Clash of Wings: World War II in the Air.* New York: Simon & Schuster, 1994.

Bradley, James. *Flyboys: A True Story of Courage.* New York: Little, Brown, 2003.

Breuer, William B. *Retaking the Philippines.* New York: St. Martin's Press, 1986.

Bruning, John R. *Indestructible.* New York: Hachette Books, 2016.

Buell, Thomas B. *Master of Sea Power: A Biography of Fleet Admiral Ernest J. King.* Boston: Little, Brown, 1980.

Bulkley, Robert J. *At Close Quarters: PT Boats in the United States Navy.* Annapolis: Naval Institute Press, 2003.

Bustin, Steven George. *Humble Heroes.* Charleston, SC: Booksurge Publishing, 2007.

Cannon, M. Hamlin. *Leyte: The Return to the Philippines.* Washington, DC: Center of Military History, United States Army, 1993.

Casey, Hugh J. *Engineers of the Southwest Pacific, 1941–45.* Vol. 4. Washington, DC: USGPO, 1959.

Connaughton, Richard, John Pimlott, and Duncan Anderson. *The Battle for Manila.* Novato, CA: Presidio Press, 1995.

Connaughton, Richard. *MacArthur and Defeat in the Philippines.* Woodstock, NY: Harry N. Abrams, 2001.

Cox, Samuel J., et al. "H-040-3: The Invasion of Luzon—Battle of Lingayen Gulf, January 1945." Naval History and Heritage Command, Annapolis, MD, January 2020. https://www.history .navy.mil/about-us/leadership/director/directors-corner/h -grams/h-gram-040/h-040-3.html.

Cutler, Thomas J. *The Battle of Leyte Gulf, 23–26 October 1944.* New York: HarperCollins, 1994.

Davison, Rear Admiral Ralph. "Action Report of Task Group 38.4, 7 October–21 October 1944." 1944. National Archives and Records Administration, Washington, DC.

Day, David. *Reluctant Nation: Australia and the Allied Defeat of Japan, 1942–1945.* New York: Oxford University Press, 1992.

Devlin, Gerard M. *Back to Corregidor: America Retakes The Rock.* New York: St. Martin's Press, 1992.

Dod, Karl C. *Technical Services, the Corps of Engineers, the War Against Japan.* Washington, DC: Department of the Army, 1966.

Drea, Edward J. *MacArthur's Ultra.* Lawrence, KS: University of Kansas Press, 1992.

Duffy, James P. *War at the End of the World: Douglas MacArthur and the Forgotten Fight for New Guinea, 1941–1945.* New York: NAL Caliber, 2016.

Dull, Paul S. *The Imperial Japanese Navy.* Annapolis, MD: Naval Institute Press, 1978.

Dunn, William J. *Pacific Microphone.* College Station: Texas A&M University Press, 2009.

Duus, Peter, Ramon H. Myers, Mark R. Peattie, eds. *The Japanese Wartime Empire, 1931–1945.* Princeton, NJ: Princeton University Press, 1996.

Early, Captain Alexander R. "Action Report for Canberra for 13 October through 27 October, 1944." 1944. United States Naval Academy, Special Collections & Archives, Annapolis, MD.

Eaton, Colonel H. O., Jr. "Japanese Defense of Cities as Exemplified by the Battle for Manila." Department of the Army, Sixth Army Headquarters, July 1945. National Archives and Records Administration, Washington, DC.

Egeberg, Roger Olaf, MD. *The General: MacArthur and the Man He called Doc.* New York: Hippocrene Books, 1983.

Eichelberger, Robert L., and Milton MacKaye. *Our Jungle Road to Tokyo.* New York: Viking Press, 1950.

Eisner, Peter. *MacArthur's Spies.* New York: Viking, 2017.

Emerson, Bill and Kathy. *The Voices of Bombing Nineteen.* 1993. http://emersonguys.com/bill/vb19.htm.

Evans, David C., ed. *The Japanese Navy in World War II: In the Words of Former Japanese Naval Officers.* Annapolis, MD: Naval Institute Press, 1969, 1986, 2017.

Falk, Stanley L. *Decision at Leyte.* New York: W.W. Norton, 1966.

Fane, Francis Douglas, and Don Moore. *The Naked Warriors: The Elite Fighting Force That Became the Navy SEALs.* New York: St. Martin's Press, 1996.

Flanagan, Edward M., Jr. *The Angels: A History of the 11th Airborne Division, 1943–1946.* Washington, DC: Infantry Journal Press, 1948.

———. *Corregidor: The Rock Force Assault, 1945.* Novato, CA: Presidio Press, 1988.

Fleming, Thomas. *The New Dealers' War: FDR and the War Within World War II.* New York: Basic Books, 2001.

———. *The Strategy of Victory: How General George Washington Won the American Revolution.* New York: Da Capo Press, 2017.

Fukudome, Shigeru. "The Air Battle off Taiwan." In *The Japanese Navy in World War II: In the Words of Former Japanese Naval Officers,* edited by David C. Evans. Annapolis, MD: Naval Institute Press, 1969, 1986, 2017.

Gill, G. Hermon. *Royal Australian Navy 1942–1945.* Canberra: Australian War Memorial, 1968.

Griffith, Thomas E., Jr. *MacArthur's Airman: General George C. Kenney and the War in the Southwest Pacific.* Lawrence: University Press of Kansas, 1998.

Halsey, Admiral William F. *Memoir.* Unpublished. Joseph Bryan III Papers, Virginia Historical Society.

Halsey, Fleet Admiral William F. "The Battle for Leyte Gulf." *Proceedings* 78 (May 1952).

Halsey, Fleet Admiral William F., and Lieutenant Commander J. Bryan III. *Admiral Halsey's Story.* New York: McGraw-Hill, 1947.

Handel, Michael P., ed. *Strategic and Operational Deception in the Second World War*. New York: Routledge/Taylor & Francis Group, 1987.

Harries, Meirion and Susie. *Soldiers of the Sun*. New York: Random House, 1991.

Harris, Brayton. *Admiral Nimitz: The Commander of the Pacific Ocean Theater*. New York: Palgrave Macmillan, 2011.

Hastings, Max. *Retribution: The Battle for Japan, 1944–1945*. New York: Alfred A. Knopf, 2008.

Hatch, Gardner N. *American Ex-POW*. Vol. 4. Nashville, TN: Turner Publishing, 2001.

Herbig, Katherine L. "American Strategic Deception in the Pacific, 1942–44." In *Strategic and Operational Deception in the Second World War*, edited by Michael P. Handel. New York: Routledge/Taylor & Francis Group, 1987.

Herman, Arthur. *Douglas MacArthur: American Warrior*. New York: Random House, 2016.

Hogan, David W. *U.S. Army Special Operations in World War II*. Washington, DC: Center of Military History, Department of the Army, 1992.

Holt, Thaddeus. *The Deceivers: Allied Military Deception in the Second World War*. New York: Scribner, 2004.

Holzimmer, Kevin C. *General Walter Krueger, Unsung Hero of the Pacific War*. Lawrence: University of Kansas Press, 2007.

Hopkins, William B. *The Pacific War*. Minneapolis, MN: Zenith Press, 2008.

Hoyt, Edwin P. *MacArthur's Navy*. New York: Orion Books, 1989.
———. *War in the Pacific*. Vol. 8, *MacArthur's Return*. New York: Avon Books, 1992.

Hughes, Thomas Alexander. *Admiral Bill Halsey: A Naval Life*. Cambridge, MA: Harvard University Press, 2016.

Hunt, Frazier. *The Untold Story of Douglas MacArthur*. New York: Devin-Adair, 1954.

Ingham, Travis. *MacArthur's Emissary: Chuck Parsons and the Secret War in the Philippines in World War II*. San Bernardino,

CA: Createspace, 2014. First published 1945 by Doubleday, Doran & Co. (original title *Rendezvous by Submarine: The Story of Charles Parsons and the Guerrilla-Soldiers in the Philippines*).

Ito, Masanori. *The End of the Imperial Japanese Navy*. New York: MacFadden Books, 1965.

James, D. Clayton. *The Years of MacArthur*. Vol. 2, *1941–1945*. Boston: Houghton Mifflin, 1975.

Japanese Defense of Cities as Exemplified by the Battle for Manila. Headquarters Sixth Army, XIV Corps, July 1, 1945.

Jordan, Jonathan W. *American Warlords: How Roosevelt's High Command Led America to Victory in World War II*. New York: NAL Caliber, 2015.

Keegan, John. *The American Civil War*. New York: Knopf, 2009.

Kennedy, Maxwell Taylor. *Danger's Hour*. New York: Simon & Schuster, 2008.

Kenney, George C. *General Kenney Reports*. New York: Duell, Sloan, and Pearce, 1949.

————. *The MacArthur I Know*. New York: Duell, Sloan, and Pearce, 1951.

King, Ernest J., and Walter Muir Whitehill. *Fleet Admiral King: A Naval Record*. New York: W.W. Norton, 1952.

Koyanagi, Rear Admiral Tomiji. "With Kurita in the Battle for Leyte Gulf." US Naval Institute *Proceedings* (February 1953).

Larrabee, Eric. *Commander in Chief*. New York: Simon & Schuster/Touchstone, 1988.

Leahy, William D. *I Was There: The Memoirs of FDR's Chief of Staff*. New York: Whittlesey House, 1950.

Luvaas, Jay, ed. *Dear Miss Em: General Eichelberger's War in the Pacific 1942–1945*. Westport: Greenwood Press, 1972.

MacArthur, Douglas. *Reminiscences*. New York: McGraw-Hill, 1964.

Mahan, Alfred Thayer. *Influence of Sea Power Upon History, 1660–1783*. New York, Barnes & Noble Books, 2004.

Manchester, William. *American Caesar*. Boston: Little, Brown, 1978.

Mann, B. David. "Japanese Defense of Bataan, Luzon, Philippine Islands, 16 December 1944–4 September 1945." *Journal of Military History 67* (October 2003): 1149–1176.

Marsden, Lawrence. *Attack Transport: The Story of the U.S.S. Doyen.* Minneapolis: University of Minnesota Press, 1946.

Marshall, George C. *Biennial Reports of the Chief of Staff of the United States Army to the Secretary of War, I July 1939–30 June 1945.* Washington, DC: Center for Military History, 1996.

McCallus, Joseph P. *The MacArthur Highway and Other Relics of American Empire in the Philippines.* Washington, DC: Potomac Books, 2010.

McGowan, Sam. *The Story of Pappy Gunn, Hero of the South West Pacific.* CreateSpace Publishing, 2016.

Miller, Donald L. *D-Days in the Pacific.* New York: Simon & Schuster, 2005.

Miller, Nathan. *The Naval Air War 1939–1945.* Annapolis, MD: Naval Institute Press, 1991.

Mooney, James L., ed. *Dictionary of American Naval Fighting Ships.* Washington, DC: Department of the Navy, 1981.

Moore, Stephen L. *As Good As Dead.* New York: Caliber, 2016.

Morison, Samuel Eliot. *Leyte, June 1944–January 1945.* Vol. 12. Edison, NJ: Castle Books, 2001.

———. *The Liberation of the Philippines, 1944–1945.* Vol. 13. Edison, NJ: Castle Books, 2001.

Morton, Louis. *The Fall of the Philippines: U.S. Army in World War II, the War in the Pacific.* Washington, DC: Center of Military History, US Army, 1953.

Murray, Williamson, and Allan R. Millett. *A War to Be Won: Fighting the Second World War.* Cambridge: Harvard University Press, 2000.

Nicholson, Arthur. *Very Special Ships: Abdiel-Class Fast Minelayers of World War II.* Annapolis: Naval Institute Press, 2015.

O'Brien, Phillips Payson. *How the War Was Won: Air-Sea Power and Allied Victory in World War II.* Cambridge: Cambridge University Press, 2015.

O'Donnell, Patrick K. *Into the Rising Sun.* New York: Free Press, 2002.

Office of Scientific Research and Development (OSRD). *Radio Countermeasures.* Washington, DC: National Defense Research Committee, 1946.

Perras, Galen R. *Stepping Stones to Nowhere: The Aleutian Islands, Alaska, and American Military Strategy, 1867–1945.* Vancouver, BC: UBC Press, 2003.

Perret, Geoffrey. *Old Soldiers Never Die.* New York: Random House, 1996.

Perry, Mark. *The Most Dangerous Man in America.* New York: Basic Books, 2014.

Persico, Joseph E. *Roosevelt's Centurions: FDR and the Commanders He Led to Victory in World War II.* New York: Random House, 2013.

Pineau, Captain Roger. *Divine Wind: Japan's Kamikaze Force in World War II.* New York: Praeger Publisher, 1958.

Pogue, Forrest C. *George C. Marshall.* Vol. 3, *Organizer of Victory, 1943–1945.* New York: Viking Press, 1973.

Ponce de Leon, Dr. Walfrido R. *The Puerto Princesa Story.* Puerto Princesa, Palawan: City Government, 2004.

Potter, E. B. *Nimitz.* Annapolis, MD: Naval Institute Press, 1976.

Potter, John Deane. *The Life and Death of a Japanese General.* New York: Signet Books, 1962.

Prados, John. *Combined Fleet Decoded: The Secret History of American Intelligence and the Japanese Navy in World War II.* New York: Random House, 1995.

———. *Storm over Leyte: The Philippine Invasion and the Destruction of the Japanese Navy.* New York: NAL Caliber, 2016.

Prefer, Nathan N. *Leyte 1944: The Soldiers' Battle.* Philadelphia: Casemate Publishers, 2012.

Price, Alfred. *The Evolution of Electronic Warfare Equipment and Techniques in the USA, 1901–1945.* Loughborough University: PhD Thesis, 1985.

Pu Yi, Henry. *The Last Manchu: The Autobiography of Henry Pu Yi.* New York: Skyhorse, 2010.

Reel, A. Frank. *The Case of General Yamashita.* New York: Octagon Books, 1971.

Reports of General MacArthur: The Campaigns of MacArthur in the Pacific. Vol. 1. Washington, DC: Department of the Army, 1966, 1994.

Reports of General MacArthur: Japanese Operations in the Southwest Pacific Area. Vol. 2. Washington, DC: Department of the Army, 1966, 1994.

Reynolds, Clark G. *The Fast Carriers.* Annapolis, MD: Naval Institute Press, 1968.

Rhoades, Weldon (Dusty). *Flying MacArthur to Victory.* College Station, TX: Texas A&M University Press, 1987.

Rielly, Robin L. *Kamikaze Attacks of World War II.* Jefferson, NC: McFarland & Co., 2010.

———. *American Amphibious Gunboats in World War II.* Jefferson, NC: McFarland & Co., 2013.

Roosevelt, Franklin D., Master Speech File, 1898–1945 (MSF). Franklin D. Roosevelt Presidential Library, Hyde Park, NY.

Roosevelt, Franklin D., Papers as President: the President's Personal File (PPF). Franklin D. Roosevelt Presidential Library, Hyde Park, NY.

Roosevelt, Franklin D., Papers as President: the President's Secretary's File (PSF). Franklin D. Roosevelt Presidential Library, Hyde Park, NY.

Roosevelt, Franklin D., Press Conferences of President Franklin D. Roosevelt, 1933–1945 (PPC). Franklin D. Roosevelt Presidential Library, Hyde Park, NY.

Rottman, Gordon L., and Akira Takizawa. *Japanese Paratroop Forces of World War II.* Oxford, UK: Osprey Publishing, 2005.

Salecker, Gene Eric. *Blossoming Silk Against the Rising Sun.* Mechanicsburg, PA: Stackpole Books, 2010.

Sandler, Stanley, ed. *World War II in the Pacific: An Encyclopedia.* New York: Garland Publishing, 2001.

Scott, James M. *Rampage: MacArthur, Yamashita, and the Battle of Manila.* New York: W.W. Norton, 2018.

Sears, David. *At War with the Wind.* New York: Citadel Press Books, 2008.

Sherman, Rear Admiral Frederick C. "Action Report of Task Group 38.3, Battle of Formosa." 1944. National Archives and Records Administration, Washington, DC.

Shin, Gi-Wook, and Daniel Sneider. *Divergent Memories: Opinion Leaders and the Asia-Pacific War.* Stanford, CA: Stanford University Press, 2016.

Smith, Robert Ross. *Triumph in the Philippines.* Washington, DC: US Army Center of Military History, 1961.

Snyder, Jack. *Myths of Empire: Domestic Politics and International Ambition.* Ithaca, NY: Cornell University Press, 1993.

Sommerville, Donald. *World War II Day by Day: An Illustrated Almanac 1939–1945.* New York: Dorset Press, 1989.

Spector, Ronald H. *Eagle Against the Sun: The American War with Japan.* New York: Free Press, 1985.

Stewart, Adrian. *The Battle of Leyte Gulf.* New York: Charles Scribner's Sons, 1979.

Taussig, Betty Carney. *A Warrior for Freedom.* Manhattan, KS: Sunflower University Press, 1995.

Taylor, John, and Richard Melzer. *USS New Mexico.* Charleston, SC: Arcadia Publishing, 2017.

Thomas, Sen. Elbert D. *Sack of Manila.* Washington, DC: Senate Committee on Military Affairs, 1945.

Thomas, Evan. *Sea of Thunder: Four Commanders and the Last Great Naval Campaign 1941–1945.* New York: Simon & Schuster, 2006.

Toland, John. *The Rising Sun: The Decline and Fall of the Japanese Empire, 1936–1945.* New York: Random House, 1970.

Ugaki, Admiral Matome. *Fading Victory: The Diary of Admiral Matome Ugaki, 1941–1945.* Pittsburgh, PA: University of Pittsburgh Press, 1991.

USS Canberra *(CA70), War Damage Report No. 54.* 1944. US Navy Department, Naval History and Heritage Command, Washington, DC.

USS Franklin *(CV-13), War Damage Report No. 56.* 1944. US Navy Department, Naval History and Heritage Command, Washington, DC.

USS Houston *(CL81), War Damage Report No. 53.* 1944. US Navy Department, Naval History and Heritage Command, Washington, DC.

Valtin, Jan. *Children of Yesterday.* New York: Reader's Press, 1946.

Vego, Milan. *The Battle for Leyte, 1944: Allied and Japanese Plans, Preparations, and Execution.* Annapolis: Naval Institute Press, 2006.

———. *Naval Classical Thinkers and Operational Art.* Newport, RI: Naval War College, 2009.

Volckmann, R. W. *We Remained.* New York: W.W. Norton, 1954.

Wahlman, Alec. *Storming the City.* Denton: University of North Texas Press, 2015.

Wells, Lieutenant Colonel Leonard E. *Military Deception: Equivalent to Intelligence, Maneuver and Fires.* Newport, RI: Naval War College, 2008.

Whitney, Major General Courtney. *MacArthur: His Rendezvous with History.* New York: Alfred A. Knopf, 1956.

Wilbanks, Bob. *Last Man Out.* Jefferson, NC: McFarland & Co., 2004.

Willmott, H. P. *The Battle of Leyte Gulf: The Last Fleet Action.* Bloomington: Indiana University Press, 2005.

Willoughby, Major General Charles A., and John Chamberlin. *MacArthur: 1941–1951.* New York: McGraw-Hill, 1954.

Woodward, C. Vann. *The Battle for Leyte Gulf: The Incredible Story of World War II's Largest Naval Battle.* New York: Macmillan, 1947.

Zaloga, Stephen J. *Japanese Tanks 1939–1945.* Oxford, UK: Osprey Publishing, 2007.

INDEX